SAGGISTICA 37

IL MIGLIOR FABBRO

Essays in Honor of Joseph Tusiani

Edited by
Paolo A. Giordano
Anthony Julian Tamburri

ITALIANA XIV

2021

Library of Congress Control Number: 2021940612

© Copyright, 2021
The Authors & The Editors

All rights reserved. Parts of this book may be reprinted only by written permission from the author, and may not be reproduced for publication in book, magazine, or electronic media of any kind, except for purposes of literary re-views by critics.

Printed in the United States.

Published by
BORDIGHERA PRESS
John D. Calandra Italian American Institute
25 West 43rd Street, 17th Floor
New York, NY 10036

Italiana • Special Issue
ISSN 0897-2583
Saggistica 37
ISBN 978-1-59954-184-6

TABLE OF CONTENTS

ix — P. A. Giordano & A. J. Tamburri • "An Introduction to Joseph Tusiani: Some Initial Thoughts"

Section I
IN HIS OWN WORDS

3 — Joseph Tusiani • "The Making of an Italian American Poet"
37 — Bea Tusiani • "The Joseph I Knew"

Section II
A COMMEMORATION

49 — Giose Rimanelli • "A Mesmeric Sculpture: Tusiani, the Humanist"

Section III
CRITICAL ANALYSES

55 — Paolo A. Giordano • "Joseph Tusiani: The Man and His Work"
81 — Luigi Fontanella • "Joseph Tusiani, collaboratore di *Gradiva* e corrispondente poetico
91 — Emilio Bandiera • "Le raccolte di liriche latine di Joseph Tusiani. Tra cronaca e curiosità"
109 — John T. Kirby • "Joseph Tusiani and The Tradition of Neo-Latin Verse"
121 — Luigi Bonaffini • "Il dialetto nell'opera di Joseph Tusiani"
147 — Gaetano Cipolla • *"Reductio ab Essentia* in Joseph Tusiani's *Envoy from Heaven*
159 — Cosma Siani • "Tusiani antico e nuovo"

165 — Ryan Calabretta-Sajder • "You Can't Go Home Again! Retro-Reading 'Exile' and 'Return' in the *Oeuvre* of Joseph Tusiani"

199 — Maria C. Pastore Passaro • "Joseph Tusiani: A Contemporary American Poet"

215 — Anthony Julian Tamburri • "Un rimpatrio linguistico ovvero un recupero culturale? *Il ritorno* di Joseph Tusiani"

239 — Ilaria Serra • "Questions on an Old Map: Joseph Tusiani's *If Gold Should Rust*"

259 — Mark Pietralunga • "*Divagando* with Giuseppe Tusiani in the *sottobosco letterario*"

279 — Contributors
287 — Index

Acknowledgements

There are always numerous people to thank when a book comes together. In our case, we need first and foremost to thank the contributors to this volume. They all had a wonderful relationship with Joseph. In some cases, those friendships were from afar (e.g., Italy, Arkansas, Florida, Illinois, Indiana), in other cases they were relationships that allowed the privilege of visiting with Joseph (e.g., Connecticut and New York).

Our friends in Italy have been his dear friends and assiduous scholars of his work over the years. Emilio Bandiera and Cosma Siani have both edited and written on his work, for the most part Latin and Italian respectively. Numerous of us here are friends — long-term and more recent — who interacted with Joseph from afar (Ryan Calabretta-Sajder, Paolo A. Giordano, John T. Kirby, Mark Pietralunga, Ilaria Serra), while others, at a more local level, had the opportunity to visit with him, and sometimes often (Luigi Bonaffini, Gaetano Cipolla, Luigi Fontanella, Maria C. Pastore Passaro, Anthony Julian Tamburri).

In a slightly different category we see Joseph's sister-in-law, Bea Tusiani, and his life-long friend of the same generation, Giose Rimanelli. Bea's contribution to this tribute provides us with insight that comes in part through a family perspective and partly through her 2001 interview. Giose's contribution dates to 1994, from the volume that Paolo Giordano had edited at that time, which figured as the first major examination of Joseph's *oeuvre*. We left Giose's text as is, in the present tense; after all, both men are still with us through their innumerable works they left behind.

Buona lettura!

Paolo A. Giordano
Anthony Julian Tamburri
Spring 2021

An Introduction to Joseph Tusiani
Some Initial Thoughts

Paolo A. Giordano
Anthony Julian Tamburri

> Two languages, two lands, perhaps two souls...
> Am I a man or two strange halves of one?
>
> "Song of the Bicentennial"
> (*Gente Mia and Other Poems*)

Joseph Tusiani has been in our respective lives for most of our careers. We each met him early on, during different moments and in different parts of the United States. Nonetheless, he had remained a constant for each of us for a variety of reasons. First and foremost, his dignity as a human being. Joseph exuded a generosity toward and a respect for all those with whom he had engaged: students, colleagues, and scholars from all parts. Second, his sensitivity as a reader of literature — as a scholar in his own right — has led him to produce an array of critical essays on English, American, and Italian writers. Third, his patience and preciseness as translator has given to the Anglophone world a plethora of important texts that otherwise would have appeared latter, if at all. We remind our reader of Michelangelo's complete poems into English, Luigi Pulci's *Il Morgante*, Torquato Tasso's *Gerusalemme Liberata*, Giacomo Leopardi's *I Canti*, and others who lived before and after these poets, from Dante to Montale. More than anything, Joseph was a poet whose production spanned seventy-eight years, articulated in four languages: Italian, Latin, dialect, and English.[1] His style could be stridently traditional in metric and register, but it was, as well, in free verse and with an expansively polyvalent lexicon. Either way, Joseph's poetry always captured, and held, his reader's attention.

---

[1] Joseph's first published books of poetry were: in Italian *Amedeo di Savoia* (1943); in Latin *Melos Cordis* (1955); in dialect *Làcreme e sciure* (1955); and in English *Rind and All. Fifty Poems* (1962).

Joseph Tusiani (San Marco in Lamas, January 14, 1924 — New York, April 11, 2020) represents a unique profile within the history of Italian immigration to the United States. He arrived with his mother on September 6th, 1947 on what could have been a short visit. Instead, they remained. Professionally, Tusiani's university teaching career began at the College of Mount Saint Vincent in 1948; then, in 1971, he moved to Lehman College (The City University of New York) where he remained until his retirement in 1983.

From a cultural perspective, Joseph worked assiduously throughout his adult life in all arenas of the literary world, and with great success as well. Over the more than seven decades he spent in New York, he developed into the polymath that he became. Poet, first and foremost, prose writer, essayist, and translator, Tusiani was the true award-winning scholar and intellectual many aspire to be. In his introduction to Tusiani's *If Gold Should Rust*, Felix Stefanile spoke about how this

> pensive drama ... though not openly representative of what he does, in his poems, in his translations (*a veritable one-man industry*), his poetry in Latin and Italian, his essays and lectures, still depict certain steady aspects of his style that have, as a matter of fact, never varied. (267; emphasis added)

We know that Joseph appreciated very much Stefanile's short commentary of him as "a veritable one-man industry." On a couple of occasions during our visits, when Felix's name came up, Joseph would smile, most appreciatively and with a good dose of modesty, as he referenced Stefanile's compliment. This is exemplary of Joseph's humility. He himself never sought fame; he did what he did for the love of his craft as writer, translator, and humanist. During any conversation about how well he might have been known and in which cultural circles, he would always revert to his books; he believed they were the true legacies of his work. Fame, for him, was secondary at best.

Tusiani's work as a poet, especially, has been recognized over the past sixty-plus years on various levels: regional, national, and international. The accolades are many, and you will read about them in the pages that follow. We would like to highlight a few of them here. In 1986, more than sixty years after it was formed, the American Association of Teachers of Italian created its Distinguished Service Award; it recognized Joseph as its first recipient. During the early 1960s then President Kennedy invited Tusiani to the White House to read from his poetry, a recording of which is housed in the Archives of the Library of Congress. The story goes that then-candidate John F. Kennedy was campaigning in the New York area and made a stop at the College of Saint Vincent, where Joseph was teaching. Not long before Kennedy's stop-over Robert L. Clements had reviewed Joseph's translation of Michelangelo's poetry, first time translated into English. Having been introduced to Tusiani, Kennedy recalled the review — "You're the Michelangelo man," Joseph once recounted to us — and he went on to promise an invitation to the White House after he won the election. That visit took place in 1963. In subsequent years other recognitions followed. Indeed, within the last decade of his life distinguished recognitions continued. In 2015, Lehman College (CUNY) bestowed upon him its Distinguished Accomplishment in Literature Award. Further still, New York Governor Andrew Cuomo named Joseph Tusiani the "New York State Poet Laureate Emeritus in Recognition of Contributions to International Literary Community." Finally, his 1960 translation, *The Complete Poems of Michelangelo*, will be re-issued in the Lorenzo da Ponte Italian Library Series of the University of Toronto Press.

Poetry, to be sure, is the genre to which Joseph has dedicated most of his literary prowess. In this regard, his books of poetry published both in the United States as well as in Europe number forty-eight; this does not include the dozen more of prose and essays. Indeed, the above-mentioned honor of New York State Poet Laureate Emeritus was bestowed on him in recognition of his achievements in American *and* Italian literature, a linguistic talent not many possess at such an aesthetic level. His prolific writing in Latin verse — eight books in this one language — and its reception among the critics have, for instance, categorized him as the greatest Neo-Latin poet who "give[s] rise to a poetic idiom *sui generis*, which, moreover, excellently voices Tusiani's own perception of our *tremenda aetas* and his search for a new language that could overcome the conflict between his native Italian and the English, the conflict between two cultures" (Sacré 167). Tusiani's poetry remains relevant today precisely because he was able to particularize the universal and universalize the particular.

In February 2014 Joseph suffered a mild stroke. During the few years that preceded his stroke, and to his own admission, he had experienced a dry spell. Remarkable, to be sure, is the aesthetic plentitude that resulted from the malady that befell him. From February 2014 until his death, Joseph composed close to 2,000 poems in four languages: Italian, English, Latin, and his Gargano dialect. His most recent publications are: in English, *A Clarion Call*; in Latin, *Lux vicit. Carmina Latina*; and in Italian, *Poesie Per un Anno (2014-2019)*.

The fact, further still, that much of his work is couched in his own experience as an Italian in America only renders his poetry more powerful, especially today, precisely because it sets up a context for the necessary comparison of past twentieth-century mobility with what we have now been experiencing in these last twenty-plus years regarding the massive migration crossing the Mediterranean. This, along with the unique multi-lingual lyrical prowess, qualifies Joseph Tusiani to occupy the position he does in our developing history of poetry in both English and Italian. His not only entertains, as some, like T.S. Eliot, say poetry should, but in the end, it inspires his reader to think, the end goal of any literary work. We cannot ask for more; we can only hope that the reader, fundamentally, engages.

Works Cited

Clements, Robert L. Review of *The Complete Poems of Michelangelo*. Translated with Notes and Introduction by Joseph Tusiani. New York: The Noonday Press, 1960. *The New York Times Book Review* (June 5, 1960): 22.

Sacré, Dirk. "Joseph Tusiani's Latin Poetry: Aspects of Its Originality" in *Joseph Tusiani: Poet Tarnslator Humanist. An International Homage*. Paolo A. Giordano, ed. West Lafayette, IN: Bordighera Press, 1994. 160-179.

Stefanile, Felix. "Introduction" to *If Gold Should Rust* in *Joseph Tusiani: Poet Translator Humanist. An International Homage*. Paolo A. Giordano, ed. West Lafayette, IN: Bordighera Press, 1994. 265-269.

Tusiani, Joseph. *Rime. The Joseph Tusiani's Classic Translation*. Edited by Gianluca Rizzo, with an essay by Glauco Cambon. Lorenzo da Ponte Italian Library Series. Toronto: University of Toronto Press, forthcoming.

Tusiani, Joseph. *Poesie per un anno (2014-2019)*. Antonio Motta and Cosma Tusiani eds. San Marco in Lamis, Puglia: Centro Documentazione Leonardo Sciascia, 2019.

Tusiani, Joseph. *Lux vicit. Carmina Latina*. Translated, edited, and with Introduction by Emilio Bandiera. Bari: Levante Editori. 2018.

Tusiani, Joseph. *A Clarion Call. New Poems*. Paolo Giordano and Anthony Julian Tamburri, eds. New York: Bordighera Press, 2016.

Tusiani, Joseph. *In una casa un'altra casa trovo. Autobiografia di un poeta di due terre*. Raffaele Cera and Cosma Siani, eds. Milan: Bompiani, 2016. 190-198.

Tusiani, Joseph. *Gente Mia and Other Poems*. Stone Park, IL: Italian Cultural Center, 1978; reprinted in *Ethnicity*. Paolo Giordano, ed. New York: Bordighera Press, 2012.

Tusiani, Joseph. *Rind and All. Fifty Poems*. New York: The Monastine Press, 1962.

Tusiani, Joseph. "The Return" http://siba3.unile.it/ctle/tusiani/the_return.htm.

Tusiani, Joseph. *Làcreme e sciure*. Preface by T. Nardella. Foggia: Cappetta, s.d. (presumed 1955).

Tusiani, Joseph. *Melos Cordis*, New York: The Venetian Press, 1955.

Tusiani, Joseph. *Amedeo di Savoia*. Poemetto in isciolti, pref. P. Ciro Soccio. Sant'Agata di Puglia: Tip. Casa del Sacro Cuore, 1943.

Section One

In His Own Words

The Making of an Italian American Poet[1]

Joseph Tusiani

An apology is in order for the use of the first person throughout the following pages, but the humility that prompts it goes with the pride that makes these very pages possible — the pride of one whose existence has been touched and crossed by too many great lives to remain uninspired or at least unproductive. Accepting, therefore, Professor Pane's invitation to make public the Italian American cultural wealth of the post-La Guardia's years — a wealth that has yet to be fully acknowledged and treasured — I will speak of some of the great people who shaped my formative years in America, thus making *Gente Mia*[2] a document of biographic as well as autobiographic history.

Some of you are, I believe, already familiar with a poem entitled "The Difficult Word." In it I described the drama, rather the trauma, of a twenty-three-year-old man who for the first time meets his father at Pier 86 in New York. If I quote here the very end of that poem, it is because I would like to remind you of that young man in desperate need of affection in a land he did not know and where his own father was now suddenly a stranger:

> Oh, we have grown apart — you with no son,
> I with no father. Emigration's last
> and most uncharted tragedy is this —
> slowly it forces people to adjust
> to want of love, anticipating death.
> A reunited family means only
> reunion of faces, not of feelings.

---

[1] ED. NOTE: With the same title, this essay first appeared in *Italian Americans in the Professions. Proceedings of the Twelfth Annual Conference of the American Italian Historical Association.* Remigio U. Pane, ed. (Staten Island, NY: AIHA, 1983): 9-40.
[2] *Gente Mia and Other Poems* by Joseph Tusiani. Italian Cultural Center (Stone Park, Ill, 1978). [ED. NOTE: Now as *Ethnicity. Selected Poetry.* Paolo Giordano, ed. (West Lafayette, IN: Bordighera Press, 2000.)]

> Or I would not with so much envy think
> of flocks of birds migrating to new climes
> yet still together in the hostile wind.
> Father, when spring is miracle again,
> the same birds fly to their remembered nest;
> but, Father, you and I cannot return
> *to* what did not exist. So call me still
> by my first name, if still your lips are slow
> to say the word you should have always said
> till it became a meaning in your soul.
> Let us (if faith begets but suffering)
> forgive each other in the name of love:
> even unnamed, a flame is warm and bright.[3]

It was September 1947. Only two years had elapsed from the conclusion of WW II. The defeated Italy I had left behind was a devastated country which, in my innocence, I used to compare to T.S. Eliot's *The Wasteland*.[4] I expected victorious America to be different of course; but never had I dreamed to find in the Italian community a literary vitality which, instead of lessening, the recent war had strangely recharged. Soon I discovered that, maybe because of the official hostilities between Italy and the United States, the Italian Americans had to an unprecedented degree succeeded in strengthening their love for their two countries.[5]

So often and so wrongly has the so-called illiteracy of the Italian immigrant been mentioned that a word must here be said about a

---

[3] The poem, "The Difficult Word," was originally published with the title "To My Father" in *Italian Americana,* 2.2 (Spring 1976): 209-12.
[4] The poetry of T.S. Eliot had been the subject of one of my courses at the University of Naples where I wrote my doctoral dissertation on William Wordsworth under the direction of Cesare Foligno in whose honor Mario Praz edited a special issue of *English Miscellany* with essays contributed by Foligno's admirers, colleagues, and former students. See my "David Gray and Sergio Corazzini: A Parallel," *English Miscellany* (Rome: Edizioni di Storia e Letteratura, 1958) 315-28.
[5] On this particular subject the Center for Migration Studies of Staten Island, New York, can provide a vast bibliography. Strongly recommended are the available studies on Vito Marcantonio and Fiorello La Guardia.

particular *sottobosco letterario* which no scholar has yet explored. I am referring to the poetic activity in Italian and in the several Italian dialects, which for many years appeared in *Il Progresso Italo-Americano, La Follia, La Lucerna,* and *Divagando,* just to mention the major publications in the New York area.[6] Especially the much-maligned *Progresso* seemed to understand a need, in our immigrants, which sociologists were still far from fathoming — their genuine, though untrained, self-expression. A distinguished feature of the newspaper was a verse column that introduced to the Italian American community sonnets or odes written by its own people — barbers, tailors, bricklayers, and even teachers and physicians.[7] Their poetry — it's true — was more often than not so poor and pathetic, so dim and devoid of the divine spark as to alienate any punctilious or supercilious "Aristarco Scannabue." Giuseppe Prezzolini, for instance, made havoc of what he apparently believed to be a threat to the awesome purity of the Tuscan "voce," but he failed to understand that, by venting their emotions in the music of their vernaculars or in quasi-Italian (that is, often ungrammatical) quatrains, those "trapiantati" lived in the blissful illusion of not being completely such. He was also unable to recognize the innate genius or a race manifesting itself in and through people who made the most of their first or second grade of elementary education. And something else and far more important Prezzolini failed to notice from the ivory tower of his Casa Italiana of Columbia University — the semi-cultural atmosphere which, unknowingly, those "poetasters" had succeeded in creating for and around themselves.[8] Indeed, men

---

[6] The birth and death — even the stillbirth — of hundreds of minor publications in Italian, in itself indicative of the intellectual restlessness of our immigrants, contradicts the theory of an absolute illiteracy.

[7] I have not been able to ascertain whether, among these categories of working people, the ratio free time-writing hobby is of any relevance. More information is needed.

[8] Utterly unknown to Prezzolini was, for instance, the existence in the Belmont area of the Bronx — precisely on Cambreleng Avenue — of a two-room apartment where, every evening, around the octogenarian Nicola Giusto, who could not offer more than a glass of water to his guests, gathered people, young and old, eager to hear him talk. With the pseudonym "Prisco N. Justus" Mr. Giusto had published

such as Italo Stanco, Rodolfo Pucelli, Giuseppe Incalicchio, Francesco Greco, Pietro Greco, Riccardo Cordiferro, Lorenzo Lucarelli, Giuseppe Zappulla, Nino Caradonna, Ario Flamma, Enzo Giustiniani, John Alifano, and women such as Lia Spezzano, "Alma Fiedlia" (sic), Mario Vecchione, and Mary Iacovella, publicly corresponded in verse with one another, to a certain extent resurrecting the time of the medieval and Renaissance *tenzone*, which, for better and for worse, rallied poets around one language, if not around one country. Thus, the poets of the Italian American *sottobosco*, whom literary Italy at best ignored, felt the need of establishing literary clubs where, in perfect mutual admiration and stimulation, those underprivileged pupils of the Muse (Sicilians, Calabrians, Apulians, Abruzzese, and even Tuscans) read and discussed their published and unpublished poems, and where entire chapters from *I promessi sposi* or full "Canti" from the *Divina Commedia* were recited by heart.[9] In other words, "roba da capitale d'Italia." So vibrant and creative was the intellectual restlessness of our immigrants that their poetic voice humbly but eloquently recorded the most memorable events of their history. One of our anonymous bards had this to say on the death of Rodolfo Valentino:

> Dallu 'spidale e sciuta la nutizia
> che tutto 'o munno agghienchie di mestizia:
> di tutti l'Italiani era conforto
> e mo Rodolfo Valentino e morto.
> 0 Pateterno 'nciele l'ha chiamate,

---

a book entitled *L'Universo fisico e spirituale* (New York: S.F. Vanni, 1941), in which his philosophical ideas, sharpened though rendered unilateral and bitter by lack of success in this country, range from an analysis of atomic energy to a study of the phenomenon of the stigmata in Saint Francis of Assisi and Teresa Neuman. I attended several of those informal gatherings and was impressed not so much with Mr. Giusto's brilliant though chaotic mind as with the attention he was listened to by humble laborers.

[9] Lorenzo Lucarelli, respectfully called "Professore," was the most spellbinding *dicitore* in the Bronx. He knew Dante and Manzoni by heart and was invited to recite passages from the *Comedy* and *I promessi sposi* even at wedding banquets. Just imagine a tarantella preceded or followed by the episode of Count Ugolino!

dove tenime 'nu sante avvucate.
Pure l'America s'ha misse 'o lutte:
figli d'Italia, chiagnite tutte!¹⁰

And there is more. Each of those clubs engendered its own artistic fervor, which, in turn, made possible the existence and triumph of several dramatic companies in the metropolitan region. Actors such as Giuseppe Sterni, Adziaro Carpi, Gino Caimi, Armando Cennerazzo, Sandrino Giglio, Nicola Paone, the Gardenias, Dino De Luca, and actresses such as Mimi Aguglia, Diana Baldi, Mimi Cecchini, and Maria Iannella were household deities. Every night, or almost, the Academy of Music in Brooklyn was filled to capacity with Italian Americans from the five boroughs for the performance of such disparate plays as *La Passione e Morte di Gesù Cristo* and *La Morte Civile*.¹¹ If we add to all this the enormous popularity of Carlo Buti, whose voice seemed to prolong amongst the Italian Americans the remembrance of the Gatti-Casazza golden age of the Metropolitan Opera House (where our immigrants were always the most enthusiastic and vociferous standees), the realization of our grandfathers' achievement will make us feel so poor in comparison as to prompt us to say that we should indeed look forward to our past.

Surely a doctoral dissertation should be assigned on our literary and artistic *sottobosco*, to determine: 1) the percentage of those who,

---

¹⁰ Hundreds of poems were inspired by Rodolfo Valentino's death. Of this particular stanza I have found several versions. The present transcription was dictated to me by my father.

¹¹ There was hardly an Italian parish in New York without its small "compagnia filodrammatica," consisting of volunteers brave enough to memorize in their free time the various roles assigned by one who, for the pleasure of presenting new plays to the "vicinato" and for the small glory of being known as "capocomico" or "direttore drammatico," sacrificed at times his own money for the rental of costumes, etc. In my possession are several posters and leaflets attesting to the vitality of "La Filodrammatica" of the Immaculate Conception Church of Gun Hill Road in the Bronx from 1945 to 1947. Its director. Michele Tusiani, my father, included in his artistic repertory Giacometti's *La Morte Civile*, an adaptation of Carolina Invernizio's *Misteri delle Soffitte*, and some of his own "farse." In general, a serious play was followed by a "farsa comica in un atto," dealing with exaggerated humorous incidents of Italian-American life.

maybe spurred by the glamor of a newspaper column, somewhat resumed their interrupted education; 2) which Italian region, and why, produced the greatest number of poets or versifiers; 3) whether or not, regardless of literary standards, their poems succeeded in capturing the two most deep-rooted feelings connected with or resulting from the history of our immigration — nostalgia and Americanization; 4) how more easily than others, and with what results, the children of those poets were encouraged to study Italian in an American school, and 5) whether the active, book-conscious inquisitiveness of our literary *artigianato* was synonymous with freedom from ignorance out of which sprang a Sacco and a Vanzetti, and in which the antifascist militancy of an Arturo Giovannitti and a Carlo Tresca could not but logically and naturally prosper.

Such was the Italian American world I came to inherit, and which, eager as I was to prove that my deracination had been preordained long before my landing in New York, I willingly called mine. How or by whom I was introduced into the inner sanctum of such a world I do not recall. But most vividly I remember a dignified old man in whose presence I stood — or almost knelt — as Dante before his Cato of Utica. He was Antonio Calitri, a former priest from a little town in the province of Foggia who had married a Jewish woman in the Bronx, had been the first teacher of Italian in a New York high school, and — what meant more to me — had dared translate Shelley (of all poets) for the benefit of the Italian Americans.[12] Calitri's *Canti del Nord-America*,[13] with a preface by none other than Cerberus Prezzolini, is an important book of verse, not because of its author's classical background, which in the

---

[12] In the "Introduction" to his translation of Shelley's selected poems Calitri refers to the skepticism of Onorio Ruotolo's *Circolo*. He points out the difficulties of Shelley's poetry but does not doubt the existence of a reading audience, so to speak, among the Italians in this country.

[13] *Conti del Nord-America. Poesie di Antonio Calitri* con Prefazione di Giuseppe Prezzolini (Rome: Alberto Stock Editore, 1925). My personal copy bears the author's inscription "Al giovin poeta Giuseppe Tusiani che sale, il vecchio che scende, Antonio Calitri."

Carduccian rhetoric had found its most congenial habitat, but because of its unprecedented choice of themes — the Italian American life and death. To be sure, the grand old man had not been blessed with the proverbial poet's wing or he would not have needed H. G. Wells's *The Future in America* as a source for the most ambitious yet least successful poem in his collection;[14] yet he was the first to understand that a typically Italian American poetry had to disentangle itself from the pathetic fetters of the Italy-America sentimentalities, and, instead, concentrate all of its energies on the life of each Little Italy and on the heroism of our pioneers.

It was Antonio Calitri who, one Saturday afternoon, introduced me to Onorio Ruotolo. Ruotolo's studio, at 15 Union Square, would certainly not have met with Titian's approval; but our Italian American sculptor had never had the good fortune of finding a Pietro Aretino for the expansion of his influence. The not exorbitantly large room was cluttered with what you might call an artist's credentials — busts, sketches, easels, plaster, modeling clay, and chaos galore. Prominently displayed above other triumphant memorabilia was Vincenzo Gemito's ungrammatical yet heart-rending inscription to his American pupil. I suddenly remembered D'Annunzio's vindication of the indigent Neapolitan Master, not knowing that it had been Ruotolo's belligerent cry to provoke the intervention of the Principe di Montenevoso. There I was in an unpretentious artist's studio where busts of Caruso,[15] Dreiser, and Keller — art, literature, and history — were commingled in one fruitfulness of life. In that very studio, every Saturday afternoon, poets and artists met, rain or shine, for their familiar yet ever unpredictable get-together. Not knowing, that day, that Jack London had sat in the very chair Ruotolo had

---

[14] *Ibid.,* "Il Cantoniere," 101-14.
[15] It was a replica of the Caruso bust still in the lobby of the Metropolitan Opera House at Lincoln Center in New York. Incidentally, when *The Great Caruso* with Mario Lanza in the title role was being filmed, Onorio expected lavish royalties for the showing, at the very end of the film, of his bust. Something, however, went wrong in the negotiations. In order not to pay him, the producers showed another bust, which, as the viewers of the film can testify, resembles anyone but Enrico Caruso.

offered me, I was invited, for the following Saturday afternoon, to read a poem of mine — any poem, free verse or whatever — provided that it be my own contribution to the vitality of the group. Before I returned to the Bronx, Onorio Ruotolo presented me with his medal of Fiorello La Guardia's Inauguration. There was, on one side, the round, cherubic face of the new mayor; on the other, appeared the turbulence of the time which the sculptor's insight had boldly captured — Hercules burning with a blazy torch the mythical Hydra's menacing heads. The easy allegory (Fiorello versus Tammany Hall) was Ruotolo's best self-portrait. Herculean, leonine, tempestuous in speech and action, in his late sixties, he was still exuberantly youthful, even if his youthfulness showed at times the preciseness of a pose.[16] His fame had waned, and he seemed to know it; but his natural fabric being of uncommon, heroic texture, he balanced the loss of his past grandeur with a volcanic resourcefulness of ideas and enterprises. He loved to talk of the Leonardo da Vinci Art School which he and Arturo Piccirilli had founded with La Guardia's blessing.[17] He relished his past association with Caruso, Valentino, Helen Kel-ler, Theodore Dreiser, and Jack London, not because he cared to bask in an alien light but simply because he knew that one important ray of that multiple splendor had truly been his. The role of "pontifex maximus", which he seemed to cherish, was made for him much easier by those in his presence who, unable to detect the limitations of his culture,[18] as if transfixed listened to his every word as well as by

---

[16] See Frances Winwar, *Onorio Ruotolo, a Monograph,* with illustrations, reprinted in the Bicentennial issue of *La Parola del Popolo* of Chicago, 1976.

[17] No thesis has yet been written on the cultural and artistic impact of the "Leonardo da Vinci Art School" of New York, founded by Attilio Piccirilli and Onorio Ruotolo. Its former students, now scattered everywhere, should be interviewed. Some of them may still have the special commemorative publication on the activity and vitality of the School, which Gabriele D'Annunzio endorsed with an enthusiastic message from his Vittoriale degl'Italiani in Gardone Riviera, Italy.

[18] Onorio's literary taste remained within the boundaries of flamboyant Ottocento rhetoric as one can easily see from the quality of verse he now and then published in *La Lucerna, La Follia,* and *Divagando.* Of classical literatures he knew very little, yet he was able to acquire a smattering of stimulating conversation topics. John Macy, the well-known American critic, invited him to illustrate his *The Story of the World's Literature,* published by Horace Liveright Co. in 1925.

those who, from the first moment aware of the perilousness of the pedestal, out of prudence and respect treated the statue gently. In sum, Onorio Ruotolo was one of those men who can even make their faults look beautiful and endearing. For he was, above all, action personified.

The regular members of Ruotolo's Circolo were Antonio Calitri, Italo Stanco of *La Follia*,[19] Oscar Mazzitelli, a former student of the Leonardo da Vinci Art School, Salvatore Viola, ever dreaming of opening up a bookstore in the Village, Pietro Greco, a poet of the *sottobosco*, and I, the youngest and the only one with a doctor's degree in letters — an insignificant detail that most likely convinced them not to take the taciturnity of my nature as a sign of mental ineptitude. And there were also the irregular members — unexpected guests, artists, writers, and even occasional models who, having come for an appointment with the sculptor, found themselves forced by him to sit through the meeting; and if they were naive enough to say that they did not understand Italian — the official language of the "Circolo" — Onorio would imperially reply: "L'italiano lo capiscono tutti: basta volere." It was as simple as that: mind over matter. Such was, indeed, the man. In one of those Saturday-afternoon sessions Onorio announced his newest plan — the publication of the "Quaderni del Circolo." He had already worked out the minutest details — printing cost, distribution, selling price, and, last but not least, the subjects to be treated. The first Quaderno would be his own Italian translation of Arturo Giovannitti's *The Walker*, preceded by a scathing invective against Emilio Cecchi, "quel farabutto che ha sempre voluto ignorare il nostro Arturo." The second would deal with the poetry of Emily Dickinson, and not only was I the one to write it but I was also instructed to present my finished product in two weeks' time — time enough for an epic, so thought Onorio. Thus, I was compelled to reread Emily Dickinson's *opera omnia*, not knowing at the

---

[19] Italo Stanco (a pseudonym meaning "The Weary, Disgusted Italian") is the author of several novels and short stories in Italian. He was still active in 1952, the year in which *Divagando* published serially his novel *Rettili d'oro* together with his caustic, bitter but always brilliant column entitled "Quest'è il mondo, folle e tondo."

time that my new, passionate research would someday bear fruit not in America but in Italy. The first "Quaderno," published by Editore Morgillo, came out as planned in the Fall of 1950. On the back cover of Ruotolo's translation of Giovannitti's "The Walker"[20] — now a collector's item — were announced the other works in progress. The series, alas, was soon afterwards relegated to the limbo of good intentions, which only meant that Ruotolo's mind had been left free for pastures new. Of his numberless plans or initiatives, I will mention three more — the three major ones, that is, without which my Italian American experience would not have been so rich as it continues to be.

Also in the same year, it was Onorio who made sure that I would remember the first centennial of William Wordsworth's death. To my amazement, he had not forgotten the poet of my doctoral dissertation. In *La Lucerna*, therefore, I published a commemorative article in which, rather hastily, I summarized the salient points of a thesis from which I had most strangely diverted my attention.[21] But something else occurred in that fateful 1950. After reading to the group an article he had just completed on the trials and triumphs of Vincenzo Gemito, his Neapolitan teacher, Ruotolo peremptorily said to me, "When you go home, start thinking of 'un poema' on Gemito." He used, I remember, the term "poema," not "poesia." The first centenary of the Master's birth was still a year and a half ahead, but Onorio had already alerted Alberto Viviani in Florence for a special issue of *Divagando* with articles, illustrations, and a "Canzone celebrativa." I did not have time to resent being treated like one of the *sottobosco* who could be given exact measurements for a poem as for a

---

[20] Onorio's translation of Giovannitti's poem came out with the title "Il Camminante," which I did not, and do not, like. I told Onorio the reasons for my objections to such an unfelicitous present participle awkwardly transmuted into a substantive which the Italian ear could hardly tolerate. Onorio, of course, did not heed my philological scruples. Asked point-blank if I had a better solution, I had to admit that "Colui che cammina" was much too long, and even prosaic, to suit our immediate purpose. "Il Camminante," therefore, remained as suggested by the translator.

[21] *La Lucerna* (gennaio 1950): 29-30.

suit. Having taught history of art as a university student in Italy, I did not have to fall in love with Gemito's "Acquaiolo and Pescatorello," nor had I forgotten D'Annunzio's magnificent apotheosis of the "vittoria" and "gemito" already prefigured in the Master's very name. The seed that had long lain deep in my mind was nearing fruition at last. My "Canzone di Vincenzo Gemito" (the employment of the terza rima was probably still linked to my admiration of D'Annunzio's Canzone in Morte di Giuseppe Verdi) appeared in the special issue of *Divagando* together with Viviani's and Ruotolo's articles.[22] All this, I know, is quite irrelevant, even considering that, at twenty-six years of age, I had not yet learned to rid my verse of the turgidity of its classical origin and training. But, in spite of its resounding richness or glittering opulence, that Canzone was noticed by an old poet living in seclusion but not unaware of the young voices rising from New York. A few days later, a letter arrived with the praise and blessing of Arturo Giovannitti, who, with a most delicate and almost anachronistic gesture of tenderness, even sent me a laurel leaf whereby crowning and welcoming me to his world of glory.[23]

Arturo Giovannitti — the poet, the legend! Of course, I hastened to thank him as a young poet would — with a wreath of sonnets, dedicated to him, in which as in a frenzy I had blended my pride, my admiration, my gratitude, and my awareness of his song and soul. The ensuing correspondence with the poet of "The Walker" made Ruotolo happy. "Ed ora che si fa?" he asked me one day, almost puzzled by his own question. I did not understand. "Andiamo o non andiamo a trovarlo?" he said, anticipating my reply. Why didn't I think of it?

My first visit to Arturo Giovannitti — with Onorio Ruotolo as my Vergil — had none of the glamor I had expected. As I had not been forewarned, I was psychologically not ready to face a spectacle of

---

[22] *Divagando* (6 agosto 1952): 19
[23] At this late reading I realize that my correspondence with Arturo Giovannitti preceded by at least one year the Gemito canzone. At least three of his letters to me are dated 1951.

suffering so reminiscent of yet so different from the sight of devastation and death that had been the unnatural background to my youth. Because it is easy, and even logical, to feign a poet as the physical embodiment of his poetry, I had envisioned Arturo as the tall, handsome, fiery fighter of Lawrence, Massachusetts. But there he lay, half-paralyzed, immobile — the ghost of his own past.[24] Had it not been for something commanding in his voice and, most especially, in his eyes, I would have failed to link that inconspicuous mound of human flesh to the battling angel of my prenatal days. I am sure I replied to all the questions Arturo asked me, but I dared ask him none. I was glad that, more than ever loquacious and torrential, Onorio monopolized the conversation. As they meandered in reciprocal delight from one topic to another (Antonini, Bellanca, Montana, Crivello, Viviani of *Divagando*, Scilla de Glauco of *La Lucerna*, Marziale Sisca of *La Follia*, etc.), I could not help seeing in Arturo a strange and almost inevitable mixture of literary and historical resemblances. If I concentrated on his roundish face to which a smooth reddish beard seemed to add distinction, I saw Garibaldi and wondered how in the world or for what inexplicable reasons he had come to rest from all his battles in a small New Jersey town. If I looked at his shoulders, which a tiny pillow propped underneath somehow made larger, I thought of Dante's Farinata "da la cintola in su." But it was that special light in his eyes that I could not at first associate with anything I had heard or read about him. It was the poet's far-reaching glance, searching for regions of superhuman serenity and peace. To this day, I knew I was not wrong in thinking of Francis of Assisi. This unsuspected facet of Arturo Giovannitti's personality I was destined to know better in future years. At the end of that first visit I sensed that a new important relationship had just begun to enrich my life. I became Arturo's last and youngest friend, almost his spiritual son and, certainly (if I am allowed to use this term), his protege.[25]

---

[24] For a fuller account of my first encounter with Giovannitti see the August 1974 issue of *La Parola del Popolo*.
[25] In one of his letters Arturo called me "figliuolo." In his latest book, *Molise, Molise* (Isernia: Marinelli Editrice, 1979) Giose Rimanelli writes of Joseph Tusiani "disce-

Joseph Tusiani • "The Making of an Italian American Poet"

Fate — or should I say Providence? — gave me the joyous privilege of comforting, if not gladdening, the last fifteen years of the poet's life.[26] Within walking distance from my house in the Bronx, every week I visited him in his new and final residence — an inexpensive basement which Florence, his never-smiling yet adoring companion and nurse, had quickly transformed into a welcoming little home. Every Wednesday evening, that is, as if performing a ritual, I sat near his bed, listening or reading poems to him. Of course, resorting to all the subtleties of my intellect, I tried to extract from him precious details of the Lawrence trial; my ever more obvious curiosity, however, never found an ally in his ever more devious postponement of the subject. I finally understood that Arturo, who was his past, did not live in the past. His mind, which had enriched an age, refused to draw sustenance from its own riches. Only the present seemed to engage his interest, and the present was now to him the poetry of the world such as Saint Francis had seen and sung. I even told him, on one occasion, that I should perhaps call him Brother Francis. "Brother Juniper," he retorted, utterly pleased, and, "Why don't you write a poem on Brother Juniper preaching in Times Square?" he added in earnest.[27] Many a time he had little things for me to take home — a flower from one of his vases, a box of candy, a tiny reproduction of Memmo's portrait of Petrarch, a first edition of *La Figlila di Jorio*, a small bunch of fresh basil, a bottle of home-made wine, etc. The exquisiteness of his giving was ever greater than the gift itself.[28] Destroyed as it was, his life had become his noblest poem. No, he had not grown accustomed to his pain, noticeably more excruciating with each passing Wednesday; but such was the fortitude

---

polo di Giovannitti che pure abitava nel Bronx, e che ha lasciato tanta parte di se fra questi alveari di case." See, 182-83.

[26] In my account, published in *La Parola del Popolo*, I even mentioned the name of the physician I convinced to visit Arturo on a weekly basis for a nominal fee.

[27] My Poem, "Saint Francis in Times Square," appears in my first collection of verse, *Rind and All* (New York: The Monastine Press, 1962).

[28] Five days before he died, Arturo sent me a Christmas gift a box of candy with a card the symbolism of which I have tried to decipher in the above-mentioned article published in *La Parola*.

of his inner life that no physical suffering, however unbearable, could subdue his spirit. Was it stoicism? Or was it faith? Was Arturo Giovannitti once again the seminarian he had been in his youth? The last ten years of Arturo's life coincided with the first ten of my literary productivity, which officially began with the publication of "The Return," the poem which won the Greenwood Prize of the Poetry Society of England. Jotted down in pencil with shaky hand, the last page Arturo ever wrote is entitled, "G. T., poeta britannico."[29] But two other important events had in the meantime happened in my life.

With the impulsiveness that was his trademark Onorio Ruotolo told me, I believe in the summer of 1951, that I was to — rather, had to — write a short introductory note to "Le Gebbie," a poem by Giuseppe Antonio Borgese which he had read in a small Italian magazine and wanted to see reprinted in *La Parola del Popolo* of Chicago. Needless to say, he had already informed Egidio Clemente, its editor, who, in turn, was already waiting for my piece. Mondadori was at the time reissuing Borgese's *Poesie* of 1922 — an event that, according to Ruotolo and Clemente, deserved public recognition.[30] I wrote my brief introductory note and sent it on to Chicago. As Onorio would put it, it was, once again, as simple as that. But I had not thought that Borgese, the author of *Rube* and *La vita e il libro*, would enter my life because of that one page I had rather hesitantly written. "Le Gebbie" was reprinted in *La Parola*,[31] and Onorio's "bollenti spiriti" were appeased. Borgese's letter came a month or so later. When it rains, do you doubt the rain? So how could I not believe my own eyes? My twenty-seven years of age leapt up with joy — to re-echo my Wordsworth — and I am sure God in heaven forgave me for memorizing, at first reading, these two sentences from that very first of Borgese's several letters to me: "Lei è critico che aggiunge pensiero

---

[29] Giovannitti's last article, whose original hand-written copy is still in my possession, appeared in *La Parola* (Fall 1957), and was reprinted in the same magazine, August 1974.

[30] See *Poesie*, Giuseppe Antonio Borgese (Milan: Mondadori, 1952). The poem, "Le Gebbie," had appeared in an issue of the Neapolitan magazine, *Realtà*, co-edited by Lionella Fiumi.

[31] *La Parola,* May 1952.

al pensiero e canto al canto," and "Spero in una Sua collaborazione."[32] Let me at once assure you that it was the second of the two phrases that made me aware of new vistas to scan and new horizons to reach. Eager to know what sort of collaboration Borgese had in mind for me, feverishly I began to study the man I did not know — the Borgese of his American exile, his antifascist activity, his association with Luigi Sturzo, Gaetano Salvemini, and Lauro de Bosis.[33] Thus a new world opened up for me. Or was it rather the world of Arturo Giovannitti, Onorio Ruotolo, and Carlo Tresca that I had come to know better and more intimately? Now I was part of that world, and even felt worthy of Borgese's trust in me. Before I opened his letter of September 8, 1952 (there had meanwhile been an exchange of unpublished poems and critical evaluations), my temerity had made me picture myself already at work on a book that was to be by Borgese and Tusiani. Giuseppe Antonio Borgese wanted to meet me, but, as I read that letter over and over again, I trembled at the thought of meeting him. I envisioned myself utterly silent or at best pathetically babbling before such a man. Little did I know that lurking death had called me to witness and record Borgese's last hour in America.

On the evening of September 11, at Rocco's Restaurant in New York's Greenwich Village, for the first and last time I met the Maestro. There was the piercing light of his glance (I had been told it reminded one of Mazzini's eyes) flashing the power of his mind ever before his word, slow and nearly stony, could reveal it.[34] Around him, at the central table sat Thomas Mann's youngest daughter Elizabeth, Borgese's wife, with their two young daughters, Angelica and Domenica, Mr. Augusto Bellanca, Mrs. Ruotolo, Onorio (in whose studio the Maestro had recently posed for a portrait-bust), and three other gentlemen whose names I have regretfully forgotten. Onorio,

---

[32] Borgese's handwritten letters to me are now in the private archives of Professor Tommaso Nardella, Preside della Scuola Media "Giovanni Pascoli" in San Marco in Lamis, Foggia, Italy.
[33] Borgese's *Goliath* is one of the most important antifascist documents in the history of our immigration.
[34] In his *Poesie*, Borgese makes reference to the hypnotic power of his eyes.

the dynamic architect of the dinner honoring Giuseppe Antonio on the eve of his return to democratic Italy and his "cattedra" at the University of Firenze, graciously (and, let me add, intentionally) surrendered his own chair to me so that I could sit next to the honored guest. Those first minutes — or were they seconds? — seemed unbearable. Giuseppe Antonio Borgese had nothing of the literary man about him. Rather short, broad-shouldered, dark· complexioned, and with his lower lip forcefully protruding, he could have passed for an anti-Savoian bandit of his native Sicily. His most noticeable feature was, indeed, the hypnotic power of his eyes, which enabled him to observe, and become, unobserved, his own observation. Had it not been for Augusto Bellanca,[35] whose remarks in perfect Sicilian made the Maestro smile, I would probably have felt utterly crushed under the magnetism of those tow eyes fixed upon me. The sound of his Sicilian dialect suddenly, almost miraculously, brought Borgese down to this world — and to me. While the other guests resumed their conversation, to which the two little girls added a silvery pitch of their own, the Maestro said, addressing me as if I were his entire audience: "Last night I wrote a poem to my Mother which I would like you to hear."

After a brief silence, looking straight ahead, and acknowledging someone else's presence — his own mother called back to life by his desperate love — he began to recite a few lines, scanning them slowly and filling each pause with subtleties of untold meanings:

> Il fotografo che ti ritrasse non disse:
> "Sorrida! S'inumidisca un poco ii labbro!"
> Perche eri pura e triste ...
> Sano passato per ii tuo corpo
> per venire a questa luce,
> ch'è già lunga ... e cala ...
> Che ne sarà? ... Mamma! ...[36]

---

[35] His more famous brother, Giuseppe, is linked to the history of American aviation.
[36] It is possible that I have forgotten a line or a hemstitch, but the lines that I quote are, to the best of my knowledge, very accurate. The slow and solemn severity

The long pause that broke the last line was heart-breaking. Though surrounded by admiring friends, Borgese was all alone at the threshold of a world one must enter alone. Fortunately, at that moment, he did not turn to me for help but to another of his own thoughts — better yet, to God:

Io non ho nulla.
Quel che ho mi fu data da Te in prestito.
Ed ecco io a Te lo rendo, Signore![37]

He himself had thus solved the problem which no one else could ever have solved for him. So, when he asked me, "Do you like it?" it was easy for me to reply, thinking of the parable of the talents, "It's a prayer." "But art is prayer," he concluded with a smile. A half hour later, as we were waiting for the taxi with Onorio, who always thought of everything, had already called, the Maestro and I knew that, although no word had been said of any collaboration, we had come to know each other well enough to speak of it on some less noisy or more intimate occasion. As his taxi pulled off toward the Fairfax Hotel where he and his family were staying for the night, Giuseppe Antonio Borgese waved at me, saying, "Mi scriva a Fiesole. Ci vedremo in aprile." I wrote to him, but when, at the end of the following November, my letter reached Fiesole, that "luce," which was already "lunga," was "calata" forever.[38]

Fate had robbed me of the opportunity to work with a glorious Master. But I did not know, in the depth of my bereavement, that the same Fate was soon to bring into my life the person that would completely and irrevocably change it — a famous writer who was

---

with which they were scanned by the author allowed me to memorize them at once before I transcribed them, that very evening, in my diary.
[37] See "Introduzione" to *Poesie*.
[38] In my last letter to Borgese I inquired whether all of his poems in English, which he had sent me still unpublished for an opinion, had already been translated by Liliana Scalero, whose name he had mentioned to me in one of his previous letters. After his death, in the commemorative issue of Piero Calamandrei's *Il Ponte*, I saw some of those poems translated into Italian.

also a stunningly beautiful woman. I must, once more then, mention Onorio Ruotolo, who — this time more appropriately though still unknowingly — was truly my Galeotto.

A few days after Borgese's death, which coincided with that of Benedetto Croce, his friend and foe, I saw Onorio so frantic as I had never seen him before. Almost literally out of his wits, he laid a tiny book in front of me, screaming, "What about this? What about this?" When lava and lapilli came to a halt, I was able to understand that a full year had passed from the publication of that tiny book and that no one had as yet reviewed it for *La Parola* of Chicago. "So, do a great job," Onorio concluded. "First, it's a book about us, and second, it's by the greatest writer we Italian Americans have." It was *The Land of the Italian People* by Frances Winwar, a book for children, one of the Portraits of the Nations Series of the J.B. Lippincott Company of Philadelphia and New York.[39] Jokingly, I said to Onorio, "Thy will be done."

My short review appeared in *La Parola* in the Spring of 1953. I did not know much about Frances Winwar. More than once I had seen her name in the Book Review Section on *The New York Times*, but of her works I had read only one, *La vita del cuore*, the biography of George Sand, in the Longanesi translation of 1946. Being, therefore, blissfully ignorant of the massiveness of her production and, consequently, unaware of the importance of her name, I did not touch, as Dante would say, "Li termini de la beatitudine" when I received from Middletown Springs, Vermont, a letter by which she thanked me for some constructive suggestions in my review. Yet the codicil to that letter ("I hope to know you when I come back to New York in August") meant to me a tacit command to learn all I could about one who "hoped to know," rather than simply see, me. Thus, I began to read, and finished by studying, her. Her first book, *The Ardent Flame*,[40] a novel based on the story of Francesca and Gianciotto da Rimini, made me discover a stylist of supreme quality long before I read that Thomas Mann had already called her "the

---

[39] It was published in 1951.
[40] *The Ardent Flame*. A novel by Frances Winwar (New York: The Century Co., 1927).

greatest English stylist of the twentieth century." In her style (a perfect combination of poetic inventiveness and elegance of diction) I recognized my most perfect and most ideal model of English prose — that of Sir Thomas Browne's *Urn Burial*. Such a discovery was a turning point in my education, for, without any doubt, but with irrepressible enthusiasm I switched from my old English classics to my new one. Of this sudden switch, let me give just one example. To understand the magic more than the mechanics of the English language, I would take a sentence by a master, split it, rearrange it, analyze it in every noun and nuance, thus to arrive at detecting the reasons why a particular word, and not another, had been used. In his *Lady Chatterley's Lover*, D.H. Lawrence introduces a hen with a chick restlessly pacing around her. But notice how, by employing monosyllabic terms, he depicts the mobility and agility of the latter, and how, by resorting to three bi-syllabic opposites, he captures the immobility and steadiness of the former: "There was a tiny, tiny perky chick, prancing round in front of the coop, and the mother hen clucking in terror." Now, this sort of critical vivisection I began to do with Frances Winwar's sentences and paragraphs. Struck by her hypnotic rhythms, I would even rewrite some of her pages in a metrical form so as to convince myself that the line of demarcation between verse and prose was, in her case, most negligible if at all apparent. For instance, this paragraph from *The Golden Round*, a novel about Pier della Vigna:

> Under the palms beside the fountain
> she twined pomegranate with orange blossoms
> in alternate hues of white and flame,
> making a chaplet of pale and fiery stars;
> and neatly she bound it
> with long strands of palm leaf.
> As she wove it she murmured
> a sad Eastern song of a maiden
> that gave her heart for a flower,

only to find in its core
the canker of death.⁴¹

I heartily agreed with what *The New York Times* had said of her: "A poet in prose. The prose has a cadence in it that would make appealing reading whatever the subject." Was it, then, the poet in her that instinctively drew me to her world? In this spirit, therefore, I read all that Franees Winwar had published until 1953: *Pagan Interval* (1929), another novel of Italian interest; *Poor Splendid Wings* (1933), the life of Dante Gabriel Rossetti and the Pre-Raphaelites, which won the Atlantic Monthly Award and gave her national prominence; *The Romantic Rebels* (1935), a biography of Byron, Keats and Shelley; *Gallows Hill* (1937), a novel inspired by the Salem witchcraft; *Farewell the Banner* (1938), a biography of Wordworth and Coleridge: *Oscar Wilde and the Yellow Nineties* (1940); *The American Giant* (1941), a biography of Walt Whitman; *The Life of the Heart: George Sand and Her Times* (1946); *The Saint and the Devil: Joan of Arc and Gilles de Rais* (1948), and *The Immortal Lovers* (1950), a biography of Elizabeth and Robert Browning. I also read, and studied, her translation of Boccaccio's *Decameron* (1950), a masterpiece that made me realize that, should I in the future ever wish to translate an Italian classic into English, there would be no other path to follow than her synthesis of faithfulness and fervor.

All this proves, I suppose, that I was ready to meet, after my long study and great love, my living classic (only the masculine gender prevents me from saying "tu duca, tu signore e tu maestro"). Years later I was to learn that Frances, too, had in the meantime done her bit of research. She had managed to find and read all my juvenilia—*Amedeo di Savoia, Flora, Amore e Morte, Petali sull'Onda, Peccato e Luce,* and the various lyrics scattered in the New York periodicals.⁴²

The fated month of August arrived, and I confess that I had numbered the hours and minutes that still severed me from the

---

⁴¹ *The Golden Round* (New York: The Century Co., 1928) 147.
⁴² See *Joseph Tusiani: A Bibliography* (On the 30th year of his Professorship in the U.S.). Compiled and edited by Pasquale Perretta. Fordham University, March 25, 1979.

source of my intellectual enchantment. When, finally, I met Frances Winwar at the Royalton Hotel in New York (in the elevator, I remember, I even rehearsed a phrase to tell her), I stood so speechless before her that I could only do what I would never have done had I been, as the Latins would say, *compos mei*: most awkwardly, that is, as if desirous to rid myself of a cumbersome object, I placed a bouquet of long-stemmed roses in her hands, simply saying, "To Frances Winwar." With a smile she accepted the gift, simply answering, "From Joseph Tusiani."

That very evening, I was categorically told what I would never have expected to hear from the Frances Winwar that I had come to idolize: "If you love and care for what the Italians are and have done in America and for America, you must say goodbye to them." I was so confused that, in order to conceal my perplexity, I asked her, half facetiously and · half impertinently, "Why did you change your name?" Her answer was disarming: "After I proof-read my first book, my publisher called me on the telephone. My name, Vinciguerra, did not fit on the spine of the little volume. So I was asked to think of a pseudonym. On the spur of the moment, I translated 'Vinciguerra' into 'Winwar,' which, you must agree, was quite a reduction in syllables." There was in her words and in her attitude such genuine love for Italy and the Italians that I still could not understand the gravity of her request. What did she mean by it? What was her fear? She meant that were I to remain within the province of the Italian American community as such, I would not have the opportunity to see its life on a larger scale. Her fear was that were I to continue being active in and for it, I would no longer be aware of the very activity around me. Frances was even more blunt in her warning: "If you remain in Ruotolo's little world — and you know how fond of Onorio I am — you will never write in English. I hate to think of you eventually playing *tressette* with your admiring *compari*." But Frances was too intelligent not to be fully aware of the painfulness of my dilemma; therefore, motivated by her boundless faith in my future, she was even ready to sacrifice part of her own future in order to hasten the liberation of myself from myself.

Before I count, so to speak, the ways by which she "Americanized" me, I must for a brief moment return to the world from which she was determined to detach me for my own sake. It is true that I felt admired in the various Italian American little clubs where *autoincensamento* seemed to be the unwritten rule — indeed a most poisonous air for a thirty-year-old writer to breathe. We must always strive for success, and never believe we have achieved it. But those wonderful barbers and tailors and bricklayers had begun to make me feel dependent on their praise and adulation, which they lavished upon me in their literary and artistic meetings. Every day, at noon, in his radio program on WOV, Giuseppe Sterni, the actor, would read a poem of mine which had appeared in *La Lucerna* or in some other magazine. It was easy for me to believe in my "mission accomplished" whereas I had not yet even discovered the fullness of my potential or where that initial restlessness was to lead me. Frances Winwar, then, came into my life at the right moment. Her praise was the only nourishment I needed, her inspiration the only driving force.

She began her work by introducing me to the literary and artistic world that was America, the America around and beyond the Little Italy of my still little dreams. Thus, other minorities arose to my ken, strengthening the knowledge of the one to which Frances and I belonged. I discovered the Little Ireland of America in our frequent conversations with James T. Farrell, the author of *Studs Lonigan*, the Jewish life on the Atlantic coast in our not less frequent visits at Gustav Davidson's home, and the WASPS of this Continent at John Gunther's elaborate and ever supercilious social parties. At one of such parties, one evening Greta Garbo, who enjoyed sitting taciturn and inconspicuous in a corner of the large living room, told Frances that she was rereading her *Joan of Arc*, whereupon the author of *Death Be Not Proud* facetiously said, "But Greta hasn't even read one of my books in its entirety."[43]

---

[43] John Gunther, the famous author of *Inside America, Inside Europe*, etc. asked me to tell him whether the Mondadori translation of one of his books was as good as he had been assured it was. Jokingly he told Frances that he would not take her word for an answer. After all, he added, I was supposed to know Italian better than she did.

Frances Winwar's literary prominence, which was still at its peak, opened many other illustrious doors to her — and to me. Thus, John Koch, the painter, and Vergil Thompson, the composer of *Mother of Us All* and friend of Gertrude Stein, became two additional sources of knowledge and inspiration in my life. I have already published my account of an incident that almost wrecked one of John Koch's lavish parties.[44] One of the many guests was Misha Elman, the famous violinist who can be heard in the background of some of Caruso's early recordings. I did not know of the enmity between the Russian-born violinist and Arturo Toscanini; but Frances did. Whatever the causes of the ancient rancor, one-glass-too-many had made the old violinist somewhat loquacious and rather ranting. As soon as I was introduced to him (obviously my Italian name caused a chain-reaction in the few molecules of his grey matter not yet vanquished by the spirits of the brandy), he began to denigrate the legendary Maestro in a falsetto voice that resembled his own instrument still unattuned before a performance. Aghast, I looked at Frances, my new Vergil, not knowing what to do in the presence of an intoxicated old man or to be more accurate, not knowing how to reconcile, in a split second, my visible anger with my invisible pity. Had the strident Charon limited his barking at Toscanini alone, the incident would most likely have ended in its own pathetic pettiness; but, as soon as, sheepishly turning to the other guests, he said, "What do you expect from Italians?" the gaiety of the party came to a halt. In the sudden silence it was as though an entire nation desperately waited for an avenging voice. "Mr. Elman," Frances Winwar said out loud, looking much higher that the five-feet-tall woman that she was, "now let me tell these ladies and gentlemen what they do not know. Your personal fury is perfectly justifiable: you were never good enough for Arturo Toscanini. But lest you make of yourself a more laughable fool than you are, leave Italy and the Italians alone. You must not sin against the second commandment." Crawling like an insignificant little worm, the famous violinist, who did know that Frances Winwar was Italian, muttered some imperceptible sounds of

---

[44] See my article, "Frances Winwar," in the Bicentennial issue of *La Parola*.

apology while Mrs. Dora Kock with the rotundity of her frame tried to re-establish the convivial festivity so unexpectedly interrupted. I whispered to Frances, "Let's leave!" "No," she replied, "he should."[45]

It was a lesson to me. My "Americanization" was not to be an end to itself. Through it, instead, I was to return, with a fully American voice, to the Little Italy of my enlarged and more radiant vision. Indeed, Frances was far more subtle than I myself could see in the white fire of that first year of friendship. She made sure that I would never lose sight of my ultimate goal — the Italian American heritage that had brought us together.

That same year, the death of Dylan Thomas kept Frances for the first time busy at something that interfered with her own research. For *The Yale Literary Review* she translated my Italian poem, "In Morte di Dylan Thomas." She liked the elegy so well that she thought other people should hear it at once. So she invited Howard Marrara and Mario Pei to her apartment near Columbia University. To this day, I wonder how much those two dear souls, so totally engrossed in a world of their own from which poetry had long been banished, could care about the Welsh poet's untimely demise, let alone my lyrical remembrance of it. But after I presented the original text of the elegy, and she read her English rendering of it, she said to them, "I assure you that from now on my translation will not be needed." Even in this she proved to be most accurate. The grub was soon to turn into a full-grown butterfly.[46]

The year 1954 was marked by a singular event — our "gita boccaccevole" to Italy, for which Boccaccio provided the money and De Sanctis the easy adjective. The Winwar translation of the *Decameron* had just been reprinted by Random House for inclusion in its Modern Library Series, and, instead of distant royalties, Frances had accepted the immediate flat-fee of $1,500 — the right amount for her trip to D'Annunzio's Vittoriale without which her new biography would not have been possible. The "gita" was my first

---

[45] *Ibid.*, 184.
[46] "For Dylan Thomas on the Day of His Death." Translated by Frances Winwar. *The Yale Literary Magazine*, CXXII, 2 (1954), Pp. 23-6.

nostos to my Gargano after seven years of severance and search.[47] Surely Frances had foreseen what I perhaps had not — that I had once more to touch and feel my own roots in order to find the best in me. When I joined her at Gardone Riviera, after a few days in my native Apulia, I could hardly recognize the Frances I knew. She had quietly ransacked the entire library of the Vittoriale. It was a joy and a constant source of inspiration to see her there, from early morning till late afternoon, going from one shelf to another, deciphering, annotating, reading, filling cards, begging for a Xeroxed copy of this or that page, discovering an important date, and always eager to detect what had possibly escaped other readers' eyes. I shall never forget the enthusiasm with which, after a long laborious day, she described to me her latest discovery — the word "Canossa" clearly legible over the door of the Priory at the Vittoriale. Not one of D'Annunzio's biographers had ever paid attention to the profound implication of that one word in the mock coat-of-arms the poet was obliged to look at whenever he crossed the threshold of his own home: a plaque showing a dog rampant with, at its feet, a bone. Her explanation is now in Wingless Victory: "The rebus is simple — *Canossa* from *can*, the Italian for dog, and *ossa*, bones. Also, in designing that coat-of-arms the Dante scholar (D'Annunzio) had not overlooked the reference in the Sixth Canto of the *Inferno* where the watchdog Cerberus is hushed by the handful of earth flung into its jaws. The bitter joke is typical of D'Annunzio's unsparing irony, particularly toward himself. Significantly, he had set up the plaque after Mussolini's visit accepting the Vittoriale for the nation. Perhaps there was also meaning in the replica of Michelangelo's "Captive" in his bedroom, whose confining band D'Annunzio had carefully gone over with gold paint. A prisoner but

---

[47] On the "Roma" of the Flotta Lauro there were two officers who gave Frances the benefit of their personal recollections of Eleonora Duse's funeral in 1924. They are duly mentioned and thanked in her *Wingless Victory*. Also, on the same ship, there were Robert Merrill of the Metropolitan Opera House and Vergil Thompson traveling with us.

with shackles of gold."⁴⁸ *Wingless Victory*, the dual biography of D'Annunzio and Duse, is dedicated to me with this Latin phrase, "To Joseph Tusiani: mentis sitim cordis gratia satiasti" — the same words, that is, with which I had already dedicated my collection of Latin poems, *Melos Cordis*, to Frances.⁴⁹ Some of my remarks had gone into the book just as some of hers were now shaping the imagery of my new poetry.⁵⁰

It was also at Gardone Riviera, I remember, that, in the excitement of a creative accomplishment, I snatched her from the Russian birth certificate of Donatella Cross⁵¹ to read to her my ode, "M'ascolti tu, mia Terra?" She listened to it, asked me to read it again and slowly, and finally commented: "This is your true voice. Now you know how Italy and America can become one in a poet's exaltation." Two years later, in her new apartment (76th Street and Central Park) I read to her the definitive draft, this time in English, of the same poem. Trying to conceal the depth of her emotions, she simply said, "May I keep this?" "Of course, you may," I replied, far from imagining what she would do with it. What she actually did with it transformed my life. Six months afterwards, precisely on March 24, 1957, *The New York Times* announced that I had won the Greenwood Prize of the Poetry Society of England for my poem, "The Return," and, also, that I was the first American poet ever to be awarded such a prize. When the telephone rang, that morning, to convey the congratulations of Father Giulivo Tessarolo, the General of the Scalabrinians

---

⁴⁸ *Wingless Victory*, a Biography of D'Annunzio and Duse (New York: Random House, 1955) was translated into Italian with the title *Con D'Annunzio di fuoco in fuoco* (Milan: Mondadori, 1956).

⁴⁹ *Melos Cordis*. Poems in Latin by Joseph Tusiani. Apud Venetian Press, 1955.

⁵⁰ At my suggestion Cesare Foligno, Alfredo Galletti, and Lionello Fiumi were asked by Frances to give their personal impressions of Gabriele D'Annunzio. Also, in her book Frances utilized the private correspondence of Angelo Pisone, my uncle killed in action in 1917.

⁵¹ It was Lionello Fiumi, whom I had introduced to Frances, that revealed to her the tragic story of Donatella Cross's last days in Paris — how he was able to suggest to the Russian countess, D'Annunzio's former mistress, the sale of his letters to a Jewish merchant. Incidentally, in her research of Vittoriale Frances discovered that, contrary to Donatella's pathetic lies to Lionello, D'Annunzio had more than once sent her money.

in Staten Island, I was, to say the least, flabbergasted. In my bewilderment I called Frances — whom else? — to tell her of what I had just heard. Only I do not recall how I told her what I had just heard. Surely, I must have been quite inarticulate, if not utterly incoherent, if, most Olympian in her serenity, she simply said "Calm down. I've seen the *Times*. It was I who submitted the poem, and it was I who knew that no one else could win." She was a miracle of faith. Still, I would not have believed *The New York Times* had I not received, that very day, a telegram from Thomas Moult, president of the Poetry Society of England. The doubting Thomas in me was finally convinced when, sometime later, I found in the mail a copy of *The Poetry Review of London* with my two-hundred lines in it, together with a check that for a few sentimental days I did not dare to cash.[52]

The Greenwood Prize, which I owe to Frances's almost blind belief in my poetry, caused other events to occur in my life — my vice-presidency in the Poetry Society of Americas[53] and my directorship in the Catholic Poetry Society of America.[54] Most especially, it gave me the self-confidence I sorely needed for the day when I would no longer be under Frances Winwar's wing. Dante's lines from *Paradiso*, "Non dei più ammirar, se bene *stimo* / lo tuo salir, se non come d'un rivo/ se d'alto monte scende giuso ad imo" suddenly became the most significant motto I could ever choose for spurring myself to more and more work, regardless of human appreciation or praise.

In *Spirit, The Catholic World, The Sign, The New York Times,* and, especially, in *The New York Herald Tribune,* I outpoured my new vitality. Needless to say, among the first poems I published after my Greenwood Prize was one entitled "To Frances." I do not really

---

[52] See *The Poetry Review*. The Official Publication of the Poetry Society of England, London. 48.4 (October-December 1957): 234-36.
[53] From 1959 to 1969. In this period, I was the recipient of the Society's highest award, the Alice Fay di Castagnola Prize, for a play in verse, *If Gold Should Rust*, based on Baretti's homicide in eighteenth-century London.
[54] From 1958 to 1969 I was director of the Catholic Poetry Society of America in whose official magazine of verse, *Spirit,* I published the best of my poems. I was the last recipient of the Society's "Spirit Gold Medal."

know if the following verses succeed in capturing a world in which two minds entrance each other in their daily enterprises, and two souls enhance each other in the fullness of their giving:

> When I was earth two worlds ago, and you,
> Two heavens ago, were light; when I was valley
> Changelessly green, and you were harmless breath
> Of godhead over me, and all was new,
> How did I thank you then? I know the sense
> Was gladness inarticulate, first creeping
> Into the soul when I awoke, that morning,
> A brief and breathing heart, a glance of wonder,
> And saw you in a bush — you, space and time,
> Transmuted into narrowness of bloom.
> Ah, worlds have gone and heavens ever since,
> And I have not yet found what word is best
> To tell the joy of your caressing hand.[55]

In the Autumn of 1956, Frances and I paid a visit to Daniel Santoro in Staten Island. Unfortunately, and unjustly forgotten, Daniel Santoro is a man to whom all Italian Americans should raise a monument. He devoted and sacrificed a lifetime and a fortune for the re-evaluation of two major Italian glories in this country — Verrazzano and Meucci. On that beautiful and mild October day (the Indian summer was making of Staten Island a particularly sparkling jewel), he placed in front of Frances and me a precious pile of papers and documents concerning Meucci and his "telettrofono." We stood there, speechless, in awe. Mr. Santoro, then, simply said: "Take it and do something. Let people know. Let people know." Through innumerable trips to Washington and other American cities he had collected the most important letters, written by Meucci himself or by some of his friends, and now the whole treasure was there before us, ours to take home and use as we pleased. We were still too stunned to accept the offer, but he insisted with such fervor that we had to

---

[55] *Spirit* (May 1957).

promise him that something had to be done to "let people know." On our way back to New York, Frances, who was at the time utterly immersed in one of her biographies, tried to convince me that I was the one to study and collate all that precious material for a monograph on Meucci. Instead, I succeeded in convincing her that, given the importance of the subject, her famous name would add to the seriousness of the project. Of course, Mr. Clemente, the editor of *La Parola del Popolo*, responded with his usual inexhaustible enthusiasm. Not only did he publish Frances Winwar's monograph but, to publicize it further, he issued reprints of it for the benefit of teachers and students here and abroad. Abroad, thanks to the vigilant attention of Cesare Basini, the monograph was translated into Italian and published by the Italian Government in one of its official Pubblicazioni dello Stato.[56] As you see, every new step into America brought me back to, instead of detaching me from, the land I had been told to forget in order to know and love more dearly.

Now, better than before, I was able to appreciate in all his greatness the solitary figure of Vincenzo di Crescenzo whose songs had been sung by Caruso, Schipa and Gigli. Timidly sitting at the piano in Lia Spezzano's home,[57] the white-haired Maestro seemed altogether unaware of his own fame as he tried to recapture on the keyboard the most popular chords of his past inspiration. Now, more than ever, I realized the charm of the ungrammatical pleasantries of a "Pasquale C.O.D." whose ethical warmth extended its radius from the daily radio programs of WOV in New York to the farthest Italian family in Connecticut. And now, only now was I able to understand why De Amicis's *Il cuore* was so popular among the Italian Ameri-

---

[56] See, Cesare Basini, *Raccolte di critiche e cronache d'arte* (Roma: Canesi, 1971) 235-39 and 255-56

[57] I was at the time romantically attached to "Cristina Garden," Lia Spezzano's beautiful daughter whose singing talent had already been recognized by Nick Kenny on several of his TV shows, and whose Italian repertory had endeared her to the Italian-speaking listeners of WOV. Maria (it was her real name) died of cancer in her late twenties. See, Lia Spezzano's *La mia Stella Caduta* (Rome: Angelo Signorelli Editore, 1970). It was in Lia Spezzano's home that I met Maestro Vincenzo De Crescendo, Cristina's mentor.

cans, and why, for instance, a poor laborer, named Nicola Testi, came to me for a preface to the work of his entire life — a verse translation of Dante's *Inferno* into the dialect of his native Foggia. Just think of it — of a man, that is, who, having spent his physical energies in a merciless factory, eagerly went home for the sole purpose of devoting his intellectual power to a task that would bring him nowhere except to the realization of a dream — Dante's first Cantica made accessible to the people of his distant Italian region.[58] Illiterate immigrants? It is not true. Those who were truly illiterate were also spiritually and mentally so dejected and debased as never to feel the need to emigrate for a better future. Those, instead, who did emigrate were people who read *Guerrino detto il Meschino, I Reali di Francia, Bertoldo Bertoldino e Cacasenno,* people like Vincent Bocchimuzzo[59] and Carmine B. Iannace who, whether or not encouraged their children, understood the importance of conveying their own *Scoperta dell'America* to others.[60] Even Frances' father knew that it was his duty to emigrate for the sake of his one- month-old baby girl.

During the next nine years of our friendship, Frances and I grew so attached to, and even so jealous of, each other's creativity that every page of her new biographies had to meet with my approval just as every line of my new poems had to be sanctioned by her sensitivity. Each spurred the other to more and better work, joyously, relentlessly, in an atmosphere of reciprocal fulfillment. When, on June 2, 1960, I presented Frances with the first copy of *The Complete Poems of Michelangelo* (the book is dedicated to her with the pentameter "And he has peace who yearns for it no more"), she said to me what only a woman of her caliber could have said, "What next?

---

[58] Poor Nicoli Testi did not see his work in print. He died suddenly while proofreading the first pages of his translation of Dante's *Inferno*. His son, of Trenton, New Jersey, realized his father's dream.

[59] Vincent Bocchimuzzo, who published several articles in *Divagando* and other magazines as "Il Vecchio della Montagna," bequeathed his papers to the Center for Migration Studies in Staten Island, NY. Maybe Vincent, Jr., should be urged to do some research on his remarkable grandfather.

[60] Carmine Biagio Iannace is the author of Uomini e *Galantuomini* (Firenze: Grafica Toscana, 1970) and *La Scoperta dell'America* (Padova: Dino Rebellato, 1971). The latter bears a preface by Michele Ricciardelli, founder and editor of *Forum Italicum*.

Why not the *Jerusalem*?" The following day she read to me the last chapter of her *Jean-Jacques Rosseau: Conscience of an Era*, and I read to her my verse translation of the first five *ottave* of Tasso's *Gerusalemme Liberata*.[61] Resting on one's laurels was not Winwar's motto. Maybe her very name, Vinciguerra, explained her vitality best.

By profession a man of Academia, I still cannot understand this phenomenon called Winwar. She did not attend any university (on the flap of some of her books Columbia is mentioned for sheer publicity's sake), did not have any classical training, was never instructed in methodology, did not study languages, and yet, at the age of thirty, she published the only American translation of the *Decameron*, which happens to be the best English rendering of Boccaccio's masterpiece. She spoke French, Spanish, German, Russian, and, of course, though with some adorable mistakes (such as *le muscole* for *i muscoli*), Italian. Her literary knowledge was vast, especially in the specific area of the nineteenth century — her forte. And almost instinctively she knew what to find in a library without ever wasting precious time. At D'Annunzio's Vittoriale, as I have already mentioned, every evening she had a new relevant discovery to share with me. Jokingly, one night, I called her "Sherlock Holmes." Yet this Frances Winwar was never truly accepted by and into Academe. The reason is simple — her style is too brilliant, and her presentation too inventive. It was exactly such brilliance and such inventiveness that ponderous pedants condemned first of all. "Quasi-novels" some of them called her biographies — but why? Her books do not lack the critical apparatus without which our dear Quintilians cannot find rest in their own little restlessness; but they — her books — are so vividly written, so clearly and magically presented in the development of every character and every chapter, that the reader becomes unaware of the line of demarcation between fact and fiction, history and legend. This is the reason why, unlike dusty scholars, creative men such as Thomas Mann, Lord Dunsany, G.K. Chersterton, Andre

---

[61] My verse translation of Tasso's masterpiece came out a few years later. See Tasso's *Jerusalem Delivered,* Translated into English verse and with an Introduction by Joseph Tusiani (Rutherford: Fairleigh Dickinson University Press, 1970).

Maurois, Padraic Colum, James T. Farrell, John Macy, Maurice Maeterlinck, and many more, praised her art.[62] And this is also the reason why Frances and I could understand each other so intimately. Or was she the Little Italy, the 'Gente Mia,' I had to discover and sing? Surely, she was the embodiment of the inborn genius of the Italian race, with its many wonders and wealth of initiatives.

Speaking of initiatives. One day, a little girl in her senior high-school year announced to her graduating class that Mr. Enrico Caruso of the Metropolitan Opera House should be asked to attend their Commencement ceremony. The same little girl volunteered to deliver a personal invitation to the great tenor. After all, she was Italian, and he was Italian. But the courageous young lady did not know that the man riding in the same elevator to Caruso's apartment was Caruso himself. "Where are you going, piccirella?" asked Don Enrico. "I'm going to invite Mr. Caruso to come to our school. I'm Italian, and he's Italian. If he refuses, I'll publish in our school paper an article that will destroy his career." "Mio Dio," Caruso replied, 'I'm sure he'll accept; he doesn't want to lose his job." You are free to imagine the little girl's surprise when, right at the door of Caruso's apartment, the same man told her, "I'm Caruso, piccirella. Will you still write that article if I say No?" "You'd better say Yes," answered the little girl, brave enough to point an intimidating finger at him. "Then I will come, and even sing at your school. But what's your name? After all, I'm entitled to know who my new manager is." "My name is Francesca Vinciguerra," replied the girl, triumphant. On Commencement Day Enrico Caruso sang the national anthem at Frances Winwar's High School.[63]

Did I say she was the embodiment of the spiritual resourcefulness of our "Italia raminga?" But the past tense should never be used in regard to the sap that nourishes the tree. Because the human spirit does not conclude itself, my report, which is a testimonial to

---

[62] It would be interesting to peruse the hundreds of reviews of Frances Winwar's work (and many foreign translations thereof) through the years. Such a study would undoubtedly reveal the width of her literary reputation in America and abroad.
[63] Frances herself told me this episode more than once. I have not, however, found any public record of Caruso's surprise appearance at her high school in June of 1918.

the past that has become the present will lead us into the future, cannot therefore have a conclusion. Let us begin anew, strengthened by what others began for us. "Itala gente da le molte vite," Carducci said of our people. The line also means that "molte vite" are needed for the full celebration of the glory we have achieved in this land. My voice is only one of the many more to come.

Joseph Tusiani with his brother Michael and his wife Bea, and their children.

THE JOSEPH I KNEW

Bea Tusiani

Like most people, I was introduced to Joseph Tusiani's poetry long before I met him. His younger brother, Michael, carried *The Rind and All* and *The Fifth Season* under his arm, rang my doorbell, sat down on my living room couch and proceeded to woo me with his sibling's romantic verses. "Never take the world for granted, for your lesson trees were planted"[1] [....] "If I say wine, am I already drunk? If I say grass, am I already spring? But oh, if I say love, I am at once the very thing I say, and am with you."[2]

No one had ever courted me with such a powerful lure.

When I eventually met the famous poet, and he learned my name was Beatrice, he quickly declared that his brother, whose middle name is Dante, had made a literary love match that was destined to survive.

Joseph, as we called him in our family, served as Michael's best man when we married, and when our children were born, they lovingly called him Jo-Jo. He never missed the opportunity to take these little ones into his study, kneel down to their level of understanding and teach them something simple, yet profound.

Beyond our family circle, I soon learned that Joseph Tusiani had more significant titles: professor, maestro, poet, translator, scholar, linguist.

That's when I came to understand the extent of my brother-in-law's unique intellect and vast breadth of knowledge.

From an early age, he was a self-taught musician, able to play the mandolin or organ without having any music in front of him. Yet, amazingly, he composed his own music to accompany some of his literary works. And he would deftly recite the libretto of most operas word-by-word. Indeed, one of his greatest joys was to

---

[1] "To A Child" in *Adventures in Reading* (New York: Harcourt Brace & World Inc., 1961) 310.
[2] "If I say wine" in *The Fifth Season* (New York: Ivan Oboloensky, 1964) 47.

listen to the same aria sung by different tenors and sopranos to determine whose voice he deemed superior to all others.

As for Italian literature, Professor Joseph Tusiani certainly amassed a fan club of former students who came up to him after his many lectures and book signings to profess their devotion — no surprise most of them were women — who fell under the spell of his melodic voice and elegant charm.

Teaching was always a very strong focus for this astute grammarian. Any student who used a verb or noun out of context received a mini-lecture on why it was wrong to do so. The difference between using "who and whom", "lay and have lain" have been particular sore spots in our family. Although we've heard the correct usage explained to us hundreds of times, we just never seemed to get it right!

The author of a multitude of translations of Italian literary classics, novels, plays, essays and articles, poetry by far, continued to be Joseph's most prolific form of expression. In fact, over a three-year period between 2015-2017, a new poem appeared in my husband's computer inbox each morning. Not surprisingly, it was "The Second Avenue Subway" written in English one day, the next it was "Ritorno alla realtà" written in Italian, and yet another was "Res Caelestis" in Latin.

"How do you know in which language to compose your poem?" is an oft-asked question. "Whatever language it is conceived in my mind, is the language I write in," replies the sure-minded poet.

I was the lucky recipient of a poem he wrote to me in 2018. It begins, "My sister-in-law (I should say sister-in-love)." Who thinks like that? One can only wonder, how to communicate with an intellectual like this on the same rarified level?

Truth be told, this uncommon man was an enigma, born out of an era in which he could have rubbed shoulders with the greatest poets of all time. He would be more at home walking along the Arno River in dialogue with Dante over *The Divine Comedy* in the 14th Century, or speaking in Latin to Virgil about the *Aeneid* in the 11th Century, or discussing sonnets with Shakespeare in the late 17th Century at Stratford-on-Avon.

Instead, as he reached the lofty age of 96, there were fewer and fewer people who could relate to Joseph Tusiani on an equal basis. He spent his last days sequestered in his New York City apartment looking down at the masses going about their busy lives. The one companion he could rely on for a daily visit was his muse, who conspired with him to write a poem a day to live on ... forevermore.

October 2020

San Marco in Lamis, circa 1966

Joseph, in the 1940s

Tusiani on Tusiani

— An Interview —

The following question and answer session with my brother-in-law, Dr. Joseph Tusiani, first appeared in *Ambassador Magazine* in the Spring 2001 edition. I share it, so readers can hear directly from the master himself.

You have been described as a humanist. What does that mean?

Today, we call humanists those who cultivate the humanities — that is, classical languages and literature — but true humanists used to be of a different breed. During the Renaissance those who deserved such an accolade had to be fluent in the language of ancient Rome, as was the case of Petrarch, Politan, Erasmus and Sir Thomas More.

Latin has long been considered a dead language. Why do you continue to write in it?

I too, ask myself what prompted me to write seven books in a language that very few people read. Perhaps there is no answer, perhaps it is a curse, or perhaps there is an answer after all. In a lyric poem from *Gente Mia and Other Poems* I say: "Two languages, two lands, perhaps two souls/ am I a man or two strange halves of one?" Since I do not know which of the two languages — Italian or English — is mine, I cling to the illusion that I can resort to my remote ancestral tongue in order to find an identity.

The days are long gone when priests said mass in Latin. Who speaks Latin these days?

In many Catholic seminaries, Latin is no longer taught, or, at best, is only optional. So, who speaks Latin then? A few scholars or humanists from all over the world. Every nation has its own group of Latin enthusiasts. There are Latin journals or magazines in Germany, Belgium, Spain and France, in which it is still possible to publish in Latin.

Who's studying Latin? Is there still much need for Latin professors?

There are nations where Latin is still much in demand; in fact, in a few countries, you cannot obtain a Ph.D. without Latin. One of the greatest satisfactions I've had was receiving a phone call in the Bronx, completely in Latin, from a man who said he was a great admirer of my Latin poetry. He said he and his friends in Belgium met one a month to discuss the works in *Melissa*, a magazine written completely in Latin, and since he was recently appointed Belgium's Ambassador to the United Nations, he wanted to know if we could meet. So, I went to the UN, and for two hours we conversed in Latin.

Much of your Latin poetry is based on modern themes — the Statue of Liberty, President Kennedy's assassination, the subway — who reads it?

I'm glad you mentioned the subway. In *Vehiculo Subviario* is my most widely read poem by high school students. Why? Exactly because the modern theme of the poem gives students the sensation that, by reading about something that is very much alive, Latin is not dead at all. All those books that were inflicted on students years ago – let's say *De Bello Gallico* by Caesar, about ancient France divided into three parts – have little relevance today. The subway appeals to modern students because they can relate to it.

Anyone can sit down and write a poem, even a child. What's so special about writing poetry?

Anyone can sit down and write words - a poem is something else. Not even a born poet can write a poem when he wants to. He can write one only when a poem is given to him by unknown superior powers to which he humbly and gratefully surrenders. With those powers he collaborates by supplying the technique he has learned from other masters.

Inspiration then is given, technique is learned?

Yes. To a child I would say, "You must study." For instance, in order to write a symphony, you must study music. My education has been a classical one, so I tend to write classical poetry, with a structure and precise knowledge of meter. When a poem is given to you, it dictates its own form, its own shape. Somehow it comes to you with the meter in which it wants to be expressed.

How many kinds of poems are there?
There is the canzone, the sonnet, the satirical poem, the idyll, madrigal, the epinician, the epithalamion, the elegy and the epic poem. Recently I translated Luigi Pulci's *Morgante*, which is an epic poem. There are as many forms and genres as there are emotions in life — well, almost.

When you sit down to write, do you consciously plan which language — Latin, English, Italian or Sammarchese dialect — to use?
It all depends on the "incipit," that is, the very first line. If it comes to me in Latin, I think Latin and so the poem is born in Latin. If the first line comes in English, then I, too, become English. This also applies to the work I've done in Italian and my Gargano dialect. Do not forget that language is but a goblet bearing the wine, the ineffable essence which gives universality – or at least identity – to a poet's thought and feeling.

Of all your works, your translation of Michelangelo's poems has received the most public attention. Do you consider that your greatest achievement?
It is the first of all my translations and is the book I'm most proud of. I'm deeply gratified to have made Michelangelo's poetry known to the English-speaking world. Nobody knew he was a poet and a great poet at that. I remember that when Democratic presidential candidate John F. Kennedy visited Mount St. Vincent College the day after my book had been reviewed in the *New York Times*, his reaction was: "Ah, you're the Michelangelo man! I never knew he was a poet."

But the book that took a greater amount of energy to translate was Pulci's *Morgante*. The length itself is staggering — almost 35,000 lines, which is the equivalent of Dante's *Divine Comedy* and Tasso's *Jerusalem Delivered* put together. It had never been translated in five centuries, though Lord Byron translated *Canto I* before he surrendered. Sometimes I wonder how I did it. It took six years.

How did you come to translate major Italian poems?

My dream was to give to America what Italy had given me. I wanted to make unknown Italian masterpieces known, or better known, to the Anglo-Saxon world. For instance, Alfieri's *America Libra* (America the Free) is the first homage that Italy paid to the new country, and I was told that the booklet of my translation was given to all the Senators and Congressmen for the Bicentennial in 1976.

Among the poets you've translated, who impressed you the most?

All of them. You have to aim high. You can't say: "At this moment I am translating Pulci. You have to say, I *am* Pulci!" You have to capture the spirt of the poem, then the letter. I always try to keep the music of the poem because with the wrong music, the wrong rhythm, you may destroy it.

Do you think you would have accomplished as much, professionally, had you remained in Italy?

I would not have written in English and would not have translated Italian classics. I probably would have translated English classics into Italian instead.

Besides reading and writing, what else inspires you?

Everything. When you least expect it, the most uninspiring thing around you suddenly becomes charged with energy. When you read a poet's entire production, you have an idea of what the major sources of his or her inspiration are. In my work, for instance, I mention music so much. You will find a poem dedicated to Berlioz's *Symphony Fantastique* – also, Wagner, Brahms. I derive pleasure from playing the mandolin and organ, and am inspired by opera and great works of art.

If you could go back in time, when would you like to have lived?

Sometimes I say, "Gee, it would be wonderful to wake up in the morning to the company of Virgil," and I wonder how would I greet him in Latin? But in reality, had I been born in another century I would not have met whom I've met and done what I've done. I'm a fatalist. I think each of us is born at the right time. It's up to us to make the best of that hour, that day, that period of time.

Arrival in America aboard the Saturnia with mother, Maria, Sept. 1947

With brother, Michael, upon his retirement from Lehman College, 1983

SECTION TWO

Commemoration

A Mesmeric Sculpture: Tusiani, the Humanist

Giose Rimanelli

How to respond to sapience if not with none too sapient observations? I recall Horace, familiar to Joseph Tusiani: "Maxima pars vatum, pater et iuvenes patri digni, decipimur specie recti." Most of us poets, old and young, are deceived by the appearance of correctness. But in your case Joseph — and allow me to address you directly — I forget Horace. You have that character, and you are that poet: better, a surviving Humanist, in the old great tradition. It is about this major aspect on your personality that I would like to address.

Instead of improvising, the good writer writes. And remembers: as I do remember today a brief article that I wrote about you so many years ago, when *La parola del popolo*, a journal printed in Chicago, wanted to honor you. You were to me an articulated sculpture at that time, Joseph, and thus you have remained: a human monument that inspires and teaches. This is what I said at that time, and it is valid now. Your magic, my dear friend, becomes flesh and blood through your sculptural observation: of things, of men, of the landscape. Solid as an ancient stump, you find the hours that others do not find. You bend over the text, you observe it, you smell it, you read it, you re-read it, you get soiled with it. The text of your attention becomes object and instrument directed by your will to possess. The love that you discover in yourself for the object of your preference inebriates itself with carnality. I noted this in your translations, excellent as the originals. In fact, to become conscious of love through the text, through your almost carnal violence of the text, finally metamorphoses in the rendition of two presences: Michelangelo-Tusiani, Tasso-Tusiani, Alfieri-Tusiani. You become, Joseph, translator and author without, however, ever taking away anything from the other, without ever taking away anything from yourself.

You are a mesmeric sculpture, Joseph. You are of today and you are of yesterday. Time has come to a halt in your eyes; and that which your eyes observe — things, men, words, landscape — assume a lustre and a vibration while preserving the film-patina of their originary structure. Your magic, Joseph, is a human angelism.

It is always with modesty that I approach your statue, Joseph. You live on Tomlinson Avenue, in the Bronx. Nevertheless, when I see you elsewhere, or I open one of your books, it seems to me that you are breathing on me. I hear your breath and your voice: perhaps it is that of Socrates, perhaps that of Caesar. Often the soul of the pilgrim, the emigrant, the notebook of thanks whines through it. But there is always a Gregorian organ that plays in you, and I imagine the vastness of the meadows, the sunken ships, the cathedral spires, the perpendicular atonal sonority of one who observes the scene around and within him on a wall. You say:

> Civilization is / what we in it destroy —
> the man that razes towns / to make playgrounds for the boy

You are a man of fate, Joseph. You are one who seeks himself and others, somewhat like Tagore, knowing implicitly that by so doing you are participating in your own realization, your epiphany. But to seek to understand as you do, Joseph, with things and me, the words, the landscape signifies naught else save to arrange all in an ordinary manner. And this need for order is born in you by the awareness that man explores in continuity seeking laws and forms, hence creating exactly that order which already exists in him.

You, Joseph, are statue but also the metaphor of this your statue. And to create — as you do with *Gente Mia* — (a likeness in your effort to discover and to remember) is an act of faith. It is this act, this movement that finally concretizes itself in image. To realize, in the final analysis, means naught else save to persist, to make oneself statue, sculpture.

> What would my life be now
> if I were still with my familiar trees?

Giose Rimanelli • "A Mesmeric Sculpture: Tusiani, the Humanist"

Thus, do you exclaim. Now let me tell you something: Heraclitus, whom you know very well, declared that every cosmology begins with self-consciousness, with self-knowledge. His is the notion that the elements are disposed in a continuous flow, and hence, in a state of constant transformation. This is man. The *anima hominis* projects itself in *anima mundi*. From oneself to others, because the flux is internal and external; from autobiography to cosmology. And the whole is enclosed in a symbolic act: that of writing, which helps to understand and to interpret, to articulate and to organize, to synthesize and to universalize human experience.

Your experience, Joseph, that co-involves the whole process of your creativity, accordingly translated itself into theory. That is how I interpret it. And this theory becomes form, volume. And form, which is the language of scholastic philosophy in close relationship with the *animus*. Form is not necessarily in the order of facts, but it is necessarily in the order of the creative process: this is an activity that is continuously exercised toward the outer from the center. And you, Joseph, know this center, that is this sculpture, that is this metaphor.

I often go walking through the Bronx where Joseph Tusiani lives and where, for a time, also lived my fellow-regionalist Arturo Giovannitti, with Tusiani's words on my lips:

> Call me whoever you are, and tell me
> whatever you please. Speak even
> of wind and heaven to
> a wounded eagle in the grass, of bread
> and fire
> to a famished beggar in the snow.
> Be cruel and be rude
> but talk to me and let me know
> that I am not alone
> in this my human solitude.

Even this human solitude of Joseph Tusiani is a metaphor. It is your metaphor, Joseph, which almost all of us have learned to love.

SECTION THREE

Critical Analyses

JOSEPH TUSIANI
The Man and His Work

Paolo A. Giordano

> To comprehend my life, I think of it
> as a translation from a flowing past
> into a flowing present, from a birth
> utterly unintelligible, into
> an altogether signifying sound
> which I call language, life and love of it.
> "Heritage" (*La parola del popolo*, 71)

> Now, only now for every suffered wrong
> I can I discover who I am at last
> the multitudinous Italian throng.
> I am the present for I am the past
> of those who for their future came to stay,
> humble and innocent and yet outcast. (*Gente Mia*, 8)

Joseph Tusiani's life is the story of a man divided between two continents and two nations, and the story of a literary odyssey. It is a journey of migration, uprooting, and, eventually, memory. It is a life that evolved from the anguish of separation and deracination to the calm and gradually accepted realization that return, going home, is elusive at best, but, most likely, impossible.[1]

Tusiani occupies a singular position in the history of Italian-American literature, but he is much more: Tusiani has written poetry and prose in Italian, English, Latin, and in the Gargano dialect, and is a translator of Italian literature to English and English literature to Italian.[2] As a scholar, he has produced numerous works of literary criticism. The whole of his work is of such complexity that to interpret him strictly from an ethnic, Italian-American perspective, as many of

---

[1] For further elucidation on the topic of the individual man divided between two continents and two nations see Cosma Siani (1999).
[2] On Tusiani's use of four languages see Cosma Siani's essay "Due mondi e quattro lingue. La poesia di Joseph Tusiani," and Luigi Fontanella's "Joseph Tusiani's Plurilinguism" in *Migrating Works: Italian Writers in the United States*: 76-94.

us have done, would indeed be a narrow and unjust assessment. Anthony Julian Tamburri justly observes that "Tusiani's rhetorical repertoire may indeed be better represented by a hyphen that would actually spin 360 degrees à la second hand of a wristwatch" (75).

A LIFE WELL LIVED

Tusiani was born in 1924 in the town of San Marco in Lamis, in the Gargano area of the Apulia region. In 1947, at the age of 23, he emigrated, with his mother, to the United States in "search" of his father, the father he had never met.

Before coming to America, Joseph had earned a degree in literature from the "Federico II" University of Naples. As a newly arrived young intellectual, Tusiani soon began frequenting Italian-American cultural circles in the area of the Bronx, where he lived. Here he met and became friend and colleague with a number of luminaries of the New York (Bronx) Italian-American community: Onorio Ruotolo, an educator, sculptor and poet;[3] Arturo Giovanitti, a union leader, socialist, political activist, and poet;[4] and Francis Winwar (Francesca Vinciguerra), who was best known for a number of romanticized biographies of nineteenth-century English literary figures and their

---

[3] Onorio Ruotolo, born 3 March 1888, in Cervinara, a small town in the Province of Avellino, and died in Greeewich Village on 18 December 1966. As a young man he studied for six years at the *Reale Istituto di Belle Arti* in Naples, apprenticing for two years under the Neapolitan sculptor Vincenzo Gemito. In 1908 Ruotolo emigrated to the United States, where he quickly made a name for himself as a sculptor. In addition to sculpting, Ruotolo wrote poetry, illustrated books, published his own journal, and was a teacher. In 1923 he founded, with Attilio Piccirilli, the Leonardo Da Vinci Art School, which "diffused among the children of workers, the Light of Art." The school, after moving to several locations, ultimately closed in 1942.

[4] Arturo M. Giovannitti (Ripabottoni, Italy 1884-New York City-1959). He emigrated to Canada in 1900 but, soon after, found his way to the United States, where he attended the Union Theological Seminary. He also began writing for *Il Proletario*, the weekly newspaper of the Italian Socialist Federation, and, in 1911, he became its editor. He is best remembered as one of the main organizers of the 1912 Lawrence Textile Strike (Lawrence, Massachusetts), and as one of the principal defendants in the famous trial that ensued from the strike. In 1914, after the trial was over, Giovannitti published his first and most important book of poems, *Arrows in the Gale*. For a more complete understanding of Giovannitti see Fontanella's *Migrating Works: Italian Writers in the United States* (19-46).

followers, as well as for being a prolific and versatile translator from both Italian and French.[5] Onorio Ruotolo and Frances Winwar were influential in the development of his artistic and personal life. Ruotolo introduced him to Giovanitti and Borgese, introductions that developed into life-long collaborations, and, most importantly, he introduced Tusiani to Francis Winwar. It was Winwar, who, through their close friendship over a span of twenty years, had the most significant influence on his life. She is the one who urged Tusiani to expand his horizons and to begin writing in English (Quoted in Capasso, 96):

> E la Winwar mi diceva "Ma tu che fai qua? Che fai qua? Vuoi passare la vita giocando a tresette? Tu non sei fatto per restare qui, te ne devi uscire!" Quindi fu lei, che era la donna di cui tutti si servivano perché sapeva l'inglese, a staccarmi da quel gruppo.

Tusiani met Francis Winwar in 1952, when she wrote him a letter regarding a review he had written about her recently published book, *The Land of the Italian People*. It all started with a conversation he had with Onorio Ruotolo (Quoted in Capasso, 96):

> "Ma io non la conosco nemmeno!" "E la conoscerai! E scriverai una recensione del libro della Winwar!" Si riferiva a un libro che lei aveva scritto, *The Land of the Italian People*. Gli dissi: "Ma non l'ho letto nemmeno!" e lui mi rispose: "E lo leggerai! E tra quindici

---

[5] Frances Winwar (3 May 1900-24 July 1985), novelist, biographer, and translator, was born Francesca Vinciguerra in Taormina, Sicily. Quickly mastering English and French and retaining complete fluency in Italian, she showed an early taste for literature, and began to publish poetry in the radical socialist magazine *The Masses* at the age of eighteen. Winwar was best known for a number of romanticized biographies of nineteenth-century English literary figures and their followers. Winwar was also a prolific and versatile translator from both Italian and French, producing, among other works, a well-received version of a translation of Boccaccio's *Decameron*, published in a luxury edition by the Limited Editions Club and in a popular edition in 1955 by the Modern Library. A widely cultivated writer, Winwar did not limit her involvement with the arts to literature. Between 1931 and 1950, she translated for the Metropolitan Opera Association in New York City Verdi's *Simon Boccanegra*, Rossini's *Il signor Bruschino,* and Verdi's *Don Carlo.*

giorni deve uscire la recensione!" La Winwar mi rispose, e cominciò la mia amicizia con lei, che fu un'amicizia completa, totale, bella. Siamo stati sempre insieme per una ventina d'anni.

Here was the beginning of a relationship which proved to be beneficial and stimulating on a number of levels. Here is Tusiani, again, in his own words (Quoted in Capasso, 96):

> Io lessi tutte le sue opere quando venni a conoscenza di questa donna. Era una bella donna; anche a cinquant'anni era bellissima. Lessi tutto e, dato che ero agli inizi e ancora non avevo pubblicato niente, avevo bisogno di chi credesse in me. Avevo letto tutto, e volevo quasi scrivere come scriveva lei; ammiravo il suo stile, era bellissimo. Questa donna non aveva studiato molto, [e ciononostante] tradusse il *Decamerone* all'età di ventun anni... Aveva un intuito speciale per le lettere; scriveva bene. E io la ammiravo per questo. Scrisse qualche articolo in cui le feci notare la bellezza della sua prosa, prosa che a volte era fatta di endecasillabi puri; era poesia. Mi ero innamorato, e quindi ogni cosa che questa donna faceva mi sembrava grande. E quindi volevo scrivere come lei. Ma il nostro rapporto era bello, perché lei leggeva a me le sue cose, io leggevo a lei le mie; perciò era un'amicizia in cui si costruiva, ci si ispirava a vicenda; e questo è bello. È bello che qualcuno creda in noi, anche uno solo. È bello ricevere uno stimolo continuo.

Joseph, together with Frances Winwar, returned to Italy and to San Marco in Lamis in 1954. During this stay in Italy, he composed a poem titled "The Return," a copy of which he gave to Ms. Winwar. Unbeknownst to him, she sent his poem to the Poetry Society of England. A few months later, *The New York Times* published the news that his poem, "The Return," had been selected for the prestigious Greenwood Prize.[6] This was the first time this distinguished literary prize was awarded to an American poet, an immigrant who had only been in the United States for nine years. Obviously, the

---

[6] See Tusiani's "The Making of an Italian American Poet" in this volume (28-29).

international recognition greatly enhanced the young professor's reputation as a poet and gave him the confidence and determination to continue writing and publishing his works in English. This is also the time that he served as Director of the Catholic Poetry Society of America and as Vice President of the Poetry Society of America. Furthermore, Tusiani was the first recipient of the American Association of Teachers of Italian Distinguished Service Award, and. in 2007, he was presented with the Keys to the City of Florence for his contribution to promoting the knowledge of Florentine and Tuscan poets, from Dante and Petrarch to Boccaccio and Michelangelo, in the English-speaking world.

In 1963 Tusiani was invited to participate in an initiative by the Steuben Glass Company titled "Poetry in Crystal," where thirty-one of Steubens sculptors were assigned to visualize in crystal the poems of 31 American poets of the time. Tusiani's poem "Standstill" was interpreted by George Thompson.[7] In the same year, he was invited by President Kennedy to record his poetry for the Archives of the Library of Congress in Washington and won the Alice Fay di Castagnola Award[8] for his work in progress, *If Gold Should Rust*.[9] This award is given annually by the Poetry Society of America to a poet that the society recognizes is at a crucial stage in his or her work.

Tusiani's most representative English poems have been published in six volumes (1962, 1964, 1978, 1983, 1999, 2004), the most recognized of which is the collection *Gente Mia and Other Poems*. He has also published ten volumes of poetry in Italian (1943, 1946a, 1946b, 1948, 1955b, 1956, 1957, 1960, 1992a, 2005), seventeen volumes of poetry in Garganian dialect collected in a 302-page volume

---

[7] *Poetry in Crystal: Interpretations in Crystal of Thirty-one New Poems by Contemporary American Poets*. Besides Tusiani, some of the poets included were Conrad Aiken, W. H. Auden, Louise Bogan, Witter Bynner, Horace Gregory, Donald Hall, John Holmes, Robinson Jeffers, Denise Levertov, Marianne Moore, May Swenson, Mark Van Doren, and William Carlos Williams.

[8] The Alice Fay di Castagnola Awarded is given by the American Poetry Society in memory of a benefactor and friend of the APS, for a work-in-progress of poetry.

[9] *If Gold Should Rust* was published for the first time in *Joseph Tusiani: Poet, Translator, Humanist an International Homage*, 271-338.

titled *Storie dal Gargano* (2006), and nine volumes of Latin poetry (1955a, 1984, 1985, 1989, 1994, 1998, 2000, 2007, 2014).

Primarily known as a poet, Tusiani's work as a translator cannot be discounted; rather, it needs further analysis. The translations constitute an important part of his opus as an intellectual and as a cultural broker. An anthology edited by Cosma Siani in 2014, *L'arte della traduzione poetica*, discusses the importance of these translation that span throughout the centuries of the Italian literature, from Dante to Montale. In the introduction to his volume, Siani informs us that Tusiani introduced the English-speaking public to the complete poetry of Michelangelo and to Vittorio Alfieri's five odes on America, *America Libera*. The volumes *Poets of the Renaissance* and *From Marino to Marinetti* contain the largest number of Italian poets translated and published in a two-volume set. His last work is the first full translation into English of Luigi Pulci's Renaissance picaresque and amusing *Morgante*.[10]

GENTE MIA AND OTHER POEMS AND THE AUTOBIOGRAPHICAL TRILOGY[11]

In the last part of this essay, I will revisit his two most important works that deal with the theme of immigration, *Gente Mia and Other Poems*,[12] and the autobiographical trilogy: *La parola difficile, La parola nuova* and *La parola antica*, works that reflect the unique dilemma migrants face, that of being divided between the Old World, their native land, and the New World, in this case America, and more specifically for Tusiani, New York. Tusiani, in his search for an answer, or, maybe, just a clearer understanding, delves into the soul and spirituality of the immigrant as s/he quests for a non-hyphenated identity and a home in his/her adopted land. In *Gente Mia* the questions

---

[10] See the list of Select Translations: following my "Works Cited."
[11] Some of the writing on *Gente Mia* and the autobiographical trilogy have appeared in previous publications. Here they are updated and expanded.
[12] *Gente Mia and Other Poems* is divided in two parts. The fourteen poems of fist part are about immigration, while the sixteen poems that follow are on different subjects. For an excellent disquisition on the second part of *Gente Mia*, see Luigi Fontanella, "Poeti italiani espatriati negli Stati Uniti: Il caso di Joseph Tusiani," 459-466.

he asks are complex and haunting. With the verses "Two languages, lands perhaps two souls / am I a man or two strange halves of one?" our poet perfectly verbalizes the plight of the immigrant.

In *Gente Mia and Other Poems,* and the autobiographical trilogy, Tusiani explores the major themes associated with migration: the spiritually and psychologically violent act of division from one's family and native land (which is the first experience of the new emigrant), the dreams of the immigrant, the prejudice he encounters, the process of Americanization, the question of language, the alienation, and the realization that the new world is not the "land of hospitality" so mythicized in the Old World.

As the immigrant begins his journey, the *expectation* is that life in the New World will be, if not ideal, at least an improvement over the life s/he left behind. As the immigrant further experiences America, the separation from the Old World, its language and its customs, becomes problematic and sets off an emotional response that leaves him with the surreal feeling of being suspended between two lands. "Song of the Bicentennial," an intensely autobiographical poem that opens Joseph Tusiani's collection *Gente Mia and Other Poems,* examines the above-mentioned themes and leaves the reader with a melancholic awareness of what it means to be an immigrant:

> Then who will solve this riddle of my day?
> Two languages, two lands, perhaps two souls…
> Am I a man or two strange halves of one?
> somber, indifferent light,
> setting before me with a sneer of glow,
> because there is no answer to my plight. *(Gente Mia* 7)

For many there is no resolution to the "riddle." The feeling of being suspended/divided between two worlds and two cultures will eventually lead the immigrant to reverse the process and idealize the Old World:

> 'Twas my presepe, full of
> tu scendi dalle stelle –

> the only song and rule of
> intime cose belle.   (*Gente Mia* 6)

The immigrant's adopted land, "the western world," the "new / mysterious Atlantis," is presented by Tusiani as cold and unfeeling, a nation of immigrants where the newly arrived are not welcomed:

> where men like me and you,
> called immigrants, are *silent*
> when Silent Night is sung
> on this Manhattan Island
> by all save those, like me
> and you, uprooted friend,
> who think of Italy —
> our lost presepe land.   (*Gente Mia* 6)

Once this "new / mysterious Atlantis" has been discovered, the mystery and myth of America dissipates and the reality facing the immigrant is one of marginalization, of being shut out, "silent," while the voices of others are being heard. The reality that was Italy, poverty and desperation, is forgotten, and Italy now is idealized in the poet's mind as a Paradise lost, the "lost presepe land," and

> My long lost land was one that,
> when snows enveloped it, did not erase a sun that
> still in my dream was lit [...]   (*Gente Mia* 6)

Tusiani looks at the question of language as a spiritual dilemma, not as a sociological problem. When the emigrant, after a long and wearisome crossing, arrives at Ellis Island, is immediately faced with the first major obstacle — a new language. The question of language, or, rather, loss of language, is of primary importance for Tusiani when discussing the experience of immigration. Tusiani introduces the language question in "Song of the Bicentennial" through a series of questions:

> Do I regret my origins by speaking
> this language I acquired? Do I renounce,
> by talking now in terms of only dreams,
> the sogni of my childhood? What has changed
> that I had thought unchangeable in me?   (*Gente Mia* 5)

The answer to these questions is that something *has* changed and that every phrase, every word uttered in English, separates him further still from his roots, from the things he loved:

> Now every thought I think, each word I say
> detaches me a little more from all
> I used to love [...]   (*Gente Mia* 4)

For Tusiani, when "sogni" becomes dreams, "cielo" becomes sky, and "mamma" is translated to mother, much more transpires than the process of Americanization and acculturation. Tusiani as poet, scholar and translator, knows fully well the importance of words. Cognizant of the fact that the ideas that words communicate go much deeper than the formal definitions found in the dictionary, Tusiani knows that the Italian "cielo" elicits mythicized visions of the old world and that the English "sky" will only remind the immigrant of the immense concrete jungle, New York, he now calls home and that when "mamma" is translated to mother a whole world of feelings is lost:

> Mother, I even wonder if I am
> the child I was, the little child you knew,
> for you did not expect your little son
> to grow apart from all that was your world...
> Yet of a sudden he was taught to say
> 'Mother' for mamma, and for cielo 'sky'
> That very day, we lost each other...   (*Gente Mia* 5)

What the poet is implying is that the loss of the emigrant's native language and the acquisition of a new, adopted idiom is the equivalent of translating oneself, growing apart from the land of origin, a betrayal and denial of one's history.

In "Ballad of the Coliseum," Tusiani tells the story of a simple, hard-working man who would have gone to his grave unnoticed like the "multitudinous Italian throng" before him, were it not for the tragic circumstances that led to his death and made the front page of New York's major dailies:[13]

> That day, he left as if in glory –
>   the father of a famous man
> The Coliseum in the sunshine
>   boasted its half-completed span –
> a lofty labyrinth of ramparts,
>   a mass of steel and wet cement
> that by no blowing wind or thunder
>   could broken be or ever bent.
> Then, if no blowing wind or thunder
>   could shake or shatter it at all,
> what sudden wrath of hell or heaven
>   struck on a hardly finished wall,
>   [...]
> How many dead? How many injured
>   Only one dead–our Angelo.[14]   (*Gente Mia* 35)

Besides recounting the tragic death of Angelo Lombardi, this poem also gives us insights into the dreams, the achievements and

---

[13] The New York Coliseum was a convention center that stood on Columbus Circle in New York from 1956 to 2000. During construction, approximately 10,000 feet of the exhibition space collapsed, injuring 50 workers and killing one. The poem is based on this event.

[14] The poem reminds us of Pietro Di Donato's 1939 novel "Christ in Concrete," which was inspired by the death of his father in a construction accident on Good Friday (thus the reference to Christ) in 1923. The novel tells the story of a bricklayer, Geremio, and his tragic death when the building he was working on collapsed.

disappointments, the values, moral and civic, of the Italian immigrant, and the importance of family. The family was essential to the emotional, psychological, and economic survival of immigrants. Tusiani makes us aware of the forces that bond this fundamental social structure: sacrifice, work, and, especially for the children, education. Insight into family life is at the heart of the poem. Forced to leave his family behind in Italy, Angelo, after the death of his mother, returns to his native village "for one who soon became his bride" (*Gente Mia* 32). Over the years, he builds a family and begins building his dream:

> Many more years went by, and seven
> boys and girls, American born,
> calling him Papà! Papà!, made him
> feel like a king a throne
> . . . .
> And so our builder every evening,
> sitting at table with his wife
> while all enrapt his children listener
> counted the blessings of his life.
>
> The pay is good — and let me tell you —
> despite my age I feel much stronger,
> well, strong enough to put through college
> (for times a \-flying) our first son.
>
> He'll be a lawyer no a doctor." (33-34)

The importance of education for immigrants is here emphasized. Angelo Lombardi works to build a better life. The cornerstone of that better life is education, a college education for his children that will assure that the dream will be fulfilled.

Reading "The ballad of the Coliseum," I came to the realization that this poem has an epic quality with biblical undertones. It does not take a stretch of the imagination to visualize Angelo Lombardi as a modern-day, immigrant Moses. Moses, who leads his people out of bondage from Egypt to Canaan — the land promised by God, where the Israelites could be free from the shackles of slavery — like our Angelo does not get to live the dream, as God does not allow it. Moses never enters Canaan, he only gets a glimpse of what the future could be and dies after the Hebrews enter the promised-land. Angelo's life in America, for all of his hard work and sacrifice, ends in the same way as it began, by being violently separated from the thing he held most sacred, his family. Angelo and his family came to America in search of the "dream," but the tragedy of his untimely death denies him that realization. as well as the pleasure of seeing his children live the dream promised by the myth of America.

For all of his hard work and sacrifice, his life in America ends as it had started, by being violently separated from the one thing he held most dear of all — family. As he was not able to be at his mother's side at the time of her death, and his tragic and untimely death denies him the realization of seeing his children fulfill their American destiny or all of his hard work and sacrifice, his life in America ends as it had started, by being violently separated from the one thing he held most dear of all — family. As he was not able to be at his mother's side at the time of her death, and his tragic and untimely death denies him the realization of seeing his children fulfill their American destiny.

In "Columbus Day in New York," Tusiani turns his thoughts to the celebrations that take place in October in urban centers all across America to honor the Genoese sailor and dreamer who "discovered" the New World by mistake and who died believing that he had found a western route to Asia. But the Columbus Day festivities have very little to do with Italian culture and traditions and, as Tusiani clearly states,

> Here is the "epic" journey of Columbus
> reduced to an innocuous parade
> where mayoral dreamers grin in competition,
> endorsed (or almost) by the Governor,
> and politicians who are neither-nor
> turn on Italian smiles as cars' ignition   (*Gente Mia* 10)

In the verses that follow, Tusiani looks beyond the superficiality of the day (the politicians' smiles, the floats, the beauty queens) and turns the poem into a hymn to the true hero of the day — the immigrant laborer with calloused hands who worked and died to make America what it is, and who still is not recognized as "one of her children":

> It does not matter. This is gente mia,
> for I can see (is there a lump in my throat?)
> dear Christopher Columbus on a float
> called for all time to come Santa Maria.
>
> How beautiful he beams! He has the eyes
> of my Grandfather, and his callous hand;
> he is the immigrant of every land
> unhappy in his happy paradise,
> misunderstood in all this understanding [...]   (*Gente Mia* 10)

In this poem, the historical Columbus, the Santa Maria, and the Grandfather are powerful signifiers that synthesize the history of Italian immigration to the United States. Columbus is the first to introduce Europe to the New World, and the New World to Europe. This act of discovery burdens the name of Columbus with an additional level of signification: being the "first" immigrant he has come to personify the destiny of all immigrants. Columbus's caravel, the Santa Maria, also has varying levels of signification: first, the ship clearly represents the ocean liners, steamers and cargo ships that brought Europeans to America, "the New Atlantis"; secondly, the Santa Maria symbolizes the Virgin Mary, the immigrant's spiritual, religious mother who will escort him safely to his destination. The third signifier, the grandfather (*the new Columbus*), represents all immigrants that came to the shores of America; he is the "conqueror" in search of the "dream":

> in all the greatness of his humble past—
> the new Columbus conquering New York:

> He brings the best credentials to be he—
> faith in his glance to win the fighting waves,
> dream of free people and despair of slaves
> to conquer a new land ultimately.
> So here he is today, today at last
> riding atop his bright Santa Maria,
> the navigator of the gente mia,
> *light of my future, darkness of his past* [...]
> 						(*Gente Mia* 10-11; emphasis mine)

The Grandfather symbolizes all the immigrants that have come to this country and, through sacrifice and suffering, made a better life possible for those who followed. For one fleeting day, they are remembered and given their rightful place.

The pomp and gaiety of the Columbus Day festivities cannot hide a bitter truth. The recognition is temporary, "he is the one no crowd will cheer/ tomorrow when the town goes back to work;" and his destiny is such that it robs him of the dignity of his existence:

> the one who came to dig (for dig we must)
> for the high glory of the subway tracks
> *the immigrant who die and yet still lacks*
> *identity with this American dust*   (*Gente Mia* 10-11; emphasis mine)

Tusiani's poem does two things: 1) it reminds America of what Italians have achieved in the new land, from its discovery by Columbus to the humble laborer, and 2) it synthesizes the despair and frustration of being a misunderstood immigrant in a land of immigrants. When this day of artificial smiles and beauty queens is over the immigrant will again be "humble and innocent," a "tragic tramp" (*Gente Mia* 13). As Tamburri points out, the "tragic tramp" reminds us of the depiction of Italian immigrants in vignettes that appeared during the late nineteenth and early twentieth centuries, "where the immigrant was indeed a beggar of sorts" and "the tragicomic figure of Charlie Chaplin, a hapless and seemingly harmless image" who made people laugh by being portrayed as a buffoon (Tamburri 87).

Between 1989 and 1992 Tusiani surprised us with the publication of his monumental autobiography in three volumes, *La parola difficile, La parola nuova,* and *La parola antica,* connected by the common subtitle, *Autobiografia di un italo-americano,* an historical event in the annals of Italian America literature. In the almost thousand pages of this trilogy, Tusiani narrates his life from the day he arrived in America, met his father for the first time, and speaks to his struggles to create a space for himself in America, in academia, and in the world of literature. On a different level, Tusiani's gives us an insight in the history of Italian immigration to the Unites States. Many of the people, famous and not famous, that grace the pages of this trilogy are the essence of Italian migration to America.

What is different in this work is that the sad tone of Tusiani's speculations on human destiny that gave an impression of mournfulness in *Gente Mia* and deepened the pathos of his verses, gives way, in the trilogy, to what I consider a serene, more joyful tone to his pages while still mindful of the uncertain future awaiting him and all immigrants. Martino Marazzi rightly points out in his excellent article, "Da un angolo di vantaggio: intorno alla parola autobiografica di Joseph Tusiani," the trilogy begins with "... un fortissimo, un vero e proprio squillo di tromba, un *trumpet call:* –Nuova York! Nuova York!... Il punto esclamativo è un indice di gioia ma in fondo anche di immane sgomento di fronte all'enormità di uno spazio e di un tempo sconosciuto e tutto da riempiere per poter ridefinire la propria identità" (Marazzi, 301-326).

Tusiani returns to his native language for his masterwork, and in the third volume, *La parola antica,* he returns to the question of language that is so dear to his heart:

> Due lingue. La realtà dello sbarbicamento (uso questo termine per indicare lo sradicamento completo) comporta diversi problemi o traumi, prima di tutto quello di un nuovo linguaggio. Progredendo nell'acquisizione della lingua straniera, si corre il rischio, per ragioni di umana vanità, di ritenere inferiore quella materna?...

Paolo A, Giordano • "Joseph Tusiani: The Man and His Work"

> Non si cade in questo pericolo se il fenomeno del bilinguismo lo si considera non come conquista ma come rinnegamento forzato delle proprie origini e di se stessi. Il bilinguismo, cioè, diventa sinonimo di disintegrata unità familiare, per cui una madre non è più in grado di comprendere il proprio figlio. Dal giorno in cui il figlio dice "Mother" per "mamma" e "sky" per "cielo", fra madre e figlio c'è già una separazione spirituale che lo studioso di linguistica non può catalogare. Se le parole sono suoni articolati che simboleggiano e comunicano un'idea, il termine "mamma", a differenza di "mother", il nuovo termine acquisito, simboleggia e comunica un intero mondo di sentimenti che nessuna espressione straniera può comprendere e rispettare. Abolirlo significa rigettare l'esistenza di una fanciullezza intimamente legata a tutti gli episodi, piccoli e grandi, e a tutte le . emozioni, importanti e non importanti, connessi ed ispirati da quell'unica parola. Non assimilazione o americanizzazzione, dunque, ma ambivalenza, un'ambivalenza di pensiero e sentimento, di dubbio e di certezza, di sogno e realtà.
>
> (*La parola antica* 143-44)

The consequence of this transformation is that the immigrant, by expressing himself in the acquired tongue, translates not only the language but his very soul, and in that process of translation he slowly and unrelentingly begins to change. He now has the language and the culture of two lands: "America e Italia; in quale ordine, però? Non dovremmo dire: Italia e America?" (*La parola antica* 143). Tusiani poses these questions because he believes that the immigrant cannot be totally assimilated into his/her adopted culture:

> Posta in termini diversi la domanda è: fino a qual punto l'emigrato può assimilare la nuova lingua, la nuova civiltà, e in che maniera dimenticare e rinnegare se stesso in mezzo alle nuove e impellenti esigenze della sua vita? Anche se la risposta sia priva di validità scientifica, il poeta ci dice che non esiste, e non può esistere, un assorbimento totale, e che non potrà mai esserci un'accettazione totale, *spirituale*, delle tradizioni della nuova terra.
>
> (*La parola antica* 143; emphasis mine)

Paolo A. Giordano • "Joseph Tusiani: The Man and His Work"

Tusiani's continuous feeling of "uprootedness" lies primarily within this context of never having fully "spiritually" assimilated into the American culture. It is precisely this sense of perpetual "uprootedness," of not belonging, and of navigating between two distinct cultural systems that pushes Tusiani to return to Italian, the language of his native land, for his autobiography. At this stage of his life there are questions that have to be resolved or put to rest.

Another important reason for writing his autobiography in Italian I gleaned from a conversation that I had with him about thirty years ago. He commented that he did not think it would be right to translate the thoughts and words of many of the people that fill the pages of the three volumes into English. These individuals, although they lived for decades in the United States, remained primarily Italian. They only learned the bare essentials of the English language, while never renouncing the "old ways," nor understanding the "new." These are individuals who did not choose to emigrate, but for whom emigration was imposed "da un capriccio del destino voglio dire, dall'inumana legge della povertà" (*La parola antica* 143).

These Italian individuals who lived in the Arthur Avenue section of the Bronx, "il cuore della piccola Italia," are very important to the autobiography. Through them Tusiani explores the phenomenon of the Italian migration to the United States. Their stories, their lives filled with memories, and their attempts to hold onto the "old ways" speak to Tusiani about the tragedy of immigration. We meet his uncle Joseph Pisano, who entered the United States clandestinely from Canada in search of work; uncle Joseph who, in his own way, continued to love Italy but never returned, and when told of the "boom economico" of post-war Italy, refused to believe it because it would have meant that all of his sacrifices would have been useless. The Italy he loved was "l'Italia terra di pietre e cardi" (*La parola nuova* 132), not the new Italy. We meet the Architect Nicola Giusto, relegated to menial jobs in America because he could not learn English and vented his anger and frustration by having a sign placed over the front door of his house: "Qui non si parla il maledetto inglese." In these books we meet the people that became so influential in his life: Onorio Ruotolo, Frances Winwar, Arturo Giovannitti.

The trilogy is the story of two generations of the Tusiani family in America. The first book of the trilogy, *La parola difficile*, traces Tusiani's life from his arrival in New York to the year he won the Greenwood prize for poetry. In addition to the factual array of events, *La parola difficile* is about the developing relationship of a man who meets his father for the first time when he arrives in America at the age of twenty-three. The father who had emigrated to America when, unbeknownst to him, his wife was pregnant. Tusiani finally utters the difficult word, "papà," but it takes the near death of his father for Tusiani to be able to resolve his conflict. The second volume, *La parola nuova*, is the story of Michael, the American brother who speaks a different language and grows up with a world view that is thoroughly different than that of his Italian family. He is the son who grows up to be president of a major petroleum company. This volume addresses the conflicts, misunderstandings, and difficulties that arise when these two cultures collide. When Michael announces his wedding plans to his mother is one of many examples that illustrate these cultural differences:

> Maichi – disse quella stessa sera a casa, – hai già fissato la data del matrimonio per luglio, e va bene. Sei ancora troppo giovane per sposarti, e va bene. Hai voluto fare di testa tua senza ascoltare né genitori né fratello, e va bene.
> Ma...alla dote hai pensato? Quali sono le usanze dei... dei siciliani in America.
> –La che cosa?
> –La dote. Ho detto la dote.
> –E cos'è la dote, Ma?
> –Vuoi sposarti e non sai cos'è la dote?
> –No, non lo so. Dimmelo tu?
> –Fattelo spiegare da Giose. In Italia si pensa prima alla dote e poi al matrimonio.
>
> (*La parola nuova* 250)

After it is explained to him what a trousseau is, Michael, with his thoroughly American point of view, explains:

> In questa terra non c'è, grazie a Dio, la povertà che tu ricordi. Qui c'è il lavoro: ecco perché non esiste quella che tu chiami dote, ed ecco perché un ragazzo di nome Maichino può sposare una ragazza di nome Beatrice senza pensare ai giorni neri di cui ho sentito parlar da quando sono nato. Mi hai dato una professione, e che altro vorresti darmi?... Penseremo a tutto noi due.
>
> (*La parola nuova* 251)

But the dialogue that follows shows that the mother does not understand her son's reasoning. It is a view of the world that is foreign to her way of thinking because she, like other immigrants of her generation, has remained anchored in the culture of her small Italian town:

> Ma io debbo fare come si faceva in Italia — interruppe mia madre — La mobilia te la farò io, la più bella e ricca da fare invidia a tutti i paesani... Devi fare una figura che non ha fatto nessuno. Una volta ci si sposa...
> In America c'è il divorzio, Ma.
> In casa mia non dire mai più questa parola.
> Scherzo, mamma bella, scherzo.
> A me questi scherzi non piacciono, Maichi.
> Ma la mobilia, io e Beatrice non la vogliamo bella e ricca; la vogliamo moderna e poco costosa perché, dopo quattro o cinque anni, intendiamo farcene un'altra e poi un'altra ancora, e poi...
> Ma figlio mio che ti hanno messo in testa questi siciliani? La mobilia deve servire per tutta la vita, e poi così pure la cucina...
> Qui siamo in America, Ma, non siamo a San Marco in Lamis...
> Non pensare a queste cose. La mobilia ce la sceglieremo noi, ioe Beatrice.
> Mia madre non parlò più. L'America non l'aveva mai capita, ma ora, più che mai, le sembrava terra incomprensibile e malvagia. Buono e intelligente com'era, quel figlio americano cominciava a trafiggerle il cuore.
>
> (*La parola nuova* 251-52)

Mother and son have culturally grown apart. The two cultures, so different from one another, have no middle ground here from which to negotiate a common language. They are destined to misunderstand each other. But what is also significant here is the mother's two-layered cultural collision. In her conversation with Michael, the incompatibilities of her Italian culture with his are clear and expected, however; within this same conversation, we see how she also feels herself in cultural disaccord with her son's future inlaws. That "questi siciliani" speaks volumes about the history of Italy and the different cultures that make up the nation state.

La parola antica, which draws the trilogy to a close, signals the end of that period of immigration than began in the late nineteenth century and continued through the first half of the twentieth century. As Italian Americans begin to assimilate into the American society, their more and more distant notion of Italy starts fading to eventually retain little or no meaning at all. The cultural differences that marked the relationships between Michael and his mother, and Michael's children and their grandmother, will disappear within a generation. As Marazzi writes:

> Si addensano le nubi della fine biologica: è la morte del padre, l'addio definitivo al proprio paese… è la prospettiva ormai inevitabile di una famiglia allargata completamente assorbita dalla vita americana e nella quale non solo la vecchia madre, ma anche il narratore ormai sessantenne, fanno risuonare le voci, i suoni della lingua delle origini, della lingua antica. (305)

For second- and third-generation Italian Americans, Italy is a place where their ancestors came from, a remembrance of cultures' past, maybe a possible tourist attraction. Such word has truly become ancient. For Tusiani, instead, *la parola* spiritually pulls him back to the land of his birth and, like many immigrants, he longs for a *return*. The problem is that decades of the American reality he has experienced have profoundly changed him and cannot be erased.

In the last chapter of the book, on his way back from Italy, Tusiani dreams that he finds himself alone with his mother in a long corridor bathed in a blinding white light, a corridor with many doors on each side and a door on each end, one marked "Entrance" the other "Exit." They begin walking towards the door marked "Exit." When they arrive, he notices that the sign had changed to "Entrance," while the sign at the opposite end of the corridor had accordingly changed to "Exit":

> Arrivai sotto quella scrittura e lessi "Entrata". Mi voltai e vidi, lì dov'era mia madre, la parola "Uscita"... Rifeci il cammino, ma quando raggiunsi mia madre, in alto, al posto di "Uscita" lessi nuovamente "Entrata"... E per quaranta volte, affannato, ansioso, con la speranza e la disperazione che mi spingevano e guidavano, corsi da un'estremità all'altra di quell'enorme corridoio...
> <div style="text-align:right">(<i>La parola antica</i> 308)</div>

On the brink of being overtaken by panic, Tusiani notices that the corridor has doors along its sides. On each door, the name of a person that has had a profound impact on his life is written: Frances Winwar, Coco, Onorio Ruotolo, Giuseppe Antonio Borgese, Louise Townsend Nicholl, Arturo Giovannitti, Martin Luther King, Antonietta Lombardi, an immigrant neighbour, and Father Walsh, a Jesuit mentor, to name a few. He knocks on all their doors but no one answers. Finally, he sees the shadow of his father, who had died a few years earlier:

> "Papà! Papà!" gli dissi, andandogli incontro, "ci siamo perduti io e mamma; non possiamo trovare l'uscita".
> "Sei proprio un bambino", mi rispose mio padre, sorridendo. "So io dov'è l'uscita: venite con me". Cominciavamo a seguirlo...
> <div style="text-align:right">(<i>La parola antica</i> 309)</div>

The dream ends abruptly when Tusiani is suddenly awakened by the flight attendant announcing the imminent landing at Kennedy Airport. No one can help him find the exit; it is an existential problem to which only he can supply an answer. The book, and the autobiography, end with this short paragraph:

Andando verso il Bronx, nella limousine della Poten,[15] notai un altro particolare: i tergicristalli, strusciando da destra a sinistra, da sinistra a destra, sembravano dire Entrata-Uscita, Uscita-Entrata, ma non sapevo più che cosa significassero quelle due parole, né a chi fossero rivolte.

(La parola antica 310)

This concluding scene of the trilogy, the confusion it evokes, is of primary importance because, after four decades, his riddle has been solved. The question posed in "Song of the Bicentennial" has become a statement.

> Two languages, two lands, perhaps two souls...
> Am I a man or two strange halves of one?

This new understanding of his human condition allows him to accept himself as being the man of "two languages, two lands, [...] two [socio-cultural] souls."

CLOSING COMMENTS

After a period of inactivity due to a medical condition, Joseph Tusiani is back, today, to writing again and experiencing a renaissance. In the spring of 2016, a new book of his poems written over the last two years, *Clarion Call,* was published; also, a one-volume, condensed edition of the three-volume autobiography has recently been published by Bompiani with the title *In una casa un'altra trovo*. In recognition of his work, the governor of the State of New York, Andrew Cuomo, has named Tusiani New York State Poet Laureate Emeritus for his lifelong dedication to poetry and the arts.[16]

---

[15] His brother's oil company.
[16] I would like to note and remember the numerous studies dedicated to Tusiani's works by Cosma Siani and Emilio Bandiera, and their work as founding members of the Centro Studi Tusiani at the Università del Salento. For a complete bibliography on Joseph Tusiani's writings and his work see the Centro Studi Tusiani.

Works Cited

Capasso, Roberta. "Emigrazione, esilio, traduzione e altro". Monografico "A Joseph Tusiani per i suoi 18 lustri". *Frontiere* 27-28 (2013): 95-119.

Fontanella, Luigi. *Migrating Works: Italian Writers in the United States*. New York: Bordighera Press, 2012.

_____. "Poeti italiani espatriati negli Stati Uniti: Il caso di Joseph Tusiani". *La letteratura dell'emigrazione. Gli scrittori di lingua italiana nel mondo*. Marchand, Jean Jacques Marchand, ed. Torino: Fondazione Giovanni Agnelli, 1991, 459-466.

Poetry in Crystal: Interpretations in Crystal of Thirty-one New Poems By Contemporary American Poets. Steuben Glass, a Division of Corning Works in collaboration with The Poetry Society of America. New York: Spiral Press, 1963.

Giordano, Paolo, eds. *Joseph Tusiani: Poet, Translator, Humanist an International Homage*. West Lafayette: Bordighera Press, 1994, 271-338.

Marazzi, Martino. "Da un angolo di vantaggio: intorno alla parola autobiografica di Joseph Tusiani". *Il Giannone* 9-10 (2007): 301-326.

Motta, Antonio, Anna Siani e Cosma Siani, ed. *Storie dal Gargano. Poesie e narrazioni in versi dialettali (1955-2005)*. San Marco in Lamis: Quaderni del Sud, 2006.

Siani, Cosma. "Due mondi e quattro lingue. La poesia di Joseph Tusiani". *Centro Studi Tusiani*. Lecce: Università del Salento. Web. 10 luglio, 2016 http://www.centrostuditusiani.com/index.php? option=com_content&view=article&id=49&Itemid=155.

_____. *L'io diviso*. Roma: Cofine, 1999.

_____. *L'arte della traduzione poetica*. Roma: Cofine, 2014.

Tamburri, Anthony Julian. *Re-reading Italian Americana: Specificities and Generalities on Literature and Criticism*. Madison: Fairleigh Dickinson University Press, 2014.

Tusiani Joseph. *In una casa l'altra trovo*. Milano: Bompiani, 2016.

_____. *Ad Maiorem Baculi Gloriam*. E. Bandiera, ed. Melpignano, Amaltea, 2014.

_____. *In nobis caelum. Carmina Latina*. E. Bandiera, ed. Lovanio, Leuven University Press, 2007.

_____. *Storie dal Gargano. Poesie e narrazioni in versi dialettali* (1955-2005). Antonio Motta, Anna Siani e Cosma Siani, eds. San Marco in Lamis : Quaderni del Sud, 2006.

_____. *Quaderno del '41. Poesie liceali (1937-1942)*. Ed. Antonio Motta. San Marco in Lamis, Fg: Quaderni del Sud, 2005.

_____. *Collected Poems (1983-2004)*, Emilio Bandiera, ed. Galatina: Mario Congedo editore, 2004.

_____. *The Return, M'ascolti tu, mia terra?* English text with Italian Translation. Apricena: *All'insegna del cinghiale ferito*, 2003.

_____. *Radìcitus (Ritorno alle radici)*. E. Bandiera, ed. S. Eustachio di Mercato S. Severino (SA), Il Grappolo, 2000.

_____. *Ethnicity. Selected Poems*, Ed. Paolo A. Giordano. West Lafayette, IN: Bordighera Press, 1999.

_____. *Carmina Latina II*. E. Bandiera, ed. Galatina: Congedo, 1998.

_____. *Carmina Latina*. E. Bandiera, ed. Fasano: Schena, 1994.

_____. *Il ritorno. Liriche italiane*. Fasano: Schena, 1992a.

_____. *La parola antica: autobiografia di un italo-americano*. Fasano: Schena, 1992b.

_____. *La parola nuova: autobiografia di un italo-americano*. Fasano: Schena, 1991.

_____. *Confinia lucis et umbrae*. D. Sacré, ed. Lovanio: Peeters, 1989.

_____. *La parola difficile: autobiografia di un italo-americano*. Fasano: Schena, 1988.

_____. *In exilio rerum*. D. Sacré, ed. Lovanio: Peeters, 1985.

_____. *Rosa Rosarum*. Oxford, Ohio: America Classical League, 1984.

_____. "New Poems". *Italian Quarterly* 24, 91 (Winter 1983): 99-112.

_____. *Gente Mia and Other Poems*. Stone Park, IL: Italian Cultural Center, 1978.

_____. "Heritage", *La Parola del Popolo* (March-April 1973): 71.

_____. *The Fifth Season. Poems*. New York: Obolensky, 1964.

_____. *Rind and All. Fifty Poems*. New York: The Monastine Press, 1962.

_____. *Alba di Gloria: Dramma Sacro in due tempi per soli, coro e orchestra*. Set to music by Michele Bonfitto, Milan: Scuola Eliografica "Figli della Provvidenza", 1960.

_____. *Odi sacre*. Siracusa-Milano: Ciranna, 1957.

_____. *Lo speco celeste*. Siracusa-Milano: Ciranna, 1956.

_____. *Melos Cordis*. New York: The Venetian Press, 1955a.

_____. "M'ascolti tu mia terra? Ode al Gargano." *Quaderni de 'Il Gargano'* 5 (1955b).

_____. *Petali sull'onda. Poesie*. New York: Euclid Publishing Co., 1948.

_____. *Amore e morte o sogni delle quattro stagioni. Liriche.* San Marco in Lamis: Giovanni Caputo, 1946a.

_____. *Flora, o primi fiori di poesia*. New York: Prompt, 1946b.

_____. *Amedeo di Savoia. Poemetto in isciolti*. Sant'Agata di Puglia: Tip. Casa del Sacro Cuore, 1943.

SELECT TRANSLATIONS BY JOSEPH TUSIANI

Luigi Pulci. *Il Morgante*. Bloomington: Indiana UP, 1998a.

Giacomo Leopardi. *I Canti*. Fasano: Schena, 1998b.

Torquato Tasso. *The Creation of the World*. Binghamton, NY: Center for Medieval and Renaissance Studies, 1982.

"Giovanni Pascoli's 'Italy,'" *Italian Americana* 5, 2 (1979). 141-59.

America the Free. Five Odes by Vittorio Alfieri. New York: Italian-American Center for Urban Affairs, 1975.

From Marino to Marinetti. An Anthology of Forty Italian Poets. New York: Baroque P, 1974.

The Age of Dante. An Anthology of Early Italian Poetry. New York: Baroque P, 1974.

Giovanni Boccaccio. *Nymphs of Fiesole*. Madison, NJ: Fairleigh Dickinson UP, 1971.

Italian Poets of the Renaissance. New York: Baroque P, 1971.

Torquato Tasso. *Jerusalem Delivered*. Rutherford-Madison-Teaneck: Farleigh Dickinson University Press, 1970.

Lust and Liberty. The Poems of Machiavelli. New York: Obolensky Press, 1963.

The Complete Poems of Michelangelo. New York: Noonday, 1960.

At age 23 in 1947

Joseph Tusiani, collaboratore di *Gradiva* e corrispondente poetico

Luigi Fontanella

> Don't tell me that those birds
> will build again their nest
> in the new May.
> You can't restore with words
> the loss of what was best
> and fled away.
>
> For I shall always mourn,
> when the new spring will come,
> the death of all
> the joy that was not born
> during the greenless doom
> of my last fall.
>
> —Joseph Tusiani

Lunga e feconda è stata la mia frequentazione di Joseph Tusiani, del cui lavoro poetico, critico e traduttorio mi sono occupato in svariate occasioni. Rimando il lettore almeno a tre miei scritti precedenti a questo: un intero capitolo a lui dedicato nel volume *La parola transfuga* (Firenze: Cadmo, 2003, poi rifluito in quello, ampliato e in inglese, *Migrating Words. Italian Writers in the United States*, New York: Bordighera Press, 2012), al saggio "Joseph Tusiani, Maestro di Lingue e di Poesia," in *Journal of Italian Studies* (XV, 1, Spring 2020) e in quello intitolato "Per Joseph Tusiani," in *Il sarto di Ulm* (n. 2, 2020).

Nelle pagine che seguono sento il dovere di rammemorare, ancorché molto schematicamente, la sua preziosa collaborazione alla rivista *Gradiva*, da me diretta per vari decenni.

Poeta quadrilingue, Tusiani è stato anche un accattivante prosatore autobiografico, agguerrito saggista, fine etimologo e "poetologo" (mi si passi il neologismo), nonché massimo traduttore fra gli italianisti trapiantati in America. Di fatto, immensa è stata la mole del suo lavoro nel campo della traduttologia, e direi che, obiettivamente, ben pochi suoi colleghi, oggi come oggi, possono affiancarlo quanto a qualità e a quantità.

Joseph è stato — insieme con Robert Hollander, Pietro Frassica, Remigio Ugo Pane, Dante Della Terza, Maristella Lorch, Olga Ragusa e Franco Ferrucci — uno dei primissimi intellettuali italiani che ho conosciuto subito dopo il mio arrivo negli Stati Uniti come Fulbright Fellow a Princeton (agosto 1976).

Andavo periodicamente a fargli visita in quella sua mitica abitazione al 2140 di Tomlinson Avenue, nel Bronx. Aveva adattato il sotterraneo della propria casa a suo personalissimo studio. Lì vi regnava un'atmosfera magica, lì c'era il suo mondo, lì il suo "rifugio", lì la sua alcova di carta, lì la sua "stanza degli spiriti", come avrebbe detto Robert Walser. Libri ovunque. Carte, ninnoli, quadri, un ampio scrittoio, qualche sedia, una poltrona, una vetrinetta speciale contenente le pubblicazioni a cui era maggiormente affezionato e, soprattutto, un organo, di fronte al quale, da me pungolato, a volte egli si accomodava per suonare qualche pezzo di Bach. Johan Sebastian Bach è stato di gran lunga il musicista da lui più amato insieme a Mozart e a Schubert, mentre fra gli italiani aveva una predilezione speciale per Pergolesi. Va ricordato che Joseph, appassionato musicologo, possedeva, per la traduzione poetica, un "orecchio assoluto". Davvero straordinaria era la sua capacità di cogliere nella poesia non solo l'anima che ne dà il senso più profondo, ma anche quelli che Gianfranco Contini un tempo aveva definito i valori "fonosimbolici" — riferendoli al Pascoli — di un testo poetico.

Fin da quei nostri primi incontri mi colpirono subito, di Joseph, la riservatezza, la signorilità, l'eleganza dell'eloquio, la sicura cultura umanistica, la sottile ironia, la straordinaria memoria. Tutte qualità che poi avrei approfondito col tempo, compresa, ovviamente, la conoscenza più circostanziata della sua poesia.

La mia frequentazione si intensificò ancor più quando si traferì a Manhattan, sulla settantaduesima strada, dopo la morte della madre Maria Pisone, avvenuta alla veneranda età di 95 anni.

Il nostro sodalizio aveva, fatalmente, come centro focale di discussione, la Poesia e la Traduttologia. Tanti e indimenticabili gli incontri e gli scambi di idee che, a tale proposito, ci hanno visto insieme sia come interlocutori sia come semplici lettori della nostra stessa poesia, o magari recitanti quella di poeti fra i più gloriosi della nostra storia letteraria. Mi vengono in mente i tanti e vari eventi tenutisi presso la mia università a Stony Brook; memorabili, p.e. alcuni memorabili *readings*: Dante, Michelangelo, Tasso (splendidamente tradotto da Joseph), Leopardi. Per quanto riguarda il versante italiano non posso assolutamente, in particolare, fra i tanti, dimenticare un evento poetico, affollatissimo, organizzato da Sergio D'Amaro, tenutosi quindici anni fa presso l'Istituto di Istruzione Secondaria Superiore P. Giannone di San Marco in Lamis, suo paese natio. Sto vertiginosamente sintetizzando.

Quando quattro decenni fa presi in mano la rivista *Gradiva* Tusiani divenne ben presto uno dei più affezionati collaboratori e fidi consiglieri. Il suo "ingresso" ufficiale in questo periodico (pubblicato e amministrato, dal 2013 dalla casa editrice Olschki di Firenze e ora diretto dal collega Alessandro Carrera) risale esattamente al 1992, allorché, insieme con Paolo Valesio, decidemmo di allestire un denso fascicolo monografico, interamente bilingue (numero doppio, 10-11), sulla poesia italiana negli USA: *Italian Poets in America*, questo il titolo da noi dato a quel volume, che comprendeva sia poeti italiani residenti negli USA sia poeti italiani-americani, che forse sarebbe meglio chiamare americo-italiani, considerato il fatto che alcuni di loro sono nati negli States o vi sono stabilmente trapiantati quando erano giovanissimi. Nelle nostre rispettive Prefazioni, che adesso ritengo superfluo sintetizzare, venivano spiegate quali — a nostro parere — erano le caratteristiche basilari delle due categorie, beninteso reciprocamente interagenti, ora più che mai.

Più importante mi sembra, per lo specifico di questo mio scritto — ripeto, volutamente sintetico — rievocare il questionario al quale ogni poeta presente in quel fascicolo (L. Ballerini, P. Carravetta, N. Condini, A. de Palchi, M. Moroni, G. Rimanelli, T. Riviello, E. Speciale, e — *si parva licet* — i due curatori: Fontanella e Valesio) era invitato a rispondere direttamente in inglese. È interessante riportare le risposte che diede Tusiani, sicuramente utili allo storico della letteratura italoamericana per individuare la poetica tusianea all'altezza degli anni Novanta, ossia quando Joseph, allo-

Luigi Fontanella • "Joseph Tusiani, collaboratore di *Gradiva*"

ra quasi alla soglia dei settant'anni, era praticamente al culmine della sua carriera. Trascrivo di seguito le quattro domande (in corsivo), approntate da me e Valesio, e le relative risposte, per iscritto, fornite da Tusiani.

Who are the poets that you have admired the most; that is, the poets against whose influence you had to fight in order to find your own voice?

Like every student in Italy, in the pre-Ungaretti age, I too was deeply influenced by Leopardi, Pascoli and D'Annunzio: three poets whose echoes are easily heard in my Italian *iuvenilia*. But, having started writing in English a few years after my arrival in this country, I had other poets to contend with and finally forget in order to feel free while still remaining in their fealty — I mean John Donne, Robert Browning, and Emily Dickinson. I do not know how singular my particular case is; but I can say that it was much easier for me to tread, so to speak, on virgin ground than to disentangle myself from the luxuriant foliage of my native forest.

Which factors of American life/society have encouraged or discouraged you in the writing of poetry?

Frances Winwar and Arturo Giovannitti were the two writers who first believed in me, and made me believe in myself. It was, incidentally, Frances Winwar's magnificent translation of the *Decameron* that perhaps inspired my entire activity as translator of Italian classics. Then, in 1956, I was the recipient of the Greenwood Prize of the Poetry Society of England, and, finally, in the anthology *Poetry in Crystal* of 1963, I found myself in the company of such poets as W.H. Auden, Marianne Moore, William Carlos Williams, Theodore Roethke, and others; and what better encouragement could I have hoped for? It was as if both Winwar and Giovannitti had told me: "Io te sopra te corono e mitrio." I cannot think of any factor that "discouraged" me, although there was a person in my life — my own mother — who always prayed for my return to "the most beautiful language in the world" — Italian.

Luigi Fontanella • "Joseph Tusiani, collaboratore di *Gradiva*"

How has your research evolved since your arrival in the United States? To what extent, and in what ways, has your stay in this country affected the expressiveness of your poetry?

Because I came to America a few days after I earned my doctoral degree from the University of Naples, it was in this country that I began to live as an adult. All my most vital experiences, therefore, are linked to the English language, which, by consequence, I now consider the primary *veste del pensiero*, the "lingua d'infanzia" remaining as a remembrance of an idyllic world beyond time itself, lyrically and maybe logically suited for Latin utterances — which was, indeed, the case.

Could you identify a "faith", a general belief, or an ideology that nourishes your poetry? Would you please provide a brief statement of your poetics?

What an arduous question this is! Do I have to tell you that I breathe, why I breathe and, by breathing, am alive? Surely you remember Archibald MacLeish. He said that "a poem must not mean but be." How, therefore, can I provide a statement of my poetics? God save me from poets who take on the role of pundits pontificating on their own poetry! They turn out to be the most pathetic and inefficient critics of the beauty of which — miraculously, *ergo* unconsciously — they are capable. It is the poem itself that proves a poet's poetics.

Si tratta di risposte che, a mio avviso, sono sufficientemente *self-explanatory* e, pur nella loro telegraficità, utili a capire il mondo poetico, diciamo pure la *Weltanschauung*, del Nostro.

Fu questo il "debutto" di Tusiani in *Gradiva*, che da quell'anno in poi, e con il suo successivo ingresso nel comitato direttivo della rivista, avrebbe "rinforzato", con le sue feconde collaborazioni, il reparto *Traduzioni* di questo periodico.

Qui mi piace ricordarne solo alcune, molto significative, partendo dai suoi precipui interessi verso la poesia rinascimentale e barocca; ad esempio la sua predilezione per poeti come Pulci, Boiardo,

Poliziano, il già citato Michelangelo, Giambattista Marino e, su tutti, il suo amatissimo Torquato Tasso. In questa fertile congerie spicca il lavoro di traduzione di Veronica Gambara (1485-1550), poetessa ammirata dal Bembo, dall'Ariosto e dal Tasso. Non poche delle rime della Gambara, stimate anche da Leopardi, trovarono in Tusiani un congeniale, perfetto traduttore. Rimando al numero doppio 12-13 di *Gradiva* (1994-1995).

Vanno inoltre ricordati: un suo delizioso mannello di versi che uscì nel n. 18, scritti direttamente in inglese, alcuni testi (nn. 31-32), uno dei quali (*Hora Solaris*) in Latino, come altri, sempre in Latino, uscirono in anni recenti, a cura di Michael Palma (n. 47, Spring 2015), e infine, *last but not least,* due sue poesie autografe a me personalmente dedicate. Mi piace citare esemplarmente, del primo nucleo, questo breve componimento, quasi una sorta di madrigale, composto di due semplici quartine di intensa forza musicale:

The rain

It rained and rained today:
surely some blossom new
already's on its way
to brightening my view.

It did, alas, not rain
on this my arid mind:
I therefore wait in vain
for buds of any kind.

Del terzo nucleo mi sia concesso per puro afflato amicale — senza voler essere narcisista — almeno questo para-sonetto che dieci anni fa *Gradiva* (nn. 39-40, 2011) pubblicò in forma autografa, e che — non vorrei sbagliarmi — è ancora oggi inedito in volume.

L'ultima foglia
a Luigi Fontanella, poeta che ammiro, amico che ringrazio

Mio caro Leopardi-Arnault, la frale
povera foglia è al ramo ancor legata,

ingiallita spettrale, ma ostinata
a vivere il suo unico Natale.

Eppure il vento la reclama e assale
con tutta la sua forza rinnovata
per portarsela lì dove già andata
è ogni altra foglia morta. Ma a che vale

un altro giorno o un'altra sola festa
trascorsa nel terror della partenza?
Ventiquattr'ore in più: sarei contento?

Guardo lassù di nuovo: nulla resta.
Gelido e derelitto, il ramo è senza
la sua ultima foglia: vince il vento.

New York, 9 dicembre 2009

Endecasillabi vibranti e delicati, questi di Joseph. Pochi mesi dopo ricambiai il suo gesto con una mia prosa poetica, anch'essa, come la sua poesia, dedicata alla natura, che Joseph mi comunicò aver apprezzato: "Carissimo Luigi, grazie dell'inatteso e perciò graditissimo dono. Come su lastra indelebile hai fissato l'ondoso vibrare dei diletti impossibili fratelli di Mount Sinai. Una poesia veramente bella e triste (ma di una tristezza che non fa male ma dà quasi riposo), una inevitabile e calma meditazione sul gorgo del tempo che si conclude in rassegnazione e ultima pace. Un abbraccio, Joseph."

Già tutta l'aria imbruna
   a Joseph Tusiani

Frusciano infiniti gli alti roveri laggiù, mentre uccelli graffiti sui vetri, fermi e sfreccianti, ne coprono talvolta le cime. È il *suono* di questo frusciare o il *movimento* in sé delle fronde che più mi attrae? Il suono è fisico e vicino, il movimento è etereo e lontano ma l'uno non esiste senza l'altro. Non smetto di guardarvi, miei impossibili fratelli, penetrando il vostro moto-suono che mi sopravvivrà…

Come può questo solo pensiero a un tratto non rattristarmi? Dolce e arcano l'ondoso vibrare dei vostri rami, ma quanto più dolce e misterioso il mio abbandonarmici mentre pian piano vanno sfumando nell'aria che imbruna. Altro tempo, altra vita, altri amori. Amici scomparsi o risucchiati nel gorgo come queste foglie impazzite d'aria e di vento. Miei insaziati spiriti, fino a quando offrirete parole insufficienti e devote? Tutto finirà, come questo giorno che ora declina e questi alti roveri me lo annunciano sommessamente con tutta la loro discrezione, con tutto il loro mistero.
Adesso sono scomparsi quasi del tutto nel buio cobalto. Resta nell'aria lo scuro profilo e solo il suono del loro fruscìo nella notte che avanza... Ne cullerete il sonno, pronti, come se tempo mai fosse trascorso, a ridare domani calmi e immemori il vostro magnifico dono.

Mount Sinai, Long Island, sera del 20 settembre 2010

Che altro aggiungere di questa nostra corrispondenza — termine da intendersi in senso letterariamente quanto spiritualmente molto ampio — che ci ha visti *compagnons de route* per ben oltre 40 anni? Fitto, variegato, ricco di risvolti e anche di pungenti curiosità poetiche-esistenziali è stato il nostro carteggio, dapprima in forma epistolare, rigorosamente autografa, poi dal 2010 in poi in forma elettronica. Anni recentissimi della sua vita in cui, Joseph-Giuseppe, benché malato, ebbe il dono, direi quotidiano, di una musa particolarmente generosa e feconda (*felix* — come s'intende in Latino).

Chiudo con una raffinatezza leopardiana che Tusiani volle regalare a *Gradiva* nove anni fa (nn. 41-42, Spring 2012). In quel tempo, a seguito della concomitante edizione di due rilevanti volumi: *Leopardi* di Pietro Citati (Mondadori, 2010) e la nuova traduzione in inglese dei *Canti*, curata da Jonathan Galassi (Farrar Straus Giroux, 2010) — contenente, sia detto per inciso, a detta di Tusiani, alcune pecche subito da lui rilevate — d'accordo con Irene Marchegiani, Managing Editor di *Gradiva*, decidemmo di lanciare un "confronto" fra le traduzioni inglesi di Galassi con quelle, ormai abbastanza numerose, esistenti nel mondo anglofono. Un'impresa talmente ardua che alla fine decidemmo di realizzare attraverso un unico *specimen*, costituito da *L'infinito*, da molti studiosi ritenuto il più celebre e forse il più perfetto degli Idilli leopardiani. Pubblicammo quindi, a titolo puramente esemplare, cinque traduzioni, diversificate nel tempo e nello stile, rispettivamente di Thomas Bergin-Anna Paolucci (1947); Joseph Tusiani (1998); Jonathan Galassi (2010, cit.); Carolyn Feleppa Balducci (2011, inedita); Luigi Bonaffini (2012, inedita).

Cito, dunque, a conclusione di questo mio breve excursus tusianeo, la traduzione di Joseph, secondo il quale era fondamentale (me lo ribadì più volte) che nella traduzione inglese si mantenesse prioritario quell'attributo leopardiano di *caro* nel verso iniziale, così come lì lo aveva concepito e collocato il grande poeta recanatese ("Sempre caro mi fu quest'ermo colle").

Infinity

Fond I was ever of this lonely hill,
And of this hedge, that from my view conceals
The farthest limit of the firmament.
But, sitting here and gazing, I can feign,
Far beyond it, still unbounded space,
And an unearthly silence, and the deepest
Quietude where my very heart is nearly
Frightened. And as this moment I perceive
The wind around me rustling through these trees,
To the unending silence soon I liken
The passing of its voice: eternity
I so recall, and all the seasons dead,
And with its lively stir the present one.
Founders in such immensity my mind,
And drowning in this sea is sweet to me.

LE RACCOLTE DI LIRICHE LATINE DI JOSEPH TUSIANI
Tra cronaca e curiosità

Emilio Bandiera

Come è noto, l'11 aprile di quest'anno 2020 Joseph Tusiani ha lasciato questa terra per intraprendere la sua ultima emigrazione, o, per usare una sua espressione, per il suo "ritorno nel regno della luce".

Mi pare opportuno, in questo momento, redigere un elenco completo delle raccolte tusianee di poesie latine, per terminare poi con alcuni dati numerici, che hanno, anche essi, la loro importanza.

1 • Tusiani, Joseph, *Melos Cordis,* New York, Venetian Press, 1955 (Pp. 24; formato cm. 13,18 x 21; composizioni 19; versi 295)

Fu stampato nel Bronx dalla piccola tipografia Venetian Press. Contiene 19 poesie latine, 16 con metrica quantitativa e 3 con metrica ritmica (2 delle quali anche rimate). È pubblicato solo il testo latino. Il libretto fu stampato in circa 200 copie; Tusiani le inviò a latinisti dei quali aveva avuto l'indirizzo. Uno di questi fu Jozef IJsewijn, che insegnava nell' Università di Lovanio – Belgio – (Katholieke Universiteit Leuven[1]), allora noto studioso di poesia neolatina. Il giudizio di IJsewijn fu ampiamente positivo. Le poesie di *Melos Cordis*, a suo parere, si distinguevano per la novità e vivezza delle immagini, per le forti emozioni che suscitavano, per la sentita musicalità. Un piccolo difetto riguardava la metrica. In realtà si trattò solo di un semplice contrattempo. IJsewijn aveva considerato che la poesia *Una donatur*, in strofe saffiche minori, avesse la prosodia completamente errata. Lo studioso e il poeta si chiarirono con lettera: *Una donatur* era poesia ritmica e non quantitativa; quindi non sussisteva il problema della prosodia. IJsewijn inserì *Una donatur* tra le poesie ritmiche di Tusiani, in un'antologia di

---
[1] Si tenga presente, d'ora in poi, che Leuven è il nome fiammingo di Lovanio.

poesia neo-latina. Dopo questa esperienza, Tusiani approfondì la sua conoscenza della prosodia latina, tanto da diventare padrone della quantità. Gli restò tuttavia la volontà di rivedere i testi di *Melos Cordis*, "perché i cultori del latino non pensassero che [egli, Tusiani] non conoscesse la prosodia latina". Oggi esistono tre "revisioni" di *Melos Cordis*. Tusiani continuò a comporre poesie latine e a pubblicarle su autorevoli riviste specializzate.

2 • Tusiani, Iosephi, *Rosa Rosarum, Carmina Latina*, Oxford OHIO, American Classical League, 1984
(Pp. 40; form. cm. 22,2 x 28; comp. 33; vv. 683)

Pubblicata per fini didattici dall'American Classical League, *Rosa Rosarum* è una raccolta di liriche latine già pubblicate su varie riviste. Chi scelse quelle liriche aveva certamente una grande finezza di gusto. Sono pubblicati solo testi latini, senza alcuna traduzione. Sono tutte liriche molto belle, composte con ottima capacità espressiva e corrette; liriche sia quantitative, sia ritmiche (e rimate). Alcune di esse sono anche tra le più note di Tusiani. Basterebbe pensare a *In vehiculo subviario*; *JFK: Obiit Nov. 23. 1963*; *De Venere Dea ac Poeta quodam Fabella*; *Spartacus Moriens*; *Epigrammata Echoïca*.

3 • Tusiani, Iosephi Neo-Eboracensis, *In exilio rerum. Carmina Latina*, collegit atque edidit Theodericus Sacré, Avignone, Aubanel 1985
(Pp. 43; form. cm. 11,5 x 18; comp. 35; vv. 394)

Tra gli allievi del già nominato Jozef IJsewijn, c'era l'allora giovanissimo Dirk Sacré. Questi, ancora studente universitario a Leuven, iniziò una fitta corrispondenza epistolare con Tusiani. Nelle loro lettere usavano la lingua latina. Sacré entrò quindi nel numero di coloro ai quali Tusiani inviava copia manoscritta delle sue poesie latine. Fu Tusiani stesso a chiedere a Sacré di scegliere alcune sue poesie latine e di pubblicarle con prefazione. Sacré compilò la sua raccolta, che fu pubblicata da Aubanel, Avignone, nella collezione "Bibliotheca Vitae Latinae", col contributo della Pegasus Ltd. Comparve, per la prima volte nei titoli, il nome dell'autore Ioseph Tusiani accompagnato dalla qualificazione '*Neo-*

Eboracensis' (Newyorkese). L'aggettivo, che si ispirava agli autori latini, (si pensi a *Catullus Veronensis*), resterà nelle successive raccolte di poesie latine di Tusiani. Il libretto è dedicato a Jozef IJsewijn "notissimo cultore delle lettere latine".

I testi sono preceduti da una *Praefatio* (pp. VII-XI) scritta in elegante latino. Sacré evidenzia subito che Joseph Tusiani ha ormai acquisito un "posto particolare" tra i poeti lirici neo-latini e le sue composizioni poetiche latine vengono pubblicate dalle migliori riviste. Le poesie di questa raccolta sono pubblicate nella lingua originale latina; ma non vengono tradotte in alcuna lingua, perché erano destinate a lettori che conoscevano il latino. Sono composizioni molto belle e ricche di significato. Dal titolo si evince che la raccolta è legata strettamente al Gargano, guardato da una persona che, trasferitasi ormai definitivamente a New York, si considera un emigrato, una persona in esilio. Qui mi basta ricordare la prima lirica, *Inviolata pulchritudo*, dedicata a un Gargano appena creato. "O Dio onnipotente, dopo aver creato il Gargano con le sue bellezze, ora riposati; se vuoi che sulla terra resti inviolata questa miracolosa bellezza, non infondere il soffio della vita all'uomo impuro". E si ripete come conclusione, il verso iniziale: "*Nunc titillatur Garganica amygdala sole*"[2].

4 • Tusiani, Iosephi Neo-Eboracensis, *Confinia lucis et umbrae, Carmina Latina,* selecta atque edita a Theodorico Sacré, Leuven, Peeters, 1989
(Pp. 62; form. cm.12,5 x 19,5; comp. 43; vv. 563)

Anche questa raccolta fu realizzata da Dirk Sacré, quattro anni dopo la prima (*In exilio rerum*, 1985). Le poesie latine di Joseph Tusiani, ormai *Neo-Eboracensis*, crescevano di numero e il contenitore dei fogli manoscritti (o di fotocopie delle pubblicazioni) diventava sempre più voluminoso[3]. Sacré aveva abbastanza testi da cui sce-

---

[2] "Ora il mandorlo garganico viene solleticato dal sole" (Tusiani avrebbe preferito "vellicato").
[3] Dirk Sacré conservava, nel suo ufficio all'Università di Lovanio, i materiali di Tusiani e su Tusiani. Ebbi la possibilità di sfogliare tutto il contenuto del grosso

gliere. Questa seconda raccolta si caratterizza per il tema della *luce* e dell'*ombra*, elementi molto importanti della poesia tusianea[4], sia latina, sia inglese.

Con una *Praefatio* (pp. 5-10) in lingua latina. Sacré introduce i testi raccolti. Lamenta che molti, che scrivono poesia latina, formalmente seguono Ovidio, Virgilio, Orazio e Catullo, tanto che la loro poesia sembra scritta in un lontano passato e non abbia niente del loro tempo. "Quanto si trovi Tusiani lontano da quelli lo può vedere *plane et aperte* uno che legge anche usa sola poesia latina di Tusiani". Il poeta italo-americano ha creato un suo stile personale e un suo linguaggio e li usa, anche se a qualcuno non piacciono. Le sue opere, in inglese e in latino, ormai vengono sempre più conosciute e apprezzate, anche perché nel suo linguaggio non solo entra il latino dei classici, ma anche tutta la ricchezza del latino degli umanisti.

Sono molte le poesie di questa seconda raccolta di Sacré, che sono diventate note. Citerei *Ripa Hudsonia* (piena di suoni, di immagini, di dottrina),[5] *Ad Pascolium poetam*, *Photographema maritimum* (breve flash fotografico pieno di suggestione), *Naenia gallinacea* (scherzosa, ma piena di sapienza pratica), *In resurrectione Domini* e *In ascensu Domini* (poesie religiose, ma piene di dottrina teologica), *Melos nocturnum* (una vera ode al silenzio).

---

contenitore, nell'ottobre 2004. Lo stesso Sacré, un paio d'anni dopo, tenne per sé le cose personali e mi donò tutte le pagine manoscritte originali di Tusiani, per il "Fondo Joseph Tusiani" che l'autore e io avevamo costituito presso l'Università di Lecce. Sul contenitore di questi manoscritti feci scrivere "Donum Theodorici Sacré Lovaniensis".

[4] I miei studi successivi hanno mostrato che, accanto alla "luce", Tusiani mette sempre il "suono", tanto che "luce e suono" sono considerati da Tusiani i motori della vita e della poesia. Si vedano Bandiera, Emilio, "*Musica vita est*. La musica nella poesia latina di Joseph Tusiani", Theodoricus Sacré, Iosephus Tusiani, Thoma Deneire, eds, *Musae saeculi XX Latinae – Acta Selecta*, Conventus patrocinantibus Accademia Latinitati Fovendae atque Instituto Historico Belgico in Urbe, Romae in Academia Belgica anno MMI habiti, Brussel-Bruxelles – Rome, (2006): 81-106; "Lucis ad fontem vehe me future". *Humanistica Lovaniensia*, 55 (2006): 195-212.

[5] Un esame di questa ode si trova in "*Lucis ad fontem*" cit. nella nota precedente.

In fondo al libretto, Sacré ha aggiunto un indice bibliografico, dove si indica in quale rivista sono state pubblicate le poesie inserite in questa antologia.

5 • Tusiani, Iosephi Neo-Eboracensis, *Carmina Latina*, Raccolta, introduzione e traduzione di Emilio Bandiera, Fasano, Schena Editore, 1994
(Pp. 407; form. cm. 11 x 21; comp. 153; vv. 2218)

Mentre IJsewijn prima e Sacré dopo, da Lovanio facevano conoscere la poesia latina di Tusiani e le varie riviste specializzate diffondevano le sue nuove creazioni poetiche, il sottoscritto non sapeva neppure che esistesse un poeta di nome Joseph Tusiani e che scrivesse anche poesie in latino. Fu durante il 1986 che conobbi il nome di questo poeta. Dopo la traduzione di 4 sue poesie latine per una rivista pubblicata a Bari, arrivò a casa mia "una grossa busta con circa 150 fotocopie di liriche latine e una lettera di Joseph Tusiani. Questi si complimentava delle mie traduzioni e «sognava» una voluminosa pubblicazione con la mia traduzione in lingua italiana delle sue poesie latine".[6] Non potevo rinunciare a una tale proposta, specialmente dopo aver letto alcune di quelle poesie già pubblicate su riviste famose. Non prevedevo ancora quale avventura stavo per affrontare. Nei ritagli di tempo liberi dai miei impegni didattici, mi misi al lavoro, anche perché man mano arrivavano da Tusiani altre fotocopie o pagine manoscritte con poesie latine. Nel maggio 1991 Tusiani venne a Lecce per la prima volta, passò la notte a casa mia, a Carpignano Salentino. Prima di cena, gli mostrai le traduzioni che avevo fatto. L'indomani Tusiani ripartì per il Gargano e poi per New York. Qualche giorno dopo mi arrivò una sua lettera, con una poesia latina in strofe saffiche minori. Titolo, *Vesper Sallentinus*. Fu una delle pochissime poesie inedite, che entrarono nel nuovo volume. L'editore Nunzio Schena, di Fasano, accettò con piacere la pubblicazione del nuovo libro, anche perché aveva già pubblicato i 3 volumi dell'autobiografia di Tusiani. Il libro, di ben

---

[6] Bandiera, Emilio, "27 anni di amicizia e affetto", *Frontiere*, 14, 27-28 (2013): 11.

407 pagine, uscì nel maggio 1994. Fu presentato dal prof. Orazio Bianco, ordinario di Letteratura Latina presso l'Università degli Studi di Lecce.

Precede i testi una "Introduzione" di 36 pagine, dal titolo "La poesia latina di Joseph Tusiani". Cercai di chiarire agli eventuali lettori quel che si poteva sapere allora di Tusiani, gli argomenti tusianei che in quegli anni erano più studiati, ossia i problemi dell'emigrazione e il suo attaccamento al Gargano. Ma cercavo anche di mostrare i vari temi affrontati da quelle poesie raccolte e il modo col quale l'autore usava il latino, — il "suo" latino —, la musicalità della sua poesia e altre sue caratteristiche. Come ho già detto, solo *Vesper Sallentinus* e pochissime altre poesie erano inedite; tutte le altre erano già state pubblicate su riviste. E aggiungo pure che in quei *Carmina Latina* entrarono le poesie latine allora più note di Tusiani.

È necessario notare che in questo volume del 1994 entrarono i testi già pubblicati e riuniti in due altre raccolte precedenti, ossia *Rosa Rosarum* e *Confinia lucis et umbrae*, che mi erano stati inviati da Tusiani. Nove testi di questo volume furono musicati da alcuni allievi compositori del Conservatorio di Musica di Lecce e dal loro insegnante di composizione, Massimo Gianfreda. Le composizioni furono eseguite per la prima volta a San Marco in Lamis, al termine del Convegno di Studi del maggio 1999 e poi in vari altri luoghi in provincia, nel Conservatorio di musica di Matera, nell'Accademia del Belgio a Roma, al termine di un convegno internazionale sulla poesia neo-latina.

Mi si può chiedere perché intitolai questo volume del 1994 semplicemente *Carmina Latina*. Pensavo che quelle fossero tutte le poesie latine scritte da Tusiani. Mi accorsi, un po' dopo, che ancora non erano arrivate a casa mia le centinaia di pagine manoscritte già esistenti e le altre poesie che sarebbero state scritte in seguito. Non avevo ancora compreso che, per Tusiani, la semplice percezione della possibilità di un nuovo libro metteva in moto la sua ispirazione e la volontà di scrivere. Questo avveniva anche quando aveva un nuovo strumento per scrivere e inviare, come il fax o il computer.

6 • Tusiani, Iosephi Neo-Eboracensis, *Carmina Latina II*, Raccolta, introduzione e traduzione di Emilio Bandiera, Galatina, Mario Congedo Editore, 1998
(Pp. 168; form. cm. 15 x 21; comp. 91; vv. 1286)

Terminate le fotocopie di poesie già pubblicate su riviste, avevo però ormai decine e decine di fogli manoscritti di Tusiani e quindi molto materiale poetico a cui attingere per un nuovo volume. Tusiani «sognava» la pubblicazione di tutte le sue poesie latine con traduzione in lingua italiana e io, avendo accettato questo compito, dovevo onorarlo. Per giunta in quel periodo Tusiani ebbe in regalo un apparecchio per fax, che costituì l'occasione di scrivere nuove poesie e inviarle agli amici col nuovo e più veloce sistema. Poi arrivò anche il computer. Le nuove poesie arrivavano quasi ogni giorno, tanto che, raccogliendole, avevo pensato di intitolare il nuovo volume *"Computatri Carmina"* (poesie del computer). Poi decisi di continuare con lo stesso titolo precedente, ma indicando anche il volume.

La scelta dei testi per il secondo volume fu tutta a mio giudizio, ossia scelsi personalmente dalla voluminosa raccolta di manoscritti, introducendo solo pochi testi già pubblicati su riviste. Nel periodo in cui il libro doveva essere stampato, erano imminenti elezioni in Italia e le tipografie erano piene di lavoro. L'editore Nunzio Schena non aveva la possibilità di pubblicare il nuovo libro entro un tempo ragionevole. Trovai nell'amico Mario Congedo, di Galatina (Lecce), l'editore disposto a stampare il nuovo libro molto prima.

Una Prefazione di 15 pagine apre il volume. La prima lirica della raccolta è chiaramente programmatica. L'autore continua a scrivere in latino: (I, 1-4, 9-12) "Io solo rimango, / legato a un'antica lingua. / A che giova scrivere, se i vocaboli di ieri / arrecano danno? // [...] Ecco la mia poesia: / ancora respirare sotto il sole, / di nuovo vedere la luce, / e vivere tra cose vive, / dimentico del dono stesso del giorno. / E mi basta." Nella III lirica invece dice che vuole cantare cose semplici.

Sono molte, in questo volume, le liriche nuove e che esprimono nuovi sentimenti e affrontano nuovi problemi. Ricordo la X "*Ad somnum inducendum*", una cantilena di 40 ottonari ritmici terminanti tutti con la rima in *-ene*, utili a indurre al sonno. La XIII "*Longe a te, Gargane*"[7] è una dichiarazione di affetto alla sua terra, perché lo stare lontano lo fa soltanto "illanguidire". Sono anche numerose, in questo volume, le poesie amorose, rifacimenti catulliani o versi dedicati a donne chiamate col loro nome. E c'è anche la poesia amorosa/erotica forse la più "spinta" scritta da Tusiani. È anche la raccolta con più poesie dedicate alla luce e a una vera e propria dottrina del *puer*. L'ultima lirica (LXXXVIII, "*Nova inscriptio cursualis*"), 'nuovo indirizzo', è dedicata alla nuova casa a Manhattan, dove Tusiani era andato a vivere dopo 50 anni di vita nel Bronx.

7 • Tusiani, Joseph, *Radìcitus.(Ritorno alle radici)*, Poesie latine con introduzione e traduzione di Emilio Bandiera, S. Eustachio di Mercato S. Severino (Salerno), 'Il Grappolo', 2000
(Pp. 108; form. cm. 15 x 20,7; comp. 40; vv. 662)

Un volumetto inatteso. Il dirigente delle Edizioni 'Il Grappolo' pubblicava volumi dedicati all'emigrazione nelle Americhe. Si offrì di pubblicare qualcosa di Tusiani. Questi indicò una mia nuova raccolta di poesie latine, dedicate all'emigrazione. Il lavoro fu eseguito velocemente e nel maggio 2000 fu edito e anche presentato a Torino, alla Fiera del Libro. Il discorso di presentazione fu tenuto da Furio Colombo,[8] il 13 maggio 2000.

In questa piccola raccolta furono incluse poesie già pubblicate nelle raccolte precedenti e anche qualche altra inedita. Per le tre poesie prese da "*Melos cordis*", ossia *Michaeli fratri*, *Daunia lutea lux* e *Redire necesse* furono usati i testi rivisti dallo stesso Tusiani.[9]

---

[7] Il manoscritto mi fu donato la prima volta che Tusiani venne a Lecce e in casa mia. È uno dei tanti *reditus* che il poeta scrisse per un certo numero di anni, al suo ritorno ormai annuale sul Gargano.
[8] Furio Colombo aveva conosciuto Tusiani e la sua famiglia a New York ed era andato a trovare i Tusiani anche nel Bronx.
[9] Nella mia biblioteca ho tre revisioni/rifacimenti delle liriche pubblicate in *Melos cordis*, ma ancora inediti.

Una Premessa di 20 pagine apre il libro e sfrutta due miei articoli sul tema dell'emigrazione nella poesia latina di Tusiani, allora in corso di stampa.[10]

8 • Tusiani, Iosephus Neo-Eboracensis, *In nobis caelum. Carmina Latina*, Raccolta, edizione e traduzione in lingua italiana con aggiunta di Prefazione e di Indici di Emilio Bandiera, Leuven, University Press, 2007
(Pp. 428, form. cm. 16 x 24; comp. 407; vv. 5256)

Maggio 2006. Ero a Lovanio per gli incontri che, per qualche anno, ebbi con docenti e studenti di quell'Università. Dirk Sacré, quando restava un po' di tempo libero, mi portava in giro per farmi conoscere il Belgio. Quell'anno eravamo diretti a Jemeppe sur Meuse, presso Liegi. Mentre andavamo in macchina, Sacré mi propose di raccogliere tutti i manoscritti ancora inediti di poesie latine di Tusiani, e di creare un nuovo volume, che la Leuven University Press avrebbe pubblicato. Accettai. Tornato a Lecce, misi insieme i manoscritti inediti tusianei delle poesie latine, rimasti in attesa di traduzione e pubblicazione. C'era da spaventarsi per il loro numero. Ma ormai, alla vigilia della pensione, avevo pochi impegni didattici. Feci conoscere a Tusiani la proposta di Sacré. Ne fu entusiasta. Mi chiese se poteva scrivere qualche nuovo testo. I patti con Sacré prevedevano che il nuovo volume non dovesse superare le 200-250 pagine. Ma Tusiani ormai "era partito" in questa nuova avventura, scrivendo nuove composizioni, come faceva sempre appena avvertiva l'odore di un nuovo libro. Nei primi mesi, inviava una poesia ogni tanto, Man mano che il tempo andava avanti, le sue nuove poesie aumentavano, aumentavano sempre di più; chi lo fermava? Fin dai primi giorni di luglio mi ero messo al lavoro, per la revisione dei testi, per l'edizione e per la digitalizzazione. Ero

---

[10] Bandiera, Emilio, "Il tema dell'emigrazione nella poesia latina di Joseph Tusiani", ora in Cosma Siani ed. *Two languages, two lands*, San Marco in Lamis, Quaderni del Sud, 2000: 29-46; id. "L'Emigrazione come esilio nella poesia latina di Joseph Tusiani", ora in Paolo A. Giordano, Anthony Julian Tamburri, eds. *Esilio migrazione sogno americano*, Italiana 10, 2001: 16-42.

nella casa di mare, ma non andavo a mare e non uscivo neppure la sera. A fine settembre era pronta la trascrizione, la revisione dei testi e la traduzione, l'esame metrico. Inviai il file a Sacré e i testi stampati a Tusiani. Dovemmo quasi ordinare a Tusiani di non scrivere più. Niente più nuove poesie, o rischiavamo che il libro non si stampasse più. Seguirono giorni di continui collegamenti Lovanio-New York-Carpignano Salentino. Sacré, sempre molto scrupoloso, non poteva permettere che in un volume dei *Supplementa* alla rivista *Humanistica Lovaniensia* (allora da lui diretta) ci fossero errori o imperfezioni. Alla prima impaginazione constatammo che il volume superava le 400 pagine. Fui costretto a scrivere una Prefazione molto breve.[11]

Il volume finito lo vedemmo nel maggio seguente. Eravamo riusciti a far venire a Lovanio anche Tusiani; questi poteva così conoscere finalmente l'Università che lo aveva consacrato poeta latino attraverso studi, pubblicazioni, letture pubbliche. Nella mattinata di martedì 8 maggio 2007, Tusiani era arrivato a Bruxelles con l'aereo da New York. Arrivai anche io nel pomeriggio; e vennero Sacré e Tusiani all'aeroporto di Zaventem, presso Bruxelles, per portarmi a Lovanio. Era maggio, ma furono giornate con freddo gelido e pioggia quasi continua; e durante il viaggio verso Lovanio ci prese il solito temporale con lampi, tuoni e pioggia. A Lovanio non pioveva più; Tusiani e io fummo ospitati nel Binnenhof Hotel a due passi dall'Erasmus Huis, ossia la "casa di Erasmo", come viene chiamata la facoltà di Lettere. In camera trovai alcune copie del nuovo volume. 428 pagine, formato bello grande.

La mattina del mercoledì 9 maggio, Tusiani tenne agli studenti di Italiano una lezione sulle sue traduzioni in lingua inglese di opere letterarie italiane. Andammo a pranzo — il mondo è proprio piccolo! — in un ristorante gestito da Sammarchesi, compaesani di Tusiani[12]. Nel pomeriggio, era previsto un viaggio ad Anversa a una

---

[11] L'aumento delle pagine fino a oltre 400, aveva reso insufficienti i fondi stanziati. Per la stampa aiutò il contributo della Pegasus Ltd.
[12] Il ristorante stava sulla Maria-Theresiastraat, che costeggia il Binnenhof Hotel, e l'Erasmus huis. Insomma tutto a due passi.

mostra di pittura. Ma il tempo non lo permise: vento fortissimo e gelido e pioggia torrenziale. Sacré ci portò nella più vicina Waterloo. Era tutto chiuso a quell'ora. Trovammo un locale aperto, un bar tutto ornato di cose napoleoniche, dove almeno potemmo gustare un caffè caldo. Tornando alla macchina, sotto pioggia e vento, vedemmo, sulle scale che portavano sulla collina artificiale, turisti coraggiosi, che bagnati fradici salivano verso il monumento in alto. Tornammo nella casa di Sacré a Herent, dove era raccolta tutta la famiglia Sacré. Dopo la cena preparata dalla gentile (e brava) signora Ingrid, Sacré ci portò all'albergo a Lovanio.

Nel pomeriggio di giovedì 10 maggio, in un'ampia aula piena di alunni, professori, ricercatori, dottorandi, presente anche il Preside di facoltà. fu presentato il libro *In nobis caelum*, un volume, come già detto, di 428 pagine, contenente 407 composizioni latine, per ben 5256 versi. L'indomani, venerdì 11 maggio, Sacré ci portò all'aeroporto di Zaventem; Tusiani ed io tornammo in Italia. E, tanto per cambiare, a Zaventem pioveva.

Il fatto che nel volume *In nobis caelum* siano contenute tutte le poesie latine di Tusiani ancora inedite, non significa che esse siano poesie di poco valore o raccogliticce. Semplicemente le poesie precedentemente pubblicate erano sembrate al poeta stesso o agli editores poesie significative in quel momento, o testi validi in base a orientamenti o argomenti specifici.

Sono state pubblicate tutte le poesie latine scritte da Tusiani fino al 2007? Certamente no. Ma di questo si scriverà in seguito.

9 • Tusiani, Iosephus Neo-Eboracensis, *Fragmenta ad Aemilium*, Italice vertit Aemilius Bandiera, Praefatus est Theodericus Sacré, Galatina, Congedo editore, 2009
(Pp. 54; form. cm. 12,6 x 19,5; comp. 20; vv. 245)

Il I novembre 2006 ero stato collocato in pensione. Per celebrare questa data,Tusiani mi donò il manoscritto di 20 poesie latine, chiedendomi di fare una piccola edizione col computer, ventitrenta copie per gli amici. E chiese anche a Sacré di scrivere la prefazione. Sacré, sempre pieno di impegni di lavoro, tardò un poco a consegnarmi la sua prefazione, scritta nel suo elegantissimo latino. Una volta pronto il materiale, contattai l'Editore Mario Congedo per la stampa; venne fuori un libretto di 54 pagine, stampato in molte copie. Il libretto fu presentato nel giugno 2009 in un piccolo convegno presso l'Accademia del Belgio a Roma. 5 degli 8 interventi furono poi stampati nella rivista *Humanistica Lovaniensia*.[13]

Le poesie di questo libretto, pur toccando molti temi caratteristici della poesia latina tusianea, fondamentalmente sono consigli al neo pensionato. Finora i libri ti hanno informato su tutto. Ora lascia i libri ed esci all'aperto. Sarà la natura a insegnarti ogni cosa. Riporto il testo, tradotto, dell'ultima lirica, in strofe saffiche minori.

> XX NON SI AVVERTE NESSUN TERMINE.
> Non si avverte alcun termine. Ora incomincia
> la nostra vera età; conosciuto l'amore,
> si prova dolcezza maggiore in un amore
>   indefinito.
>
> Soavemente ora noi siamo portati attraverso le ombre
> verso i prati mirabili della nuova Aurora,
> come sotto le onde va il mormorio continuo del mare,
>   che sarà domani musica ampia.
>
> Domani la musica riempirà, occuperà
> ogni spazio del mondo e, insieme beati,
> vivremo, Emilio, evviva! i doni
>   di una seconda vita.

10 • Tusiani, Iosephi Neo-Eboracensis *Ad maiorem baculi gloriam*, Scelta, presentazione, traduzione di Emilio Bandiera, Melpignano, Amaltea edizioni, 2014
(Pp. 24; form. cm. 15 x 21; comp. 12; vv. 147)

Nel febbraio 2014, Joseph Tusiani fu colpito da *ictus*. Fortunatamente si riprese abbastanza presto e potè tornare a casa. Ma già in

---

[13] "*Acta Tusianea*", Proceedings of the International Colloquium 'Joseph Tusiani as a Neo-Latin Poet', Roma, 5 may 2009, *Humanistica Lovaniensia* 59 (2010): 304-358.

ospedale i medici gli avevano permesso, anzi lo avevano spinto a scrivere. Iniziò una ricca produzione di testi poetici nelle lingue che anche in passato aveva usato, italiana, latina, inglese, dialettale.

In occasione delle feste natalizie del 2014, pensai di far pubblicare alcune delle poesie latine scritte *post ictum*, come omaggio e auguri natalizi. La pubblicazione fu dedicata "A Joseph Tusiani — amico risanato — con la stima e l'affetto di sempre". Ne risultò una pubblicazione di 24 pagine, comprendente 12 liriche latine, stampate col testo latino in alto e la mia traduzione in basso ad ogni pagina.

Una piccola prefazione illustra le 12 composizioni. Facevo subito notare che il titolo in italiano, "*A maggior gloria del bastone*" non era una irriverente variazione di "*A maggior gloria di Dio*", frase di San Gregorio Magno, diventata poi motto della Compagnia di Gesù. "Dal v. 1 si comprende immediatamente che lo stesso 'bastone' potrà dare i suoi benefici con l'aiuto del cielo". Il bastone comunemente è di legno e Gesù, morendo sulla croce di legno, ha reso questo materiale "nobile, amato e almo".[14] Già in queste prime poesie si notano i mutamenti di cui parlerò nel prossimo titolo.

11 • Tusiani, Iosephus Neo-Eboracensis, *Lux vicit. Carmina Latina*, Edizione, introduzione e traduzione italiana a cura di Emilio Bandiera, Bari, Levante editori, 2018
(Pp. 144; form. cm. 17 x 24; comp. 83; vv. 984)

Man mano che Tusiani mi inviava (o mi faceva inviare)[15] le sue nuove poesie latine, le andavo raccogliendo e a un certo momento decisi di incominciare a tradurle; prima o poi avrei cercato un editore. All'inizio del 2016 furono pubblicate le poesie di Tusiani in lingua inglese, scritte *post ictum*.[16] Mi applicai con maggiore lena alla traduzione delle nuove poesie. Per giunta avevo notato che qualcosa era cambiato dopo l'*ictus*. Dovevo controllare con molta atten-

---

[14] Dalla prefazione, 5.
[15] Si faceva aiutare, anche per il computer, dalle 'badanti' che lo accudivano. Tusiani consegnava loro il manoscritto e dettava i testi.
[16] Tusiani, Joseph, *A Clarion call. New Poems*, Paolo Giordano, Anthony Julian Tamburri, eds, New York, Bordighera Press, 2016.

zione il testo, la metrica e la prosodia. Come ho sempre fatto, quando trovavo qualcosa che non andava, inviavo il testo all'autore ed egli interveniva per risolvere il problema. Per queste ultime poesie, Tusiani non sempre trovava la soluzione; decideva in questi casi di non far pubblicare tali poesie difettose e non pochi testi sono stati esclusi e distrutti per volontà dell'autore. Per il nuovo libro, proposi a Tusiani il titolo "*Lux vicit. Carmina Latina*"; egli fu d'accordo.

Intanto pensavo alla stampa. Avendo conosciuto il giornalista editore Gianni Cavalli della Levante di Bari, mi rivolsi a lui[17]. Egli stesso, esaminato il testo, lo passò al Prof. Francesco De Martino, (professore ordinario di letteratura greca all'Università di Foggia e direttore editoriale di Levante), che accettò di includere il nuovo volume nella collana da lui diretta KLEOS, specializzata in "studi e testi sulla fortuna dell'antico". Il libro uscì nei primi giorni del gennaio 2018 e, nel giro di pochissimi giorni, fu accolto subito con molte e importanti recensioni, e non solo in Italia.

Nel nuovo volume *Lux vicit* ho incluso le 12 liriche già pubblicate in "*Ad maiorem baculi gloriam*", sistemate all'inizio. Seguono altre 71 liriche, per un totale di 83 composizioni.

Una Introduzione di 19 pagine precede i testi con mia traduzione a fronte. Spiego il perché del nuovo libro ed evidenzio subito le novità della "nuova" poesia tusianea. Essa si distingue molto dalla precedente. E soprattutto si nota un maggiore sforzo compositivo. Risultano, a mio parere, almeno 3 elementi nuovi. 1) Tusiani si rende chiaramente conto che qualcosa è cambiato con l'*ictus* ed è convinto che inizia un periodo nuovo per la sua vita e per la sua poesia. 2) È evidente un approfondimento del sentimento religioso. 3) Il pensiero, in queste nuove poesie, è, "involuto", come lo definisce l'autore stesso. Cerco di chiarire che forse "involuto" vuole dire 'più profondo, che ha bisogno di maggiore sforzo per la sua comprensione' (20).[18]

---

[17] Gianni Cavalli aveva pubblicato nel 2015 il romanzo di Tusiani "*Dante in licenza*" (Tusiani, Joseph, *Dante in licenza*, a cura e con saggio di Delio De Martino, Bari, Levante Editori, 2015).
[18] Si veda l'Introduzione, 21.

"Qui il discorso diventa più complicato, certamente più delicato. Gli 83 carmi di questa raccolta presentano un tipo di poesia latina con non poche differenze rispetto alla precedente produzione latina del Tusiani. Sono rinvenibili i noti temi o argomenti; sono rispettati modi di pensare e di vedere caratteristici della produzione tusianea in generale […]. Ma si nota qualcosa di diverso. C'è un modo di esprimersi nel quale spesso manca la serenità espressiva e la chiarezza di stile e di pensiero di Tusiani latino".

Chiudono l'Introduzione alcune osservazioni sulla metrica, anche questa ricca di novità. Tra queste, vanno ricordate non solo alcune varianti metriche, di schemi classici quantitativi, ma anche qualche altra novità. Tusiani ha qui introdotto e usato più volte gli *haiku*, nella forma di strofa di versi di 5/7/5 sillabe o more. Però varia il genere, usando gli *haiku* come strofe di composizioni più lunghe.

&

Una domanda, che spesso è stata rivolta a Tusiani o a me, è stata: "Quanti versi latini ha scritto Joseph Tusiani?"

La risposta apparentemente può sembrare semplice; ma non lo è. Forse sarebbe più logico chiedersi quanti versi di Tusiani sono stati pubblicati e in questo caso basterebbe misurare i versi dei vari libri, tanto dei volumi che superano le 400 pagine, tanto le pubblicazioni con numero minore di pagine, comprese le piccole raccolte di 19 o 20 composizioni. Ma anche in questo caso rimarrebbe valida la prima domanda: "Quanto ha scritto Tusiani in latino?" Non è possibile rispondere con precisione. Si è già accennato in questo lavoro alle poesie latine "ripudiate/non accettate" più dall'autore stesso.

In questa categoria sono da inserire a) poesie rimaste inedite anche dopo decenni dalla composizione e; b) poesie già pubblicate su riviste o in altre pubblicazioni, fin da quando Tusiani ha iniziato a scrivere in latino. Moltissimi sono i testi ancora inediti, che sono stati esclusi dalla pubblicazione dallo stesso autore (non mi permettevo di farlo io!) perché, ripresi magari dopo anni dalla loro composizione, non sono stati considerati più significativi, oppure validi, oppure con qualche difetto non emendabile o che con l'emendamento cambiava tutto. In questa categoria a) entra un buon numero di versi scritti *post ictum*. C'è poi anche un altro buon numero di versi già pubblicati (comunemente su riviste), ormai da decenni. Quando queste composizioni sono state riprese per l'inserimento in raccolte e per la traduzione, l'autore (sempre lui direttamente!) qualche volta si è anche messo a ridere, esclamando: "Ma come ho fatto a pubblicare versi così inutili, senza significato?" E anche questi versi già editi sono stati eliminati.

Poi si arriva a un'altra categoria di versi. È noto che Tusiani molto spesso improvvisava poesie (e non solo latine). Cercava un pezzo di carta e una penna o matita e scriveva. Aggiungeva, magari, anche l'indicazione del luogo, la data e la dedica. E poi regalava queste composizioni a quella persona presente, per la quale aveva scritto. Ho sentito moltissime persone che si vantano di possedere poesie scritte da Tusiani (e non solo latine, ripeto), con dedica. Ho chiesto di farmi una copia, ma mi è stato risposto, quasi sempre, che non era più possibile ricordare dove era stata sistemata quella poesia (evidentemente conservata anche troppo bene!, tanto da non ricordare più dove). Perciò in quest'ultima categoria ci sono testi ormai irreperibili o che torneranno alla luce (se avverrà mai) chissà quando.

Il sistema più sicuro per misurare i versi latini tusianei credo che sarebbe quello di misurare i versi delle varie raccolte, che sono 11. Ma è necessario tenere presente che le poesie delle raccolte *Rosa rosarum* e *Confinia luci set umbrae* sono confluite nel volume *Carmina Latina* del 1994. Le poesie della piccola raccolta *Ad maiorem baculi gloriam* sono entrate in *Lux vicit*. Questo significa che dal conto è necessario togliere le poesie che già sono state inserite in altri volumi (che sono quelli con traduzione). Perciò sono da conteggiare a parte solo *Melos cordis* e *In exilio rerum*.

Melos cordis	versi	295
Rosa rosarum	"	683
In exilio rerum	"	394
Confinia luci set umbrae	"	563
Carmina Latina	"	2218
Carmina Latina II	"	1286
Radìcitus	"	662
In nobis caelum	"	5256
Fragmenta ad Aemilium	"	245
Ad maiorem baculi gloriam	"	147
<u>*Lux vicit*</u>	"	<u>984</u>
Totale versi scritti e riconosciuti dall'autore		12,733 -
Da togliere[19]: *Rosa rosarum* + *Confinia lucis* + *Ad maiorem*		<u>1393</u>
		11,340 -
Da togliere[20]: *Melos cordis* + *In exilio rerum*		<u>689</u>
	Versi tradotti	**10,651**

Al totale dei versi scritti e riconosciuti dall'autore, **12,733**, aggiungerei (approssimati molto per eccesso) più o meno altri 2000 versi ripudiati/non accettati più dall'autore, o perduti. Si arriverebbe a circa **15,000** versi latini scritti da Joseph Tusiani.

---

[19] Perché già inseriti nei volumi con traduzione.
[20] Perché ancora da tradurre.

In front of his home, 35 Via Palude,
in the historic district of San Marco in Lamis

JOSEPH TUSIANI
AND THE TRADITION OF NEO-LATIN VERSE

John T. Kirby

Good morning to you all. I should begin by saying what a tremendous honor it is, as well as a very great pleasure, for me to be on this panel.[1] I am grateful to the Italian Cultural Institute, and to the John D. Calandra Italian American Institute, for including me in today's festivities in honor of Professor Tusiani.

I have thought for quite a long time about what I have wanted to put before you today. The topic I have chosen, 'Tusiani and Neo-Latin,' is not a simple or even a single subject. Rather it is like a braid of many strands, which I will try and bring together for you in the next few minutes. Let us consider these, one strand at a time, and then try to see how they braid together.

[1] I would like to begin by asking you to think about your own life, your self, the pursuits that make you the happiest, and the achievements of which you are most proud. Then think about how readily comprehensible or appreciable these are to those in the world around you, the circles in which you move. We may be talking about your prowess on the tennis court, or in the stock market, or your ability to play the violin, or to bake the perfect pie. What are these things for you? How do they affect your life, as you live it in the world around you?

---

[1] This lecture was delivered in September 2012 as part of 'Finding Joseph Tusiani: The Poet of Two Lands,' an international symposium sponsored by the John D. Calandra Italian American Institute of Queens College/CUNY; the Italian Consulate General, New York; Hunter College, CUNY; and the New York Italian Cultural Institute. Thanks are due once again to those institutions for hosting the event. The *honorandus* was in attendance for the entirety of the event, and indeed sat directly facing the podium, just a few feet away. To preserve the happy *ambiente* and festivity of that day, in a time when Joseph was still among us, I have reproduced the text just as it was delivered; the only changes I have made are an expansion of the title, the addition of some suggestions for further reading, and a few asides in the form of footnotes.

[2] Now I want you to think on a much broader scope, moving from the personal or the individual to the cultural. What are the benchmarks of civilization? What indices do we use to measure the greatness of a society? When we peer down the long corridors of time past, what do we consider the greatest gifts of our forebears to those that followed them — the noblest and best achievements of prior civilizations, the touchstones of their excellence? (Bear in mind that as a classicist I spend a lot of time thinking about the past, about the legacy of ancient peoples and cultures to later generations, and about loss: what does not survive the ravages of time, and what, miraculously, manages to make it through, whether by sheer chance or by the determination of a grateful posterity to preserve and protect what they most prize about their inheritance.)

This constant erosion, and the concomitant heroic process of preservation, is an ongoing pattern through recorded history. Already in the works of authors like Plato and Aristotle, we see the ancient Greeks treasuring, almost fondling like talismans, the inherited texts of Homer and the Attic tragedians. Already by the fourth century BCE they are acutely aware of the erosion I am talking about, and of their incredible, good fortune in having the works of these great poets to hand.

[3] Thus far, two strands: the achievements in your life that are the most important to you personally; and (on a macro-level) the cumulative achievements of the world's cultures that have throughout history proved to have the most substantial and lasting value. As the third strand of our braid, I ask that you ponder how much your personal or individual achievements mirror, or partake of, or contribute to the overall achievements of our society in such a way that it is likely to be memorable, hundreds or thousands of years from now. This third measure, for each of us and for our culture, puts us a long way toward understanding more deeply what it means to speak about 'the classics.' That concept, or cluster of con-

cepts — 'classics,' 'the classical,' and 'classicizing'[2] — has proved notoriously difficult to define in a way that satisfies everyone. A fool's errand, some might say. But in my book, *Secret of the Muses Retold*,[3] I myself rushed in (where angels fear to tread), and tried to offer a definition of 'classic' along these lines:

[a] A classic is something that is the best of its kind
[b] A classic is something that has withstood the test of time
[c] A classic is something that embodies the mythic or symbolic values of its culture.

I have not, despite much contemplation of the matter, significantly revised this definition in the intervening years.[4] A measure of my foolishness, perhaps. But you may be able to hear how these ideas resonate with what I was saying previously: if what we spend our time doing is important, of lasting value, and widely appreciated, and if it turns out to be a brick (so to speak) in the larger edifice of our culture, we are in touch with *the classical*. We ourselves may even be producing *classics*, of one sort or another — whether these be works of literature, of the visual or plastic arts, of performance, of gastronomy or science or technology. And in so doing, we take

---

[2] I discuss *in extenso* what I have termed the 'Three Ages' of the verbal arts, and specifically the phenomenon of 'classicizing,' in §2 of John T. Kirby, 'The Notion of Comparing and the Meeting of Fragments,' pp. 14–29 in Lisa Block de Behar et al., eds. *Comparative Literature: Sharing Knowledges for Preserving Cultural Diversity*. Volume 1. Oxford: EOLSS Publishers Ltd., 2009; see especially pp. 19–24). This essay is also published in digital format as Entry 6.87.1.2 in the Encyclopedia of Human Sciences and Humanities (a part of the Encyclopedia of Life Support Systems [EOLSS] published by UNESCO; accessed online at www.eolss.net).
[3] John T. Kirby, *Secret of the Muses Retold: Classical Influences on Italian Authors of the Twentieth Century* (Chicago: University of Chicago Press, 2001).
[4] For more on 'the classics' as a concept, see John T. Kirby, 'The Great Books,' pp. 273–282 in *The Routledge Companion to World Literature*, eds. Theo D'haen, David Damrosch, and Djelal Kadir (New York and London: Routledge 2011), and 'An Ancient Greek *Journey to the West*: Reading the *Odyssey* through East-Asian Eyes,' *Sino-American Journal of Comparative Literature* 2 (2016) 46–108. On canons, see John T. Kirby (ed.), *The Comparative Reader: A Handlist of Basic Reading in Comparative Literature* (New Haven: Chancery Press 1998), especially xvii–xxv.

our place conspicuously in the Great Chain of Being (*conspicuously* being a key term here, as every human participates in this eternal dance, however long or briefly); and that means that we are in touch with the most deeply-cherished values of our species — both before us, in that we sustain and celebrate what our ancestors have bequeathed us; and after us, in terms of what we bequeath to those generations yet unborn.

If you have followed me this far, you are in a position to understand what is at stake when we speak of the particular form of *classicizing* known as 'neo-Latin.' With your permission I will spirit you back to a momentous occurrence in the history of the West: to what is generally known, in French, as the 'Renaissance' (or, *nella lingua degli dei*, as 'il Rinascimento').[5] In the United States one generally hears the French term, but I think it is important for our purposes today to insist on the Italian, because the particular place and time to which I am taking you is in Toscana — in Firenze itself, in fact, in the year 1439. Firenze had just been the site of an extraordinarily hopeful meeting: the so-called 'Council of Florence,' which convened in 1438 with the astounding ambition of reconciling the Roman Catholic and Eastern Orthodox branches of Christianity. I need not tell you how that turned out for them; but along the way, a neoplatonic philoso-

---

[5] Technical terms may denotatively signify the development of scholarly focus, method, and systematization; but connotatively, they may also serve as the emblazonments of disparate theoretical approaches. The terms *Renaissance* and *Rinascimento* are no exceptions. At least since the publication of Jacob Burckhardt's *Die Cultur der Renaissance in Italien* (Basel, 1860; translated by S.G.C. Middlemore as *The Civilisation of the Renaissance in Italy*, London 1878; continually reprinted), the 'Renaissance' has been conceptualized in terms of its *discontinuity* with the Middle Ages. But many thinkers of more recent vintage would prefer to emphasize the *continuity* of the 'Renaissance' with the rest of the mediaeval period. Eugenio Garin, a scholar of the latter category who deserves to be much better known outside of Italy, published prodigiously on the Renaissance, specifically using the term *Rinascimento*; a short list of his relevant works would include *Giovanni Pico della Mirandola* (Firenze: Vallecchi, 1937); *Il Rinascimento italiano* (Milano: Istituto per gli Studi di Politica Internazionale, 1941); *Dal Medioevo al Rinascimento* (Firenze: Sansoni, 1950); *Medioevo e Rinascimento* (Bari: Laterza, 1954); *L'educazione in Europa 1400–1600* (Bari: Laterza, 1957); *La cultura filosofica del Rinascimento italiano* (Firenze: Sansoni, 1960); *Scienza e vita civile nel Rinascimento italiano* (Bari: Laterza, 1965); and *La cultura del Rinascimento* (Bari: Laterza, 1967).

pher called Georgios Gemistos, later known as Plethon,[6] spoke to Cosimo de' Medici, the great 'Cosimo il vecchio' that is, and other elite Florentines about Plato and the Alexandrian Mystics (thinkers such as Plotinus and Proclus). Gemistos presented his fascination with these thinkers in such a way that the hunger for Greek learning was kindled as never before in Florentine culture. And I mean specifically *Greek* learning: the ability to read Greek authors in Greek. Hitherto, even the most learned in the West were principally reliant on Latin renditions of Greek authors and traditions: thus if you wanted to know about Plato, and could read Latin — a big 'if' in itself, I might add — you went and read Cicero's redaction of Platonic texts. If you wanted a good compendium of Greek mythology, you read Ovid's *Metamorphoses* or *Heroides*. And so on.

But suddenly, this was not enough. Educated Florentines became suddenly and acutely aware that there were people who could read Greek authors *in Greek*; and that meant that perhaps such people could also teach *them* to do the same. The proposition, and the prospect, were irresistible.[7] It may not be quite fair to compare Florentine intellectuals of the *quattrocento* to the average modern New Yorker, but the quickest analogy I can draw here is to imagine stepping outside this building and announcing, 'If you win this lottery, you will receive tens of millions of dollars. And I am about to show you all where to get the winning tickets.'

By 1459, a Greek scholar from Constantinople named Ioannes Arguropoulos had come to Firenze to hand out a fistful of winning lottery tickets: that is to say, he began teaching Florentines how to read ancient Greek. The effect was electrifying. The seeds that Georgios Gemistos had sown in 1439 — the desire to have unmediated

---

[6] Γεμιστός *gemistos* and Πλήθων *plêthôn* both mean 'full,' but *plêthôn* appears to be much the older word, attested in Greek as early as Homer's *Iliad*. Plethon's adoption of the older word as a sobriquet was a deliberate, consciously classicizing move. The formal resemblance to the name Plato (Πλάτων *Platōn*) doubtless pleased him, but appears not to have been the principal motivation for the change.
[7] A vivid and memorable narrativization of the coming of Greek learning to fifteenth-century Firenze is presented in George Eliot's *Romola* (first published in serial format in *Cornhill Magazine*, in 1862–1863; compiled into book format in 1863 by Smith, Elder & Co., a London house).

access to the Greek classics — began to sprout and grow under the hand of Arguropoulos. On 7 November 1468, a group of scholars and poets, which included Marsilio Ficino, Antonio degli Agli, Cristoforo Landino, and Bernardo Nuzzi, met at the villa de' Medici in the hills of Careggi,[8] to discuss classical thought. Ficino immortalized the event in his commentary on Plato's *Symposium*, which stands in a larger literary tradition that includes the *Symposium* itself, along with a *Symposium* by Xenophon, the *Deipnosophistae* of Athenaeus, and (in comedic distortion) the 'Cena Trimalchionis' in the *Satyricon* of Petronius.

Ficino (and doubtless some of the others) studied Greek with Arguropoulos and went on to produce editions and translations of Greek authors. Under the patronage of Cosimo 'il vecchio,' and then of Piero 'il gottoso' and Lorenzo 'il magnifico,' this *Accademia neoplatonica*[9] generated tremendous excitement about what they were learning, and about the doors such knowledge might open for those who would learn it. They made a concerted effort to recuperate the splendor and majesty of classical Greek literature in its original language. And of course they were aided in this by the simultaneous achievements of a number of other remarkable people who either complemented their own work in textual and literary studies, or facilitated the wide and rapid dissemination of it. Examples of the former would include artists, architects, and engineers such as Michelangelo Buonnaroti, Leonardo da Vinci, Donato Bramante,

---

[8] This beautiful villa, acquired by the Medici in 1417 and passing through many hands in the following 600 years, is now a UNESCO World Heritage Site. It may still be visited (by appointment) at Viale Gaetano Pieraccini, 17 (50134 Firenze; tel. +39 055 212245).

[9] Whether or not Ficino and his associates would have used the word *ac(c)ademia* to describe this gathering of literati, is the subject of scholarly debate; see e.g. James Hankins, 'The Myth of the Platonic Academy of Florence,' *Renaissance Quarterly* 44 (1991) 429–475, who thinks not. Federico Giannini ('Marsilio Ficino e lo sviluppo del neoplatonismo nella Firenze medicea tra realtà e invenzione,' published in 2016 on www.finestresullarte.info), is cautious ('l'ipotesi rimane comunque molto affascinante'). Certainly Cosimo's patronage of Ficino long antedates 1468, going back (if we may believe Ficino himself) to 1452. As Ficino was born on 19 October 1433, he would have been just 19 or 20 in 1452.

and Filippo Brunelleschi, who themselves recuperated, celebrated, and indeed extended the achievements of their ancient forerunners in those fields. In the latter category I am thinking principally of Johannes Gutenberg, whose development of movable metal type made possible the production and publication of printed editions of the classical authors, and Andreas Heilmann, who owned the paper-mill that supplied Gutenberg's press. One must never lose sight of the fact that before this time, if you wanted a copy of any author, ancient or modern, you had to have it made as a manuscript — a document written by hand, with pen and ink made by hand, on a writing surface (such as papyrus or parchment) that was also made by hand. Again, the effect was electrifying.[10]

So I propose to you that this was the very moment and place — Firenze, 7 November, 1468 — at which the *Rinascimento* began as a self-conscious cultural movement.[11] From that fertile soil, the crop was harvested and replanted all over Europe, and eventually in the New World as well.[12]

---

[10] On the epoch-making importance of the printing press, see e.g. Elizabeth L. Eisenstein, *The Printing Press as an Agent of Change: Communications and Cultural Transformations in Early-Modern Europe* (Cambridge: Cambridge University Press, 1979, 2 volumes). This book was written in the modern era, but just antedates the development of the internet as we know it today. The value of broad *dissemination* must be weighed against the cost (real or perceived) of *uniqueness*, a problem foregrounded by Walter Benjamin in his famous 'Das Kunstwerk im Zeitalter seiner technischen Reproduzierbarkeit' ('The Work of Art in the Age of Mechanical Reproduction'), first published in 1935 and itself almost immediately disseminated widely, including in French and English translations.

[11] The proposition may be, I recognize, to romanticize somewhat. The most hardened sceptic will insist that Ficino's *Commentarium in Convivium Platonis de Amore* is so closely modeled on Plato's *Symposium* that the dramatic setting could be pure fiction. Moreover, 7 November was thought of in Ficino's time as the birthday of Plato himself, so to describe the banquet as having occurred on this particular date could itself be a symbolic gesture. But Ficino refers to the event separately, in a letter to Jacopo di Poggio Bracciolini, as having actually occurred. In any case, the narrative is more than symbolic: these epoch-making developments really did occur at some point in the mid-15th century, and specifically because of the work of Ficino and his associates.

[12] What is usually called 'Renaissance Humanism' has its roots in the preceding century, also in Tuscan soil: Francesco Petrarca, that great lover of classical learning, was born in Arezzo in 1304. The topic is gigantic, but for readers of English, a

One very memorable moment of this *fioritura* in Italy was Ficino's publication, in 1484, of his monumental translation of Plato — from Greek into Latin. It is important to bear in mind that while our modern Romance languages — Italian, Spanish, French, Portuguese, Romansch, Romanian — developed from Latin, they did not spring, Athena-like, fully-developed out of the classical tongue. Nor did the Latin of the classical period immediately die and ossify: Latin itself continued to develop and grow as it was spoken throughout the Middle Ages, in both literary and vernacular registers. As such, mediaeval Latin evinces every possible degree of clarity, elegance, and beauty — or their opposites. Ficino himself writes a very lucid, workmanlike Latin, but no one would mistake it for Cicero or Caesar or Livy, or even Augustine. But even before the time of Ficino, we find mediaeval writers plying an elegant, sophisticated, and classicizing Latin — have a look, for example, at the *De uulgari eloquentia* of Dante Alighieri, written in around 1305, which ironically is a pamphlet canvassing for the use of a vernacular tongue in literary writing.[13] And very soon after the appearance of Ficino's translations, humanist scholars across Europe were paying close attention — sometimes slavishly so — to the vocabulary and

---

solid start in understanding it may be made by delving into the published research of two modern scholars: Nigel Wilson and Anthony Grafton. Wilson's many books include *Scribes and Scholars: A Guide to the Transmission of Greek and Latin Literature* (Oxford: Clarendon Press, 1968); *Scholars of Byzantium* (Baltimore: The Johns Hopkins University Press, 1983); and *From Byzantium to Italy: Greek Studies in the Italian Renaissance* (Baltimore: The Johns Hopkins University Press, 1992). From Grafton's prodigious œuvre, one might begin with *Commerce with the Classics: Ancient Books and Renaissance Readers* (Ann Arbor: University of Michigan Press, 1997); *Joseph Scaliger: A Study in the History of Classical Scholarship* (Oxford: Clarendon Press; 2 volumes, 1983 and 1994); and (with Lisa Jardine) *From Humanism to the Humanities: Education and the Liberal Arts in Fifteenth- and Sixteenth-Century Europe* (Cambridge MA: Harvard University Press, 1986).

[13] Even apart from the quasi-divine stature of it author, it would be hard to overstate the historic importance of this document. Its very title tells some of the tale: *eloquentia* was, even in the classical period, the Latin word for rhetorical prowess; but elite Romans of Cicero's day sent their sons to Greece for their training in rhetoric — a training they received, of course, in Greek. So this 'classicizing' gesture, embodied in a reverence for Greek learning specifically, was not historically limited to mediaeval Italy.

syntax of their Latin prose. In the most extreme cases, the type lampooned by Erasmus in his dialogue the *Ciceronianus*, they seem to have insisted upon restricting themselves purely to words that can be found in the extant works of Cicero. But even those who, like Erasmus himself and his great friend Thomas More, wrote a more flexible Latin prose, were increasingly conscious of what it means to write a classicizing Latin.

On the verse side (and I use the word 'verse,' not 'poetry,' in an attempt to avoid a long argument over what constitutes *poetry*), this movement was also in full cry by the 1300s, as we see in the stunning classicizing verse of Francesco Petrarca. As the Rinascimento burst into full blossom, in the 1400s and 1500s, the fashion for classicizing verse in Latin, and sometimes even in Greek, became a craze. Writers such as Lodovico Ariosto, Baldassare Castiglione, and Pietro Bembo all tried their hand at this art, as a way not only of expressing their creativity and exhibiting their erudition, but also in order to salute their illustrious predecessors of the classical era.[14]

It is as part of this long tradition and lineage that we must understand the astonishing achievement of Joseph Tusiani, in the twentieth and twenty-first centuries, who produces original work, not only in Italian, his natal *dialetto garganico*, and English, but also in Latin verse of the most impeccable classicizing authenticity.

I am at pains to stress to you what an extraordinary accomplishment this is. Quite apart from whether one's verse qualifies as 'poetry,' which is perhaps to say 'artistic' or 'beautiful' or (to toss yet another cultural hot potato) 'literature,' one must be equipped with a 'skill-set' (if I may smuggle that somewhat inelegant term into this context) that very few people now living possess. Above and beyond a basic knowledge of the grammar and syntax of the Latin language, one must:

---

[14] For a sampling of Neo-Latin verse from the *Rinascimento*, see Alessandro Perosa and John Sparrow (eds.), *Renaissance Latin Verse* (Chapel Hill: University of North Carolina Press, 1979). A standard modern *florilegium* of older mediaeval Latin, in both prose and verse, is Karl Pomeroy Harrington (ed.), *Medieval Latin* (Boston: Allyn & Bacon, 1925), second edition by Joseph Pucci (Chicago: University of Chicago Press, 1997).

[a] know the metrical quantity of each syllable in each line
[b] be familiar with the metrical patterns of classical Latin verse, which are traditional, highly codified, and governed by strict and arcane rules of composition
[c] be able to position each syllable and each word in a sequence that will be semantically intelligible *and* will conform to the metrical requirements of the verse-form
[d] know which vocabulary is deemed more appropriate for prose than for verse, and vice versa
[e] be able to tap into the rich mother lode of the classical Greek and Latin literatures by alluding to them, overtly or covertly, in one's verse.

Only then can one hope that one's work has enough artistic value to some readership that it will merit reading and perhaps even re-reading.

It does not take much charity to grant that even without such artistic value, any poetaster's work that satisfied these formal criteria would be something of a *tour de force*. But I am here today, ladies and gentlemen, as something of an expert witness, to testify to you that Joseph Tusiani's Latin verse is more than this.

I have dealt at some length, in print, with the ways in which his neo-Latin poetry — I am now going to use that word without reservation — is not only skilful and noteworthy, but also beautiful and moving.[15] I have also said a few words about why it is biographically important for him. What I want to emphasize today is that it also situates him in a very long and massively important tradition that goes back at least to Dante and Petrarca, in their consciously classicizing use of Latin for a contemporary audience. What this gesture does, above all, is to reinscribe and underscore the enduring importance of these classical forms *for today*. It buttonholes the

---

[15] John T. Kirby, 'The Neo-Latin Verse of Joseph Tusiani,' pp. 180–204 in Paolo A. Giordano (ed.) *Joseph Tusiani: Poet, Translator, Humanist* (Bordighera, 1994); 'Fresh Air from Helicon: The Neo-Latin Verse of Joseph Tusiani,' reprinted (in revised form) as chapter 3 of *Secret of the Muses Retold: Classical Influences on Italian Authors of the Twentieth Century* (Chicago: University of Chicago Press 2000).

unsuspecting reader, shakes him (if only gently) by the lapel, and reminds him that Catullus and Horace and Vergil and Ovid are not mere fossils or dinosaurs: their artistic fire burns on among us, even today, if we will only fan the flames.

For Joseph Tusiani this is something of a compulsion. When I first began to focus intensively on his Latin verse, he would send me poems fresh from his pen — sometimes scribbled literally on a napkin.[16] *Difficile est saturam non scribere*, said the ancient Roman poet Juvenal: It is hard not to write satire.[17] For Tusiani, the parameters are much broader, much more congenial and less dyspeptic: simply put, for him, 'It is hard not to write verse.' This is the surest sign of a true artist: the creative force wells up exuberantly in him like a mountain spring. And this force is not restricted to his recondite and learned pursuit of Neo-Latin poetry: in every dimension of his creative work, it springs afresh. It brings life and strength and hope and joy to everyone who reads it. And that is why we are here to celebrate him today.

---

[16] My chapter on Tusiani in *Secret of the Muses Retold* includes the *editio princeps* of five such poems. But for a fuller perspective on Tusiani's Neo-Latin verse, one must consult the meticulous editions, sensitive translations, and perceptive criticism of Emilio Bandiera, including *Carmina latina* (2 volumes, Fasano, 1994, 1998); *Joseph Tusiani: Collected Poems (1983–2004)* (Lecce, 2004); *In nobis caelum: Carmina Latina* (Leuven 2007); *Fragmenta ad Aemilium* (Lecce, 2009); and *Lux vicit: carmina Latina* (Bari, 2018).

[17] Juvenal, *Satires* 1.30.

Bronx, NY, preparing for a graduation ceremony, 1950s

IL DIALETTO NELL'OPERA DI JOSEPH TUSIANI

Luigi Bonaffini

Il problema della subalternità del dialetto e della sua dipendenza da altri codici, in cui, specialmente di fronte alla scomparsa del suo universo antropologico e la conseguente contrazione della dialettofonia, cerca gli strumenti del proprio arricchimento, si complica notevolmente quando alla diglossia italiano/dialetto si aggiunge un terzo codice (ed in questo particolarmente consiste l'*eccentricità* di Tusiani), la cui presenza è inglobante, determinante, e minaccia pertanto di sopprimere qualsiasi espressione diversa da sé. Forse il significato più profondo della poesia dialettale, come osserva Brevini[1], sta proprio nella sua lotta mortale contro l'imposizione di una superlingua livellatrice, che a livello nazionale (l'italiano) emana dai mass media e dai centri produttivi del Nord, portatrice di valori legati esclusivamente alla produzione ed al consumo, ed a livello internazionale (l'inglese) mirante al monoculturalismo globale, all'azzeramento di qualsiasi particolarismo etnico e culturale, alla massificazione totalizzante. Da una parte, quindi, l'inglese come lingua imperiale, planetaria, irrinunciabile; dall'altra, in Tusiani, è lingua d'elezione e di studio, la lingua di Wordsworth e di Milton, delle grandi traduzioni dei classici, delle poesie di *Rind and All*, *The fifth Season*, *Gente mia*. E infine, per lui, anche lingua veicolare e strumentale, della quotidianità e del lavoro.

Al centro della vasta opera di Tusiani si colloca quindi una lunga ricerca dominata dal problematico *interplay* di diversi codici linguistici, che interagiscono e si complementano non senza inevitabili conflittualità e disagi, ma sempre nello spazio di una sorvegliatissimma sensibilità linguistica: l'italiano, lingua dei primi studi e della prima formazione culturale; l'inglese, non lingua acquisita per semplice processo di acculturazione, cioè lingua dell'emigrazione, ma oggetto di ricerca e di studio già prima dell'evento traumatico,

---

[1] Franco Brevini, *Poeti dialettali del Novecento* (Einaudi: Torino, 1987) X.

della separazione, e in seguito assurta a strumento espressivo privilegiato; il latino, lingua dei classici, ma anche di una essenziale *romanità*, che come osserva Fontanella, potrebbe rappresentare in chiave linguistica-subliminale il superamento di quell'*impasse* tra italiano e inglese, "ossia una 'lingua' usata come strumento complessivo, unificante, liberatorio, sublimante".[2] Aggiungerei che nel latino Tusiani scorge la possibilità di ritrovare una pronuncia originaria, salda, "antica", nel senso pascoliano di lingua ideale, inedita:

> A farla breve, ho pubblicato in tutte le riviste classiche d'Europa e d'America... e insomma io stesso ho finito col prendere sul serio le *nugae* o *nugellae* che mi ritornavano tradotte in più lingue. Sì, in latino, nella lingua pudica e solenne dei pochi, sono riuscito a dire cose che forse non avrei mai detto, o saputo dire, né in inglese né in italiano. Forse il latino è la *parola antica* di chi, avendo due lingue e due patrie, non sa quale di esse più gli appartenga o lo contenga. Indubbiamente esso è la base solida (e profondamente italica) su cui poggia la mia *ars poetica*.[3]

Ma se le patrie rimangono due, le lingue che Tusiani possiede, oltre al latino, sono inevitabilmente *tre*; anzi il dialetto è la prima lingua, la vera lingua originaria, la più profonda, la lingua materna, sulla quale si sono successivamente sovrapposte le altre, ma senza poterla sopprimere e nemmeno scalfire nella sua unicità, nella sua ricchezza affettiva, nel suo ruolo insostituibile di veicolo memoriale. La scelta del latino e del dialetto, anzi, seguono strade parallele, volte entrambe, ma in modo diverso, alla ricerca di una purezza espressiva impossibile nei due codici dominanti, saturi come sono di letteratura e contaminati da infinite stratificazioni culturali: il latino offre la promessa di un linguaggio antico, preromanzo, non compromesso dal processo di omologazione e di appiattimento che

---

[2] Luigi Fontanella, "Poeti italiani espatriati negli Stati Uniti", in *La letteratura dell'emigrazione*, a cura di Jean-Jacques Marchand (Edizioni della Fondazione Agnelli, Torino, 1991) 465.
[3] Joseph Tusiani, *La parola difficile. Autobiografia di un italo-americano* (Schena Editore: Fasano, 1988) 3.

caratterizza le lingue delle società post-industriali, al cui livellamento espressivo il dialetto oppone invece una parola concreta, fortemente connotata, sovraccarica di significati affettivi, pura di impronte letterarie; il perfetto antidoto, idealmente, ad una sovraeccedenza di cultura. Il regresso del dialetto come lingua strumentale davanti all'inarrestabile dilagare dell'italiano standard è in effetti un fenomeno complesso e, per certi versi, apparentemente contraddittorio, in quanto è proprio nel momento di più forte contrazione che esso assume una sempre più spiccata funzione letteraria, accelerando un processo già in corso al principio del secolo con di Giacomo, e poi maturatosi con Marin, Giotti, Noventa. Che il dialetto, lungi dall'essere considerata lingua "bassa", sia da tempo stato elevato a "lingua profonda" dai dialettali, è anch'essa nozione ormai pacifica, come del resto attestano le numerosissime testimonianze di poeti contemporanei:

> Per me il dialetto non è una lingua *bassa* (come qualche volta si sottintende quando si dice che non se ne ha nostalgia), ma una lingua *profonda*, non perché abbia delle caratteristiche speciali in quanto sistema linguistico, ma perché è stata la lingua delle prime, più vivide fasi della mia vita. E questo vale per milioni di italiani che hanno avuto un'infanzia dialettofona, anche se col passare dei decenni il loro numero continuerà a diminuire[4]

Questa affermazione di Meneghello mette in risalto il bisogno fondamentale di qualsiasi poeta, e che naturalmente interessa tutti i poeti che scrivono in dialetto o anche in dialetto, e cioè quello di esprimersi nella propria lingua nativa, "naturale", in cui il mondo originariamente gli si offrì.[5] Necessità che non poteva non sentire anche Tusiani:

> Il pericolo o nemico maggiore della poesia è proprio la letteratura, e noi riusciamo ad essere noi stessi solo quando, in pochi e rari

---

[4] L. Meneghello, *Il tremaio* (Lubrina: Bergamo, 1986) 124.
[5] F. Brevini, *Le parole perdute* (Einaudi, Torino, 1990) 86.

> momenti di grazia, dimentichiamo quanto ci è stato imposto di ricordare attraverso gli anni. Orbene, ricorrere al dialetto è forse un *nostos* liberatorio, un ritorno alla verginità del vedere e del sentire. Non ammette orpelli il dialetto e, perciò, l'espressione deve essere pura e genuina, direi *elementale*. (Brevini, *Le parole perdute*, 406)

Il ritorno ad un linguaggio *elementale*, che possa risolvere il dimorfismo culturale ed estetico dell'autore, lacerato tra la compostezza ed eleganza classica delle sue composizioni in inglese e in italiano ed il bisogno di massima comunicabilità, di servirsi di uno strumento assai meno diaframmato delle due lingue dominanti, che tendono a guardare le cose dall'alto, a frapporre tra lingua e realtà il peso e la mediazione di una cultura che mira ad appiattire differenze e particolarismi, rappresenta d'altra parte un tentativo di ricongiunzione tra memoria personale e collettività, io soggettivo e comunità, in una ricerca inquietante, necessaria, della patria perduta dopo lo strappo, la lacerazione, il dislocamento culturale. Ernesto De Martino ha fatto notare come il rischio della perdita di una patria culturale riguarda non solo le società arcaiche o primitive e gli emigrati, ma tutto il mondo borghese moderno, come conseguenza del disagio provocato dallo "spaesamento", dalla "perdita di domesticità", dal "naufragio del rapporto intersoggettivo"[6] Per Tusiani, come per tutti gli emigranti, questo disagio rimane invece un trauma originario mai risolto, una ferita profonda solo in parte medicata dall'orgoglio che nasce dall'appropriazione di un'altra cultura e di un'altra lingua, dall'ampliamento degli orizzonti culturali, dalla crescita intellettuale ed artistica. L'inglese viene riscoperto in un lungo processo di acculturazione, ricordato dall'autore nella sua autobiografia:

> Il bagaglio scolastico, di cui dovevo disfarmi, era tutto italiano; la lingua inglese non solo non mi aveva in alcun modo contaminato (forse non ho usato il verbo giusto) ma ero io a scoprirla e quasi inventarla gioiosamente nello studio dei classici, in

---

[6] F. Brevini, *Le parole perdute*, 406.

quello studio paziente e amoroso che mi avrebbe consentito il passaggio dalla conoscenza tecnica all'intimità creativa del nuovo idioma. (Tusiani, *La parola difficile*, 1)

Ma il nodo esistenziale di Tusiani ha origine proprio nello scompenso che si crea tra ampiezza di esperienze culturali ed il vuoto lasciato dalla frattura originaria, dall'impossibilità di sanare l'incrinatura che si è formata là dove c'erano stati l'appartenenza, l'identificazione, il riconoscimento, il collegamento con la comunità dei vivi e dei morti. È da questo scompenso che nasce l'esigenza di riscoprire il legame comunitario, che tanto più cresce quanto più se ne è allontanati, e di recuperare a tutti i costi un proprio autentico radicamento culturale. Il dialetto si offre quindi come lingua comunitaria, legata al vissuto, al concreto, ad una reale collettività di parlanti in senso antropologico, e come il mezzo più idoneo a rappresentare l'esperienza di partecipazione ad una coralità. La scelta del dialetto non costituisce una scelta solamente estetica, ma è una dichiarazione sullo "stato caotico del cosmo, inafferrabile e incomprensibile nella sua totalità estesa, ma ancora in qualche modo decifrabile in una economia *curtense*[7]". Il dialetto pertanto garantisce al poeta la possibilità di ritrovare un'autentica specificità culturale, di coniugare vicenda individuale e destino collettivo, e concede il rassicurante riconoscimento che non tutto il mondo deve essere esperito come estraneità e separazione, perché esiste un mondo *suo* in cui la ferita originaria può, almeno per qualche attimo, (nei momenti di grazia, dirà poi l'autore), rimarginarsi, e dove l'alienazione può trasformarsi in partecipazione, anche se questo mondo esiste ormai solo nella memoria dell'io poetante.[8]

È indicativo quindi che la prima raccolta dialettale, *Làcreme e sciure* (Lacrime e fiori, San Marco in Lamis, 1955) — le altre due so-

---

[7] È quello che dice F. Franchi dell'uso del dialetto da parte di Zanzotto, in *Lingua, dialetto e culture subalterne*, a cura di G. Di Biasio (Longo Editore, Ravenna, 1979) 95.
[8] Per la necessità del dialettale di riappropriarsi di un suo mondo privato, *cfr.* Brevini, *le parole perdute*, *cit.*, 149-150.

no *Tìreca tàreca*, Quaderni del sud, 1978 e *Bronx, America*, Lacaita Editore, 1991 — inizi con un poesia in cui questo legame comunitario viene riaffermato, una dedica alla gente del paese natio: "Ei bona gente, bona gente mia, / te done a te tutte lu core mia .../ I' vogghie sule che me recurdate / come se fosse nu figghie, nu frate" (Ei, buona gente, buona gente mia / ti do tutto il cuore mio... / Io voglio solo che mi ricordiate / come se fossi un figlio, un fratello). La "gente mia" a riconferma dell'incondizionata centralità di questo tema nell'opera di Tusiani, diventerà poi il titolo della maggiore raccolta di poesia inglese. Non a caso è proprio nel primo componimento di *Gente mia* che viene introdotto il motivo dello sradicamento, nell'immagine della pianta violentemente divelta, lasciando al suo posto il deserto, l'erosione, l'abisso e la notte: "Deracinated — / is this the word that somewhat hides the grief / of one uprooted and no longer young? // What would my life be now / if I were still with my familiar trees?" Lo strappo è non solo inizialmente straziante, ma presto rivela la sua misura di tragicità, in quanto condanna l'emigrante a privarsi per sempre di tutto ciò che dà un significato all'esistere, tutto ciò che forma la sua cultura ed il suo mondo, e soprattutto quei legami affettivi di cui si nutre la vita del gruppo, della comunità, della famiglia: "Emigration's / last and most uncharted tragedy is this — slowly it forces people to adjust / to want of love, anticipating death".[9]

In Tusiani questo senso profondo di spaesamento provoca un attrito continuo e tenace, una resistenza residua, in un certo senso retroattiva, all'acculturazione, che spesso si manifesta con dei contraccolpi violenti, proprio perché acculturazione, paradossalmente, significa il contrario di appartenenza e di radicamento, e nemmeno un sovraccarico di cultura può proteggerlo dall' "antica ferita" dell'emigrante, se è vero che la permanenza dell'emigrante all'estero cambia solo superficialmente il suo modo di porsi davanti alla realtà, ma "le strutture profonde della visione del mondo rimangono pressoché intatte":[10]

---

[9] J. Tusiani, *Gente mia* (Stone Park, IL: Italian Cultural Center) 44.
[10] U. Bernardi, "L'antica ferita", in *Lingua, dialetto, e culture subalterne, cit.*, 16.

> ... doppe quarant'anne de 'sta Mereca,
> na cosa sola è certa: quasa quasa
> me pare che non zo' manche partute
> e che ddu bastemente l'ej sunnate
> o viste inte li libbra de lla scola.[11]

A questo impossibile tentativo (subito riconosciuto come tale nella stessa poesia) di ribaltare il rapporto sogno/realtà si accompagna l'altrettanto impossibile impulso a sconfessare la lingua inglese, quasi fosse una colpa da disconoscere, un peccato originale da espiare, come rito iniziatico preludente alla reinserzione nella comunità originaria:

> Chi te l'ha ditte che m'eve scurdate
> di quiste dialette paiesane?
> Non è llu vere. Trenta verne e 'state
> i' non èi maie parlate 'merecane.[12]
>
> ****
>
> ...seppure stegne luntane,
> i' so ssempe paiesane;
> che, seppure parle 'nglese,
> i' so ssempe santemarchese.[13]

Questa insistenza dell'opposizione dialetto/inglese, per tanti versi la più significativa e determinante delle tante possibili opposizioni operanti nell'universo plurilinguistico e multiculturale di Tusiani (dialetto/italiano, inglese/italiano, latino/inglese ecc.), proprio perché nasconde conflittualità molto profonde (identifica-

---

[11] ...dopo quarant'anni d'America / una cosa sola è certa: quasi quasi / mi sembra che non sono nemmeno partito / e che quel bastimento l'ho sognato / o visto dentro i libri della scuola. *Bronx, America*, 48.

[12] Chi te l'ha detto che mi ero scordato / di questo dialetto paesano? / Non è vero. per trenta inverni ed estati / io non ho mai parlato americano. — *Tìreca tàreca*, (San Marco in Lamis: Quaderni del Sud, 1978) 15.

[13] ...seppure vivo lontano / io sono sempre paesano; / e, anche se parlo inglese, / io sono sempre sammarchese. — *Tìreca, Tàreca*, 27.

zione/estraniamento, patria/esilio, comunità/globalismo, appartenenza/massificazione, passato/presente, cultura dominante/cultura "subalterna") si fa ancora più urgente quando i trent'anni d'esilio diventano quaranta, cioè nella raccolta dialettale *Bronx, America*, del 1991, e si profila di nuovo come motivo incombente proprio *in limine*, in "Cercàteme perdone" (Cercatemi perdono):

Che? V'avessite ccrede che pe' quisti
quarant'anne de' Merica
me so scurdate quidde che i' viste

cu quist'occhiera meia
prima de parte pe' dda terra trista?[14]

Il dialetto è soprattutto la lingua della memoria, il tramite necessario tra passato e presente, tra il dentro e il fuori. È l'unico strumento con cui l'autore può testimoniare un universo antropologico perduto non solo attraverso il distacco, ma obiettivamente scomparso, una civiltà cancellata eppure ancora superstite come sistema di valori e di contenuti umani, come struttura profonda ancora operante. In effetti, il dialetto per Tusiani si costituisce fatalmente come sistema segnico due volte rimosso dalla realtà che vuole esprimere, non solo per l'allontanamento geografico del parlante, ma soprattutto perché, e questa è la sua dimensione tragica, i suoi referenti sono ormai addirittura estinti, assenti. Di quell'universo cancellato rimangono, anch'esse minacciate, solo le parole, come nota ancora Meneghello: "le lingue scompaiono più lentamente delle cose, e quindi c'è un periodo in cui le cose scomparse non sono più accessibili altro che attraverso i loro spettri presenti nella lingua in via d'estinzione."[15] Attraverso la parola dialettale, per un po' di tempo ancora, si possono quindi ritrovare

---

[14] Che? credete voi che per questi / quarant'anni d'America / mi sia dimenticato di ciò che ho visto / con questi occhi miei / prima di partire per quella triste terra? — *Bronx, America*, 9.
[15] Citato da Brevini in *Parole perdute*, 46.

le cose perdute. Ma se le tre raccolte di poesie dialettali rappresentano un ritorno alle origini, l'autore non può tuttavia annullare l'aleatorietà del suo sforzo, ed è ben consapevole che il mondo che la parola dialettale tenta di evocare nella sua piena concretezza è segnato dal fantasma della sua propria inconsistenza, "ed il suo tendere verso di esso, in una condizione di tragica solitudine, è simile al gesto con cui Ulisse nell'XI dell'*Odissea* tenta di abbracciare la madre, che 'volò dalle mani simile a un'ombra / o a un sogno'"[16]

> Me vè da chiagne dope quarant'anne
> de Mereca, me vè da chiagne penzanne
> a questa terra che non è cchiù mia,
> mo cche me porta qua la fantasia[17]

Questo pianto del poeta, che percorre tutte e tre le raccolte, ma si fa più frequente nell'ultima, non è, come potrebbe a prima vista sembrare, soltanto archeologia sentimentale, nostalgia etnica, *homesickness*, ma è un pianto cosmico, una sorta di epicedio universale, un lamento funebre per un mondo scomparso per sempre ed irrecuperabile al di fuori della dimensione memoriale. L'unico ritorno possibile può avvenire soltanto nel ricongiungimento finale con gli avi, con i morti della sua terra, come lamenta il poeta nella solitudine del suo scacco esistenziale:

> Non sacce chija sònne; sacce sule
> che, iune de quisti iurne,
> j'a ì a ffà pe sempe cumpagnia
> a di vecchiune de la terra mia..[18]

---

[16] F. Brevini, in *Parole perdute, cit.*, 150, con riferimento alla condizione del dialettale contemporaneo.
[17] Mi vien da piangere dopo quarant'anni / d'America, mi vien da piangere pensando / a questa terra che non è più mia / or che mi porta qui la fantasia.
[18] Non so chi sono; so solo / che uno di questi giorni, / devo andare a far compagnia / a quei vecchioni della terra mia. *Bronx, America*, 27.

Questo nodo fondamentale si pone al centro di un folto campo semantico, fortemente connotato, che ne esplora la molteplicità di implicazioni e ramificazioni: la nostalgia, l'esilio, l'emigrazione, il paese, il distacco, le feste, il ritorno, il ricordo, la gente. Inutile dire che l'emigrazione è uno dei temi dominanti in tutta l'opera di Tusiani, ma nelle raccolte dialettali viene vista da una angolazione diversa, *dall'altra parte*, come attraverso i ricordi dei quattro vecchietti che pensano a *Loangailanda e Brucculine* in "Lu mure 'li grazie", o nei disoccupati che sognano *Bronx e Brucculine* in "La strata 'lu ponte", o nell'emigrante che ritorna al convento di San Matteo (uno dei luoghi *sacri* nella memoria di Tusiani, come la *montagna*), o ancora nel ricordo del porto di Napoli in "La lettera ma' 'mpustata". La sua condizione di emigrante e di emarginato s'incarna nella parola chiave *furstier*[19], anche titolo di una delle liriche di *Tìreca tàreca*:

"So menute culla scurda:
cumpà Pé, non te recurde?
Me canusce? So Tusiane,
so menute da luntane".

Cumpà Petre trainere
no' responne a nu frustere.
Tutte li spine sonn'asciute,
tutte li stelle so fernut[20].

---

[19]. Per una discussione della figura del "forestiero} nella poesia dialettale, vedi Brevini, *Le parole perdute, cit.*, 154: "È tutt'altro che casuale che Baldini, non senza il ricordo di *L'étranger* di Camus, intitoli la più recente raccolta [1988] *Furistìr*. L'estraneità si è insinuata anche nel cuore dell'universo dialettale...Contro ogni estetica della nostalgia e del rifiuto, Baldini ha dimostrato come il disagio dell'uomo contemporaneo non conosca eccezioni geografiche. Il testo che intitola il libro può anche essere letto come un apologo della condizione del poeta neo-dialettale. Lo occupa il monologo di un vecchio che non riconosce più il paese nel quale è sempre vissuto."
[20] Sono venuto di notte: / compare Pietro, non ti ricordi? / Mi conosci? Sono Tusiani?, / son venuto da lontano. // Compare Pietro carrettiere / non risponde ad un forestiero. / Tutte le spine sono spuntate / tutte le stelle son finite. *Tìreca tàreca*, 14.

Il dramma che si nasconde dietro la cantabilità dell'ottonario è quello del non-riconoscimento, del non-ritorno, della mancata identificazione, ed è sintomatico che sia proprio il carrettiere, un leit-motif ricorrente e figura emblematica nella poesia dialettale di Tusiani, a non riconoscere più il poeta che viene da lontano. Infatti, in "La morte 'lu trainere" (La morte del carrettiere), l'uccisione del carrettiere da parte de "lu tomòbbile" (l'automobile) preannuncia anche la morte dell'antica civiltà contadina soppressa dal progresso tecnologico dell'età postindustriale, che ignora le aspirazioni più intime dell'individuo, del carrettiere che "sunnava stelle e nide / e nu funne de sucamele..." (che sognava stelle e nidi / ed una valletta di narcisi). Il dialetto, che si propone di salvaguardare queste aspirazioni, è quindi "testimone di una realtà umana che non è soltanto il passato o la nostalgia, ma è ancora storia delle emozioni e delle esperienze di un popolo, e si propone come futuro proprio nella sua qualità di lingua conservatrice, portatrice di valori comuni dispersi o dimenticati, nella sua capacità di mettere in luce aspetti dell'uomo dimenticati o respinti..."[21] Alter ego del poeta, alternativa umana e sofferente all'impersonalità ed alla estromissione, il carrettiere è una figura antica, mitica, legata alla luna e al vento, con cui l'io poetante s'identifica profondamente, fino a sprofondarsi in essa:

> Lu trajenere è quiste penzere,
> e llu traìne
> è llu destine:
> iè llu destine de lla vita mia
> che ffa sempe,
> sempe la stessa via,
> Sante Marche e San Severe...
> Ammèn e cusissìa[22]

---

[21] F. Loi, "Il paradiso perduto", in *La maschera del dialetto*, a cura di A. Foschi e E. Pezzi Ravenna: Longo, 1988) 110.
[22] Il carrettiere è questo pensiero, / e il carretto / è il destino: è il destino della vita mia / che fa sempre, sempre la stessa via, / San Marco e San Severo... Amen e così sia! *Bronx, America*, 26.

Oltre al carrettiere, la memoria del poeta è popolata da molte altre figure e luoghi che assumono un aspetto sacrale, mitico, archetipo, veri e propri grumi esistenziali dai quali il processo memoriale non può prescindere, nodi semantici ed affettivi intorno ai quali si ricompone la patria perduta del ricordo: il convento di San Matteo, la montagna, la campana, la chiesa di Sant'Antonio, i vecchi del paese, le parole infantili. Alla montagna sarà infatti indirizzata "La lettera ma' 'mpustata" (La lettera mai imbucata), l'ultima poesia di *Bronx, America*, che riassume un po' tutto il destino dell'emigrante:

> Gargane mia, te scrive questa lettera
> pe' ffarète capì che, dallu iurne
> che sso' partute, me vì sempe 'nzonne
> come vè 'nzonne allu zite la zita,
> come vè 'nzonne allu figghie la mamm[23].

È chiaro che la montagna conserva intatto il suo significato archetipo di amnios protettivo a cui tende l'io emarginato, che può riconquistare il suo status originale solo attraverso il sogno o la memoria. Ma la montagna, il paese, il convento sono i luoghi privilegiati dalla memoria, profondamente radicati nella psiche con tutta la loro ricchezza di significati emozionali, soprattutto perché sono i luoghi dell'infanzia, e la poesia dialettale di Tusiani è anche, e forse principalmente, una riscoperta, un ritorno, un regresso verso il mondo dell'infanzia, (e quindi, come esperienza collettiva, ad uno stadio anteriore all'industrializzazione). Quello del "ritorno" è uno dei *topoi* più tenaci nella poesia dialettale contemporanea, innanzitutto per la sua carica salvifica di fronte alla *malaise* dell'uomo moderno, e lo troviamo in Pierro (ritorno all'infanzia mitizzata, ma anche ad un mondo sotterraneo, ctonio); in Loi (all'adolescenza ed agli anni della resistenza); in Zanotto (ad una

---

[23] Gargano mio, ti scrivo questa lettera / per farti comprendere che, dal giorno / in cui son partito, mi vieni sempre in sogno / come viene in sogno al fidanzato la fidanzata, / come viene in sogno al figlio la mamma.

civiltà scomparsa o che sta per scomparire); in Calzavara (ad una mitica età primordiale, anteriore ad ogni alfabeto); in Zanzotto (ad uno stadio pre-razionale, al grembo materno).[24] Il dialetto si rivela quindi anche una via per una personale regressione verso le proprie radici esistenziali, nel suo ruolo di lingua "originaria", lingua ancestrale, lingua materna, facendo sì, nel contempo, che alla pagina approdino contingenti di realtà infinitamente più densi di quelli rintracciabili sulla pagina del poeta italiano... I caratteri storici e culturali del proprio strumento fanno sì che il dialettale dica in primo luogo quell'essere radicato, infitto nelle cose ... quel mantenersi ancorato alla vita nella sua greve, materica umiltà".[25]

Il *nostos* liberatorio del dialetto, a cui accennava l'autore, si afferma sia sul piano linguistico sia su quello esistenziale (la psicolinguistica, tra l'altro, sottolinea gli stretti rapporti che intercorrono tra le due sfere), permettendo un ritorno ad una situazione evolutiva pre-culturale, se non addirittura pre-razionale:

Sciò sciò! Musce muscille! Sciò!
'Ndi 'ndò! 'Ndì 'ndò!
La campana de Sant'Antó!
None none! I' non stegne sbalijanne:
me stegne 'mbrijacanne
de quiddi sóne che senteva 'ntanne,
quande teneva sett'anne,
fore lu Puzzeranne.
Scì e nno! Scì e nno! Cicche ci vò!
Cicche ciacche, cicche ciacche!
Petre Mola e vacchevacche!
Nucenzie e Nespolone!
Tirolò e Trufelone[26]

---

[24] Sul motivo del "ritorno" nella poesia dialettale contemporanea, cfr. M. Chiesa e G. Tesio, *Le parole di legno* (Milano: Mondadori, 1984) 24-25.
[25] Brevini, *Le parole perdute*, 113.
[26] *Sciò sciò! Musce muscille! Sciò! / 'Ndi 'ndò! 'Ndì 'ndò! / La campana di Sant'Antonio!* / No no! Io non sto farneticando: / mi sto ubriacando / di quei suoni che ascoltavo allora, / quando avevo sette anni, / fuori il "Pozzogrande".

Questi versi, costruiti sull'insistenza fonica ossessiva di filastrocche infantili, slegati da qualsiasi razionalità discorsiva e da qualsiasi coerenza logica, puro abbandono al processo memoriale in atto, si snodano sul filo di una singolarissima energia espressiva, di ebbrezza ditirambica, e sono indubbiamente tra i più *liberi* e immediati che il poeta abbia scritto, e sarebbero certamente impensabili sia in italiano, sia in inglese, sia in latino. Che la filastrocca, come linguaggio infantile, pre-grammaticale, svincolante, grumo esistenziale asemantizzato, sia uno dei nodi essenziali della poesia dialettale di Tusiani (significativo, in questo senso, che sia una filastrocca a dare il titolo al secondo libro, *Tìreca, tàreca*) è evidenziato dalla sua ricorrenza sistematica nelle tre raccolte, non solo nel suo significato di sedimentazione antropologica e culturale (per esempio la filastrocca sul pane, in "Lu parrozze", che ricorda un componimento del siciliano Vincenzo D'Ancona sulla mietitura), ma come nucleo emozionale riaffiorante nei momenti più impensati sotto la spinta del ricordo prorompente, sconvolgendo spesso la regolarità metrica e sintattica del testo, e minandone dall'interno lo status di discorsività:

> Iame a cogghie mericule, uagliò,
> sope la cima de Monte Celane
>
> e, se pùnceche, *cicche ci vò*,
> sagne de rosa te tegne le man[27].

Se il tentativo di recuperare l'innocenza dell'infanzia è intenzionale, cosciente, espressamente dichiarato, come in "Lu refuge" e "Nustalgia", è nella capacità di riscatto della parola che ha ritrovato la sua verginità, affrancata da qualsiasi stratificazione culturale, nel suo potere consolatorio, che fa affidamento il poeta, come

---

/ *Scì e nno! Scì e nno! Cicche ci vò! Cicche ciacche! / Pietro Mola e Vacchevacche! / Nucenzio e Nespolone! / Tirolò e Trufolone!* — *Bronx, America*, 11.

[27] Andiamo a cogliere more, ragazzo, / sopra la cima di Monte Celano, / e se ti pungi, ti sta bene/ sangue di rosa ti tinge le mani. — *Tìreca tàreca*, 16.

appunto in "Nustalgia" dove gli oggetti dell'infanzia vengono evocati più per le loro qualità sonore, o meglio per l'intensità della loro risonanza interiore, palese anche nell'infoltirsi delle rime, che per la loro realtà fenomenologica:

> Se i' nen penze a tutte questi cose,
> che cce rumane de 'sta vita mia -
> sette iurnate corte e ventelose?
> Li dice, sti parole, e tte chenzul[28].

La virtù magica, apotropaica, della parola, si rivela tutta nell'atto stesso del dirla, nella sua forza di ripercussione psichica ed emotiva, come nella bella poesia "Petrusine 'gne menestra", dove il ritorno di "Tusiane" dalla "'Mereca remota" si fissa sulla ricerca di una parola superstite, "la parola Cannelora" (la Candelora è una festa paesana, diventata poi proverbiale: "Cannelora, Cannelora, la vernata è sciuta fora"). È inevitabile, a questo punto, un raffronto con la poesia dialettale di Zanzotto, che per strade diverse, nella sua ricerca della fonte originaria della lingua, approda ad un dialetto arcaico, paleoveneto, che si trasforma poi in glossolalia infantile, il *petèl*, "mezzo originario omogeneo alle radici lontane per esprimere il rapporto affettivo 'insanabile' con la Madre".[29] Straordinario è poi, in ambedue gli autori, lo scarto tra profondità di cultura e umiltà del mezzo linguistico. Ma se il *petèl* di Zanzotto nasconde la promessa di un linguaggio arcaico, pregrammaticale ed universale nella sua essenzialità, il regresso di Tusiani per molti versi prende spunto dal Pascoli dei *Nuovi Poemetti* e di *Myricae*, dalla sua poetica del fanciullino, ma anche dalla sua apertura a contaminazioni plurilinguistiche, come del resto il poeta stesso è pronto a riconoscere:

---

[28] Se non penso a tutte queste cose, / cosa resta della vita mia / sette giornate corte e ventose? / Le dici queste, parole, e ti consoli. – *Bronx, America*, 13.
[29] Sul *petèl* di Zanzotto, vedi l'interessante saggio di F. P. Franchi, "Clausole di una memoria infelice", in *Lingua, dialetto e culture subalterne*, op. cit., 78.

> Ecco riascolto le parole che dicevo alla mamma e che la mamma diceva a me, e—dimmi—non sono di nuovo lo stesso fanciullino di quegli anni lontani? E non È forse vero che, per tutta la vita, noi ci portiamo dietro, anzi dentro, il bimbo che siamo stati? (Tusiani, Lettera, *cit.*)

E si vedano certe inserzioni nel corpo del testo dialettale per un diretto raffronto con la famosa "Italy" di Pascoli:

> Li scappa cacche *yesse* e *bisinisse*,
> ma, cchiù de tutte, dìcene *monì*,
> la parola che 'mpara e dice spisse
> chi mette pede inte quidde *contrì*[30]

Pascoli è naturalmente un punto di riferimento obbligatorio per la poesia dialettale e neodialettale del Novecento, valga per tutti Pasolini, per le sue suggestioni di una lingua vergine "che più non si sa", in cui trasferire una cultura perfettamente aggiornat[31], ed il richiamo suona ancora più opportuno per Tusiani, con la sua riscoperta di una "lingua antica" nel latino. Resta da chiedersi, specialmente in vista della rilevante fioritura di poesia dialettale attualmente in corso, dove possa situarsi Tusiani nel variegato panorama della poesia dialettale del Novecento, ed in particolare quale posto venga ad occupare nei confronti della rigogliosa poesia neodialettale.

Sotto il profilo della metrica, pur nell'ineccepibile costruzione ed eleganza formale del verso, le composizioni dialettali abbondano di ottonari, endecasillabi, doppi senari ed ottonari, decasillabi, distici a rima baciata, con rare incursioni nel verso libero, e privilegiano la regolarità metrica, le forme chiuse, fino al recupero di forme popolari o popolareggianti, come la ballata e il dialogo amoroso. Siamo cioè nell'ambito di una poesia apparentemente impo-

---

[30] Ci scappa qualche *yes* e *business*, / ma pù di tutto dicono *monì*, / la parola che apprende e dice spesso / chi mette piede in quel paese. *Bronz, America,* 22.
[31] Per l'importanza di Pascoli nella poesia dialettale di questo secolo, vedi Brevini, *Le parole perdute, cit.,* 199-202 e F. Loi, *La maschera del dialetto, cit.,* pp. 67 e 121.

stata in modo tradizionale, che risente maggiormente delle esperienze dialettali della prima metà del secolo. Lo stesso si potrebbe dire per i temi, che registrano i topos abitualmente legati alla poesia vernacolare: la nostalgia del paese nativo, che però è una componente centrale a tutta l'opera di Tusiani, così struggente in quella in inglese, e diventa dominante, ossessiva nella poesia dialettale, colorando di sé tutte e tre le raccolte, con il peso di tutte le implicazioni esistenziali ed antropologiche discusse sopra; l'importanza data alle feste, alle processioni, ai funerali, iniziazioni e cerimonie che perpetuano arcaici riti di primavera con abbondanza di cibo e di vino, ed "in tutte viene esaltato il ricordo mai spento nella memoria collettiva di una società di eguali, dove l'identità culturale del gruppo era più forte delle tensioni sociali."[32] (riaffermando così l'aspirazione a riacquistare uno specifico culturale); il ricorso a forme e motivi popolari, la ballata, la canzone, la filastrocca, la ninna nanna, la fiaba ed anche — sulla scia di Meli, di Cima, di Trilussa — la favola; la mitizzazione dell'infanzia, dei suoi luoghi e dei suoi oggetti, la montagna, la campana, il convento, la campagna, la chiesa, i giochi infantili, il paesaggio; la frequenza dei proverbi e detti popolari; la tendenza al dialogo teatralizzante da parte dei numerosi personaggi che popolano il mondo della memoria (specialmente in *Bronx, America*), i vecchi del paese, i parenti morti, il riconoscimento cioè della comunità come aggregato di *persone*, — uniche, irriducibili, irripetibili nelle loro radici metastoriche come nella loro identità storica.[33]

DIALETTO E TRADUZIONE

Tempo fa ho chiesto a Tusiani se la traduzione della poesia dialettale ponesse dei problemi particolari, perché ritenevo che una sua testimonianza diretta fosse importante. Ecco la sua risposta:

> Mi è stato chiesto se il tradurre dall'italiano [cioè dal toscano] sia meno difficile del tradurre da un dialetto non toscano; se, cioè,

---

[32] U. Bernardi, *op. cit.*, 19.
[33] U. Bernardi, *op. cit.*, 39.

qualsiasi altro dialetto della nostra Penisola presenti per il traduttore ostacoli più scabrosi da affrontare e superare. Non è facile la risposta. Anzitutto, bisogna prima vedere con quale dei dialetti italiani (e sono più di quanti non ne abbia registrati Dante nel suo *De Vulgari Eloquentia*) avrà a che fare il traduttore, e qual è la provenienza linguistica dello stesso traduttore. Un dialetto meridionale presenterà un minor numero di problemi a uno che dall'infanzia abbia parlato il medesimo dialetto. Ed è anche questione di preparazione, dirò, alloglotta del traduttore. Valga questo esempio, anche se di natura personale. Avendo io parlato il dialetto garganico fin dall'infanzia, ed essendo il dialetto garganico altrettanto meridionale quanto il napoletano e il siciliano, sono in grado di comprendere napoletano e siciliano più di quanto non possa un traduttore di formazione linguistica settentrionale, a prescindere da singoli vocaboli o singole strutture idiomatiche che richiedono studio e approfondimento. Tutti i dialetti meridionali hanno un legame più solido col latino, a differenza dei dialetti settentrionali, geograficamente ed intrinsecamente più vicini alle lingue d'oltralpe. Orbene, a meno che non ci troviamo dinanzi a un traduttore versato in dialettologia e, di conseguenza, capace di affrontare e risolvere problemi di immediata comprensione ed assimilazione, il traduttore di origine meridionale riuscirà a dominare qualsiasi dialetto meridionale perché tutti i parlari del Meridione d'Italia, anche se divergenti per varietà di pronuncia e peculiarità di terminologia, sono identici per ceppo e ramificazione etimologica. E questo mi porta alla domanda più pertinente: Quali difficoltà ho dovuto affrontare nel tradurre poeti napoletani, dallo Sgruttendio al Nicolardi? Rispondo: non molte, e sempre di natura lessicale, ma mai sì gravi da sprofondarmi in un abisso di assoluta incomprensione del testo, voglio dire dello spirito del testo. Ed è infine la stessa preparazione culturale del traduttore la chiave per una lettura più attenta e feconda. Prendiamo i primi due versi della celebra lirica natalizia di Sant'Alfonso de' Liguori "Quanne nascette Ninne a Bettalemme /jeva notte e pareva mezejurne," Sono due endecasillabi di una sorprendente facilità che, però, un traduttore del tutto ignaro di dialetti meridionali non riesce a vedere, credendo termini incomprensibili "nascette," "jeva" e "mezejurne" che, invece, sono locuzioni italiane lievemente travisate per "nacque" "era" e "mezzogiorno." Certamente mi è a volte toccato ricorrere all'ausilio di un glossario approntato dallo specialista in materia per accertarmi del significato di vocaboli quali "paputo" e "sciaureia" (Nunziante Pagano) o "acrisante" (Edoardo Nicolardi) o "cacciuttella" (Rocco Galdieri). Ma questo è avvenuto nel caso di tutti i testi medievali e rinascimentali che ho tradotto in inglese. Ed ora l'ultima domanda, la più difficile e pericolosa: Che cosa succederebbe se io volessi affrontare, diciamo, il dialetto bergamasco o valdostano? Anzitutto, non potendo a prima lettura rendermi conto dell'importanza o vitalità poetica del testo, rimarrei inceppato nella stessa mancata comprensione di una frase o dell'intera pagina, più che di una singola parola: il che già crea un distacco fra traduttore e lirica da tradurre, un senso di sfiducia o paura, insomma una alienazione spirituale. Tra me e i miei poeti napoletani, grazie appunto alla lingua meridionale in comune, non è esistito alcun divario d'intelletto o di spirito. Alla loro presenza mi sono sentito come dinanzi al Pulci, al Tasso, a Michelangelo, ed agli altri poeti da me volti in verso inglese.

Per l'antologia trilingue di poesia napoletana *The Bread and the Rose. A trilingual Anthology of Neapolitan Poetry from the Renaissance to the Present*, Legas, New York 2005, curata dal poeta napoletano Achille Serrao e da chi scrive, Tusiani ha tradotto otto poeti napoletani: Giulio Cesare Cortese, Giambattista Basile, Filippo Sgruttendio da Sclafani, Nicola Capasso, Nunziante Pagano, Alfonso Maria De' Liguori, Rocco Galdieri, Edoardo Nicolardi. Li ha tradotti partendo da un concetto fondamentale e a mio avviso imprescindibile, e cioè che questi poeti scrivono nella loro lingua, senza riserve e senza preconcetti, nello stesso modo in cui Tasso e Leopardi scrivono nella loro. Viene subito così eliminato il pregiudizio più pernicioso verso i dialetti, che inficerebbe irrimediabilmente qualsiasi tentativo di traduzione, e cioè che si tratta di linguaggi gergali, substandard, che richiedono una forma gergale nella lingua in cui si traduce. Il problema della traduzione si pone allora, ad un livello più alto, come una questione di resa stilistica, attenta ai valori formali dell'originale, e non come semplice problema lessicale e semantico.

Le prime poesie tradotte da Tusiani per l'antologia sono alcune ottave di *La Vaiasseide* (1612), di Giulio Cesare Cortese (1570?-1640?). *La Vaiasseide* è un poemetto in cinque canti in ottava rima (la tradizionale ottava eroica è il metro cui il Cortese si manterrà fedele in tutti i suoi poemi) i costumi e gli intrighi amorosi delle serve napoletane. Ha la dedica di Giambattista Basile: "A lo re de li viente". Ogni canto inizia con l'*Argomiento:*

Canto secondo

Argomiento

Figliai Renza e facette na figliola
che lo marito n'appe a spantecare.
Ogne vaiassal n'have cannavola
e se ne sbigna pe se sgoliare.
Vace lo hanno; Preziosa sola
scrive a Cienzo e se vole mmaretare;
nce la dà lo patrone, e Carmosina
non pò fuire, e posta è a na cantina.[34]
Renza campaie commo na Segnora
e 'scette prena 'n capo de no mese.
Ogne uno le diceva: «A la bon'ora!
Te vea mamma de Conte e de Marchese».
A Mineco parea mille anne onne ora
che la mogliere trasesse a lo mese,
ped avere no ninno o na nennella
che la portasse a màmmara-nocella.[35]

---

[34] Argomento. Partorì Renza ed ebbe una bambina / che il marito aveva atteso a lungo. / Ogni serva ne ha desiderio / e se ne fugge per togliersi la voglia. / Si diffonde la notizia: solo Preziosa / scrive a Cenzullo e si vuole sposare; / percossa dal padrone, Carmosina / non può fuggire ed è segregata in una cantina.
[35] Renza campò come una Signora / e restò incinta in capo a un mese. / Ognuno le diceva: «Alla buon'ora! / ti veda mamma di Conte o di Marchese». / A Menico

Luigi Bonaffini • "Il dialetto nell'opera di Joseph Tusiani"

L'ottava, con la sua struttura metrica così rigida (rima abababcc), pone dei problemi notevoli al traduttore che voglia riprodurla, o almeno avvicinarsi ad essa. Tusiani è uno dei pochi traduttori che cerca sempre, quando è possibile, di rispettare le caratteristiche formali dell'originale nella traduzione. Ciò richiede un impegno ed una sensibilità linguistica che possono sfuggire al lettore poco attento, ma che non sfuggono alla maggioranza dei traduttori, per i quali affrontare l'endecasillabo o la rima è un'impresa pressoché impossibile, per cui spesso traducono anche il sonetto con il verso libero. L'ottava in particolare, con il suo schema inesorabile ed austero, offre una forte resistenza alla riproduzione mimetica, ed in questo caso è comprensibile se il traduttore non insiste sulla rima a tutti i costi, quando ciò portasse ad una traduzione arzigogolata o stucchevole. Tusiani affronta così il problema (p. 30):

Summary

Renza gave birth at last to a baby girl
for whom her husband waited long, too long.
All servant girls were seized by the same urge
and all sneaked out to make their wish come true.
News travels fast: Preziosa, all alone,
writes to her Vincent, whom she wants to marry;
impeded by her boss to run away,
Carmosina is doomed in a cellar to stay.

Like a true lady Renza lived her life,
and she got pregnant after just one month.
"Good luck!" everyone said, "May you become
the mother of a Count or a Marquis!"
To Dominic each hour seemed countless years
before his wife into her ninth month came:

---

ogni ora sembrava mille anni / che la moglie entrasse nell'ultimo mese, / per avere un bambino o una bambina / da portare a màmmara-nocella.

> if not a boy, a girl he craved so much
> he dreamed of children playing just as such.

Prima di tutto è da notare che l'endecasillabo, verso canonico della poesia italiana, viene tradotto, e questa è una costante in tutta l'opera di traduzione di Tusiani, nell'unico verso inglese possibile, cioè il pentametro giambico, anch'esso verso canonico della poesia inglese e molto simile all'endecasillabilo per struttura ritmica e numero di sillabe. Dico questo perché la maggior parte dei traduttori raramente fa questa scelta, optando spesso per un verso variabile che va dalle otto alle undici sillabe. Tusiani decide di non riprodurre lo schema della rima in tutti i versi, ma lo conserva negli ultimi due, traducendo il distico a rima baciata con una "heroic couplet", dando così la sensazione della rima che, applicata a chiusura della strofa, sugella ogni ottava in modo formalmente preciso. Questa, per inciso, è la soluzione adottata da Tusiani anche per altre opere molto più impegnative, come la traduzione del *Morgante* di Pulci. L'attenzione ai valori formali non si limita però alla struttura metrica ed alla versificazione, ma interessa anche il registro linguistico ed il tono, per rendere la tonalità piana e colloquiale del tema popolare (la storia della servetta) con espressioni altrettanto familiari: *and all sneaked out, impeded by her boss.*

Per Filippo Sgruttendio Da Scafati, certamente il più grande poeta napoletano del Seicento, valgono considerazioni diverse, forse anche perché egli adotta il sonetto, la forma metrica più ampiamente diffusa nella poesia italiana e poi europea. L'intento primario del suo capolavoro, *La Torbia a taccone* (1646), appare quello di liberare la scrittura napoletana dalla gabbia della lirica convenzionale, oramai stereotipa, proponendo — sulla base della tradizione popolare dialettale locale e sulla scorta dei canzonieri berneschi di soggetto amoroso — un testo che, se accetta l'immissione del toscano letterario, tutto lo adegua alle esigenze di una cultura squisitamente dialettale, della parodia e del sarcasmo (12). Sgruttendio ripropone quindi, ma in chiave parodistica, la tradizione "alta" della lirica amorosa, con relativo scarto stilistico verso un linguaggio anch'esso apparentemente "alto", ma continuamente screditato e scalzato dall'interno tramite la sistematica alternanza e contrapposizione di espressioni "basse", come nel sonetto III:

"Dechiara lo nomme e la bellezzetuddene cosa de la sdamma soia"

Cecca se chiamma la Segnora mia,
la facce ha tonna comme a no pallone;
ha lo colore fusto de premmone
stato no mese e cchiù a la vocciaria.
Ha l'uocchie de ceféscola o d'arpia,
ha li capille comme l'ha Protone;
no pede chiatto ha dinto a lo scarpone
che camminanno piglia meza via.

È cchiù vavosa che non è l'anguilla,
cchíù saporita che non so' le spere:[1]
bellottola cchiù assai d'Annuccia i Mulla.

S'hai desederio de guadagno avere
tienela, Ammore, a na gaiola, e strilla:
"A tre tornise chi la vò vedere!"[36]

In questo sonetto predomina nettamente il lessico 'basso', popolare, che mina irrimediabilmente la parvenza di decoro classico del titolo. La faccia della Dama è come un pallone e ha il colore di un polmone, ha gli occhi di civetta, il piede grasso e così via. D'altra parte, però, la struttura classica del sonetto viene conservata, compreso il perfetto assetto rimico *abba* per le quartine e *aba*,

---

36 "Dichiara il nome e ricama le bellezze della sua Dama" – Cecca si chiama la Signora mia, / la faccia ha tonda come un pallone; / ha il giusto colore del polmone / che è stata un mese e più in macelleria, // Ha gli occhi di civetta o di arpia, / ha i capelli come li ha Plutone; / un piede grasso ha dentro lo scarpone / che camminando invade mezza via. // È più bavosa che non sia l'anguilla, più saporita che non sian le spere: belloccia molto più di Annuccia e Milla, // Se hai desiderio di guadagno avere / tienila, Amore, in una gabbia e strilla: / "A tre tornesi chi la vuol vedere!"

bab per le terzine. La traduzione di Tusiani è notevole non solo in quanto segue lo schema metrico dell'originale – due quartine e due terzine di pentametri giambici con una semplice variante dello schema rimico, *abba, cddc, efe, gfg* – ma cerca anche una perfetta corrispondenza stilistica, cioè lo scontro tra tono alto e lessico basso. Quindi appare anche in inglese la serie di espressioni popolari: *her face resembles a balloon, just like lamb's lung, More than an eel she's slavering and wet,* mentre l'originale viene reso con grande precisione nella traduzione, che non si scosta mai dal testo napoletano. Sottolineo questo fatto perché nella traduzione di schemi metrici chiusi come il sonetto, se il traduttore ardito si accinge a riprodurre le caratteristiche formali come la rima, il primo elemento a farne le spese è inevitabilmente la precisione, perché la ricerca della rima costringe a manovre funamboleshe che possono facilmente compromettere la naturalezza e l'esattezza del testo. Ma questo in Tusiani non avviene:

"Declares the Name and Praises the Beauty of His Lady"

My lady's name is Cecca. Look her up:
her face resembles a balloon, her hue
is just like lamb's lung that has been in view
one month, and longer, at the butcher's shop.

Like owl's, or harpy's, her bright pupil glows,
her hair is just as black as Pluto's soot,
and a large foot she hides in a big boot
that takes half of the road as out she goes.

More than an eel she's slavering and wet,
and more delicious than a clam or trout,
much prettier than Millie or Annette.

God Love, if it is cash you care to reap,
keep her locked tightly in a cage, and shout:
"Only three dollars, folks — but just to peep —"

Mi pare si possa concludere da quanto si è detto che Joseph Tusiani, grande traduttore e poeta in quattro lingue, autore oltre che di numerosi libri in lingua inglese e in italiano anche di una notevole produzione di poesia in dialetto garganico, e quindi profondo conoscitore sia dell'inglese che del dialetto, rappresenta forse il modello ideale di traduttore dal dialetto.

Entertaining his students with mandolin, circa 1975

"REDUCTIO AB ESSENTIA" IN JOSEPH TUSIANI'S *ENVOY FROM HEAVEN*

Gaetano Cipolla

The memory of the collectivity is un-historical.[1] Historical events and figures of individuals tend to lose their specific characteristics, even after just a few decades, to conform to categories of thought and to archetypes. The popular memory of a person who belongs to history seems to be shaped, not by the total of the deeds performed by such an individual but by a process of selection that rejects what is personalistic in favor of what is timeless. Such a process of reduction to archetypal models is easily observed in mythology and folk tales. But it is also present in the works of poets and writers who deal with historical people.

This *reductio ab essentia* is similar to the concept of "figure," first adopted by Erich Auerbach[2] in an exegesis of the characters of the *Divine Comedy*. This process, by which a person becomes totally identified, frozen one might say, in a gesture, an action, or a thought that sums up the significance of an entire life, is accomplished by a selection of those aspects of an individual's life that conform to and indeed enhance an "a priori" view which time and men have contributed to shape. Arising from an unconscious desire to see the present as an imitation of the past, to see modern figures repeat heroic gestures and deeds, archetypes can account for the similarities in the lives of heroes and saints.

The processes that I have briefly described can be observed in Joseph Tusiani's novel, *Envoy from Heaven,* published in 1965.[3] It is in this book that the figure of Francesca Saverio Cabrini, the beloved Madre Cabrini known 'to all Italian-Americans, appears for the first time, as far as I have been able to ascertain, as a fictional

---

[1] Mircea Eliade, *The Myth of the Eternal Return* (Princeton, NJ: Princeton UP, 1971) p. 44.
[2] Erich Auerbach, *Mimesis* (Princeton, NJ: Princeton UP, 1968) pp. 174-202.
[3] Joseph Tusiani, *Envoy from Heaven* (New York: Ivan Obolensky, 1965). Translated into Italian as *Dal Cielo Inviato Speciale* (Rome: Ed. Presenza, 1966).

character. The transformation of Francesca Cabrini, the frail-looking but iron-willed founder of the Missionary Sisters of the Sacred Heart into Madre Cabrini, saint and protectress of the Italian-American community in the United States, is the subject of this paper.

To better understand such a transformation, a brief outline of the novel is necessary. Following a council in heaven, the saints agree to send someone to earth on the occasion of the Second Ecumenical Council convened by Pope John XXIII, not so much to judge modern man's behavior but to comfort him during a difficult time. Dante Alighieri is chosen.[4] Since his mission will last one full year, he is charged to prepare a monthly report of what he sees on earth to be given to heavenly messengers. As Dante sets out to fulfill his mission, he is confronted with examples of greed, corruption, and evil. But he witnesses self-denial, goodness, and love as well. At the end of his journey, Dante is unable to fathom the mystery that is man. The book, conceived as a humorous portrait of our times, offers a somewhat critical view of the world, tempered with understanding and compassion.

The heavenly messengers who visit Dante each month are, in the order of their appearance a Cherub,[5] Tertullian, Mother Cabrini, Thomas Aquinas, Savonarola, Michelangelo, Brother Juniper, Saint

---

[4] The idea of Dante's reincarnation is the obvious subject of Tusiani's earlier novel *Dante in licenza* (Editrice Nigrizia, 1952), written in Italian. In this book, which antedates the author's first affirmation in English (Greenwood Prize, 1956), Dante's one-year pilgrimage on earth, though not motivated by the Ecumenical Council of the Catholic Church, is nonetheless spurred by religious circumstances, judging by the variety of incidents in which the Divine Poet finds himself. It would be interesting to compare the hilarious if not absurd vicissitudes of *Dante in licenza* with those of *Envoy from Heaven,* not only to see to what manner certain literary problems of Dante scholarship are preserved by the same author in the span of thirteen years (and, more importantly the transition from one language to another, and, better still, from one *forma mentis* to another) but also to discover in what measure some of the author's most vital fixations have been transferred from one book to another.

[5] Apropos of this Cherub, who plays a rather conspicuous role in the novel, it is Madre Cabrini who hands Dante his amusing letter from heaven. I wonder if this detail is meant to suggest another maternal trait of the nun, who, in her numerous journeys from country to country, delivered immigrant's messages entrusted to her.

Catherine of Siena, Martin de Porres, Machiavelli, and Dante's own guardian angel. The list itself is somewhat puzzling not only because it contains names of men one would hardly consider "heavenly" material (Machiavelli, for example), but also because one would not expect a humorous book to contain conversation with saints. The choice may be justified, however, by what seems to have been one of the author's intentions: to offer a view of Italy and of Italians as exemplified through the actions or thoughts of some of her more famous sons and daughters.[6] The book, in fact, offers a vast amount of information on the life and works of Dante, as well as on the other historical figures. The author possesses many other qualities that cause me to recommend the book: a polished, elegant, and poetic use of the English language, an imaginative interweaving of fiction with known facts, and an ability to move into the very hearts of the people he portrays.

The book is also an important document in the context of Italian-American studies in that, as early as 1964, that is, when the plight of the Italian-Americans was just beginning to be recognized and discussed outside of the Italian community[7] — Joseph Tusiani had understood it clearly and was depicting it with compassion. Indeed, Tusiani's concern for the problems of Italian immigrants dates back to his *Dante in licenza,* published in 1952. While there is no mention of Mother Cabrini in that novel, I believe that the theme of Italian emigration is, *in nuce,* in the following paragraph:

---

[6] Some comments on the choice of messengers is in order. While the figures of the nine messengers other than Madre Cabrini are consonant with the author's desire to recount some of the highlights of Italian history and civilization, the figures of Mother Cabrini (the only representative of the twentieth century) and of Martin de Porres (the only non-Italian) seem to have been chosen out of a desire to focus the reader's attention on the plight of the "have-nots" of the world. The choice of Porres, a humble and little-known saint, and protector of slaves, can be explained only if one considers his presence as a development of the theme explored with the old immigrant and Mother Cabrini.

[7] Tusiani's novel preceded the publication of such bestsellers as Mario Puzo's *The Godfather* (New York, 1969) and Gay Talese's *Honor Thy Father* (New York, 1971), which, while focusing on one particular aspect of Italian-American life contributed greatly to the growing dialogue on the subject of Italian-American life, history, and contributions to this country.

Avevo una famiglia, non mi mancava niente, dovevo essere felice, e invece no. Pensavo sempre a quei poveri emigrati che, cani randagi, si aggiravano per le strade dell'immensa città in cerca di chi li mettesse a lavorare. fosse pure per pochi centesimi al giorno. Me li immaginavo stanchi, spauriti, senza un amico che li comprendesse od aiutasse, cacciati da un'agenzia all'altra, sfruttati, vituperati, e senza un prete italiano che li assistesse. Per la prima volta, dopo tanti anni, io credevo alla missione del ministro di Dio. (116)

(I had a family; I lacked for nothing, I should have been happy, but I was not. I always thought of those poor immigrants who as stray dogs wandered the streets of the immense city looking for someone to put them to work, even for a few cents a day. I imagined them tired, frightened, without any friend who could understand or help them as they were driven from one agency to the other and exploited as well as vituperated, with no Italian priest to assist or console them. For the first time, after so many years, I believed in the mission of the ministers of God.)

Undoubtedly, Tusiani was aware, early in 1952, of the immigrant's plight. But whether he was at the time thinking of the Scalabrinian fathers or of Madre Cabrini, as *ministri di Dio,* it is not possible to ascertain. The fact, however, remains that, long before the Dante of *Dante in licenza* became the more modern and sophisticated Dante of *Envoy from Heaven,* Tusiani considered Italian immigration as a theme worth developing in a story, dealing, after all, with a poet whose greatest regret was to have abandoned his land and the things *più dilette.* It is my belief that Tusiani's well-known friendship with Arturo Giovannitti, which began at the time of *Dante in licenza,* was amply responsible for the development of the immigration theme as framed in *Envoy from Heaven.* Tusiani's growing concern for the plight of the immigrants is made evident by the greater emphasis that he placed on the theme in his second novel. In fact, he devotes almost two full chapters to it.

The episode of Dante's encounter with Madre Cabrini is preceded by a scene in which an old Italian-American seated in a coffee house in Rome tells the poet about the problems of Italian immigrants in the United States. The two encounters, conceived as a natural and logical development of the theme, should not be considered as separate entities, especially since Madre Cabrini will be presented as the mother of all immigrants.

The elderly man, who has returned to Italy after forty years in the United States, is an embodiment of so many *trapiantati*, who felt the special agony of being men without a country: they are neither truly American, because their country of birth, by now embellished by absence and memories, still occupies a place of honor in their hearts, nor are they truly Italian, because the many years of toiling in American factories — indeed, their mere presence in a foreign country — have slowly but surely altered, without their realizing it, their language, their manner of dress, and even their facial expressions:

> You see, my friend, you come back to your own land after almost forty years, and how do they treat you? Like a dog! They almost tell you you're not Italian anymore. And over there they tell you you're not American. So, you are nothing. Believe me, if you leave your country for more than five years, you're lost. You don't belong anywhere. (*Envoy*, 115)

America emerges from the words of the immigrants as a land in which one "works like a dog and dies like a dog." The special loneliness of the immigrants, so many of whom had to leave their families behind to work in badly paid, dangerous, and demeaning jobs, is captured in this brutal and yet eloquent statement: "You work and work, you rush and rush, and then, one day, you drop dead and the police bring the news to your family, if you have one, and if you're alone, goodbye Jack" (*Envoy*, 116).

While the old man's words reflect the general attitudes of the *diseredati* of this world and possess, therefore, a quality of timelessness, it is interesting to note that, more than the historical reality of 1963, they are reminiscent of the condition of life that prevailed among the immigrants around the turn of the century.

Thus, a more precise link is established between the immigrant and Mother Cabrini, based not on historical accuracy (Mother Cabrini's work did not directly touch the immigrant's life), but rather on a symbolic level, which accepts the old man as the representative of an oppressed group and Mother Cabrini as the protectress of such a group. Tusiani's immigrant identifies himself with the Cabrinian era and with the condition that existed then, and even more specifically with the views expressed by Giovanni Pascoli in the poem "Italy."

> Vanno serrando i denti e le mascelle,
> serrando dentro il cuore una minaccia
>
> ribelle, e un pianto forse più ribelle.
> Offrono cheap la roba, cheap le braccia,
> indifferenti al tacito diniego
>
> e cheap la vita, e tutto cheap; e in faccia
> no, dietro mormorare odono: DEGO!

The coffeehouse scene, in which Dante, is almost a silent but sympathetic listener, seems to have been written from a dual point of view. The author has succeeded in making the immigrant somewhat obnoxious at first (he talks loudly, he is offensive to waiters, he is boisterously generous and dresses tastelessly), which seems to be the view Italians have of returning Italo-Americans. The appearance of the two young Roman bullies, who taunt the old man with mindless cruelty, ridiculing the flashiness of his clothes, his presumed wealth, and his being an americano, serves to underscore this view. But under the crude facade, there lies the grief of a man who has been rejected, who belongs nowhere, and whose dreams have been a disillusionment. When the immigrant discloses his plan to return to America, where no one awaits him, Dante, who at times is the author's alter ego, places his hand on the man's shoulder, realizing the utter insignificance of words.

This chapter serves as an introduction to the Mother Cabrini episode. The Mother Cabrini who comes alive through Tusiani's imagination, is different from the woman for whom "the world was too small a place" to fulfill her aspiration for missionary work. The real mother Cabrini, at least as she appears in the already mythicizing world of biographers, was a woman driven by a passion for the creation of an ever-expanding network of hospitals, orphanages, and convents with which to serve God. She also possessed an uncanny ability as a businesswoman. According to Theodore Maynard, author of one of the best-written biographies of the saint, Mother Cabrini would have made a great real estate speculator if that had been her calling. Her extraordinary drive and determination to work on behalf of the needy and her considerable charm opened avenues for her that seemed beyond reach to less gifted individuals. Mother Cabrini's guiding precept was, in fact, "I can do all things in Him that strengthens me."[8]

In Tusiani's portrayal of her, Mother Cabrini is not the businesswoman who ran a vast enterprise with efficiency and business acumen, nor is she the foundress of a large order that has spread over the world; finally, she is not the woman who considered the whole world as the arena for her work. Although she was Italian and believed hers to be an Italian enterprise, she was not interested in helping Italians exclusively. Her efforts were aimed at the world, at the well-to-do in Brazil, at the American Indians, at the poor in South America, at the Eskimos, and at the Chinese. Her original plan, in fact, had been to go to China, until Leo XIII convinced her that she was needed more in America.[9]

---

[8] Theodore Maynard, *Too Small a World: The Life of Francesca Cabrini* (Milwaukee: Bruce Publishing Co., 1945). Two other biographies may be mentioned: one by Mother Antonietta della Porta, who became Mother General of the Missionary Sisters of the Sacred Heart after Mother Cabrini's death, and a more recent one by Pietro di Donato, author of *Christ in Concrete*.

[9] The pontiff of the "Rerum Novarum" is mentioned more than once in Tusiani's *Poesia missionaria in Inghilterra ed America* (Edizioni Nigrizia, 1952), in which the author studies the most important poems of a "missionary" nature in the English language. Judging by his critical evaluation of Longfellow's "Evangeline," in which the role of Father Felician as spiritual assistant and comforter of the perse-

The Madre Cabrini who shines through Tusiani's novel is indeed a *figura matris*. However, before she assumes this unmistakable identity, she speaks with a voice that is not hers. Tusiani, who seems at first more interested in illuminating certain aspects of Dante's character uses her in a supportive role, neglecting to focus his attention on her character. The night before the appearance of the Saint, Dante had witnessed a cruel killing by a band of children. This episode, which had provoked Dante to a furious invective against the seed of man, is the starting point of the dialogue between the poet and Mother Cabrini. Seeing the despair and the anger of Dante's heart, the saint urges indulgence:

> "My dear, impulsive son, I know your thoughts," said Mother Cabrini. "If God, our merciful God, had listened to your prayer there would be no children now on earth, there would be no earth at all. Oh, yes, that was typical of you. In your Comedy — do you remember? — because of four innocent children thrown into the tower of Hunger you wanted to destroy the entire city of Pisa. And now, because of a small number of noisy, cruel boys, you would like to see not only the children of Rome, but all man's children destroyed forever." (*Envoy*, 129)

It is obvious that Mother Cabrini's words are not uttered to display some of her inner qualities. Any of the other ten messengers could have spoken them without altering the significance of the passage. It is also obvious that Tusiani was more interested at this point in highlighting Dante's hatred of injustice and cruelty as well as to remind those readers who have also read Dante of the piteous death by starvation of Conte Ugolino and his children in

---

cuted, wandering Acadians is firmly and consistently stressed Tusiani's predilection for discovering and presenting the plights of migrating group appears obvious. In a rather important detail (pp. 122-123) and after a rapid analysis of Theodore Maynard's poem "Ruined Temples," he states that Maynard's 1945 life of Frances S. Cabrini is, in his opinion, superior to all his poetic production. Tusiani's documented awareness of and fascination with the "figura" of Madre Cabrini may, consequently, be traced back to the early 1950s.

the infamous tower, and the poet's wrathful invective against the Pisans.[10]

The clue as to how the character of Mother Cabrini will be treated is, however, present even in the passage just quoted. While many of the characters of the novel have difficulty in deciding how to address Dante (Pope John, for example, as the father of all Catholics could easily use the appellation "son" but he hesitates), Mother Cabrini, extending her spiritual "maternity" onto Dante as an exile, addresses him immediately as "My dear, impulsive son." Mother Cabrini will emerge from Tusiani's characterization not only as the saint protectress of the Italian-American immigrant but also as their spiritual mother.

Tusiani has, in other words, chosen one aspect of her multi-faceted life to Illustrate and define her essence. And it is in this aspect, as the mother of all those poor and bewildered men and women for whom she did so much, that her true calling shines through. With compassion, she chronicles the plight of "all those children" of hers. As the weight of the sad memories slowly sinks into her consciousness, making her stagger, she offers a moving account of her activities among the Italian-American immigrants, accompanying them on the voyage across the ocean, recounting their aspirations, feeling with them the anxiety, the fear, and the humiliation that the new world held in store for them. The entire passage is worth reading.

"No, no poet, not even a man called Dante of Florence, could ever have described what I saw in my brief stay on earth. There is some sordidness that escapes the naked eye, and there are tears that can never be mentioned. You see hundreds of people lying at the bottom of a ship, their heads resting on their few belongings, and their thoughts terrified by the uncertainty of their future. You

---

[10] Ahi Pisa, vituperio delle genti
del bel paese la dove il "sì" suona,
poi che i vicini a te punir son lenti,
movasi la Caprara e la Gorgona,
e faccian siepe ad Arno in su la foce
sì ch'egli anneghi in te ogni persona. *(Inferno,* XXXIII, 79-84)

put this entry in your diary. 'Hundreds of men going to America to better their economic lot,' and you think you have done your duty. But you have already sinned against them, for you have used but words, and words are not worlds. What is the real meaning of 'hundreds'? You cannot add as mere cyphers hope and despair, poverty and illiteracy, homelessness, and terror. You have written 'men,' but do they look like men to you? They look like meek, frightened lambs on their way to the slaughterhouse. And yet they are men, good, honest, simple men. Why are they there then? Who has starved them? Who had made them so desperate as to force them to leave wives, children, and the one bit of earth they knew and loved — their little native village? And then you say 'America,' and you think you have described in one little word the cold of their landing in an unknown country, the humiliation of their first dumb contact with men they cannot understand, for the daily search for work and more work, the anxious waiting for a letter, the sleepless nights, and things of this sort. And, finally, you say, 'to better their economic lot!' Yes, you are right. They have sent their first money home: they have paid their debts, they have received word that their children can even go to school now. But, sir, have you seen how these people live? They live in squalid cellars, they count every cent, and shall I tell you? They, the illiterate, the uneducated people who speak neither English nor Italian, are now capable of a pun: they say 'dolor' instead of 'dollar'" (*Envoy*, 132).

Mother Cabrini speaks with the eloquence of a mother pleading for her desperate children.[11] She is no longer the frail bride of

---

[11] Mother Cabrini's impassioned description reminds the reader of certain pages from Emma Lazarus diary depicting the plight of Jewish immigrants (see *The World of Emma Lazarus,* New York, Schocken Books, 1949). But this is more than a mere coincidence. Between *Dante in licenza* and *Envoy from Heaven* there is Tusiani's chapter "Emma Lazarus" in his book *Sonettisti Americani* (Chicago Edizioni Clemente, 1954). The author presents the genesis, together with a critical appraisal, of Lazarus' famous sonnet "The New Colossus," engraved on the pedestal of the Statue of Liberty. The inclusion of Lazarus in Tusiani's evaluation of the most important American sonneteers (from David Humphreys to Thomas S.

Christ who wrote in her diary: "Oh Jesus, I grieve with love of you.... I am languishing and dying, why don't I die for love of you?" And "From the first moment I became acquainted with you, I was so enchanted by your beauty that I followed you.... The more I love you, it seems the less I love you, because I want to love you more. I cannot bear it any longer. Expand, expand, my heart!" (Maynard. *Too Small a World,* p. 242).

The aureole which men have placed around Mother Cabrini's head has somehow congealed her multi-faceted personality into a fixed image: a motherly saint who worked endlessly, without regard for herself for the welfare of her children, and who still grieves for them in heaven. Of all her activities on earth, one has emerged as the measure and breadth of her life. Just as Farinata in the *Divine Comedy* will always be remembered for his magnanimous defense of Florence: a gesture that reflected with unmistakable clarity the essence of his being — Madre Cabrini will always be seen as compassionately heeding the plea of her immigrant children. Indeed, the appellation "Madre" seems to reflect in full the significance of her life.

Jones) is, I am sure, indicative of his spiritual kinship to the author of such lines as

> Give me your tired, your poor.
> Your huddled masses yearning to breathe free,
> The wretched refuse of your teeming shore.
> Send these, the homeless, tempest-tost to me.
> I lift my lamp beside the golden door.

Joseph with his father, Michele,
at the wedding of Michael and Beatrice, 1971

Two brothers walking toward the sunset in San Marco in Lamis
on one of his last trips overseas

TUSIANI ANTICO E NUOVO

Cosma Siani

Dicendo "Tusiani antico" mi riferisco a una sua passione di sempre, la musica, e anche a certi suoi testi antichi, e ignoti ai lettori perché mai pubblicati. I due articoli che seguono vertono infatti su questi due aspetti. Il "Tusiani nuovo" si riferisce alla recente pubblicazione di un suo inedito "antico", un lungo romanzo che letto oggi suscita grande interesse. Ecco allora il Tusiani "musicologo" e "giovane narratore".

IL MUSICOLOGO

Tusiani amava ripetere i versi dannunziani della Francesca da Rimini "Fin dall'infanzia prima / la musica piegò l'anima nostra / come l'acqua del rivo piega l'erba". Infatti, la musica è sempre stata una passione profonda della sua vita. Albeggiò quando era bambino nel suo ambiente di paese. Con voce di soprano, divenuta basso in età adulta, all'età di sei anni faceva parte della *schola cantorum* di Don Matteo De Cata, sacerdote il cui nome era divenuto proverbiale e ritornava in filastrocche locali. In paese imparò a suonare il mandolino da Michele Daniele, ovvero "Mechèle lu cecate", come era inteso. E in seminario apprese a diteggiare sull'organo — e in America ne ha sempre avuto uno elettrico in casa.

Musica di voce, di strumenti e di parole per lui sono inscindibili. Una sua poesia in *The Fifth Season* si chiama "Italian Serenade", e comincia: "Window, guitar and mandolin, and what / is music if my darling's still asleep!" ("Finestra, chitarra e mandolino, e che cosa / è la musica se la mia bella ancora dorme!"). La musicalità come ritmo regolare ha sempre legato Tusiani alla metrica tradizionale, tenendolo lontano dalla più sfuggente melodia del verso libero. Egli ha provato si può dire tutte le misure canoniche della prosodia italiana e inglese. E proprio dove la cantabilità più è accentuata, spesso abbiamo la sorpresa di un Tusiani lieve e allo stesso tempo carico di pensiero (tratto qualificante della sua produzione poetica).

La passione per l'amalgama inseparabile di musica e parola culmina con una lunga composizione intitolata "Marsyas, or the Supremacy of Music" (come non pensare all'ode di John Dryden "Alexander's Feast: or the Power of Music"?), che è letteratura, sì, ma compare su una rivista di musicologia (*Ars Lyrica*, 1994). Comincia con una movenza di pensiero tipica di Tusiani, il rovesciamento di prospettiva: "È stata la divinità a tentare me / non io lei"; prosegue sfruttando il mito di Marsia, che sfidò Apollo e dovette soccombergli in una gara musicale, e continua meditando sul rapporto umano-divino, per identificare il creatore d'arte, il "fabbro", *the maker*, con la stessa divinità – altro tema caro a Tusiani.

Se la musicalità è parte irrinunciabile dell'estetica di Tusiani, la passione per la musica è un aspetto talmente costitutivo della sua sensibilità, che non saprei se appunto "passione" sia parola adatta. Usiamola solo per dire che Tusiani non è musicista o musicologo di professione; e tenendo ben in mente che è comunque stata sempre una passione "attiva", non semplicemente musicologica. Fra le carte che conservo ci sono gli spartiti di due canzoni: "Il tuo sorriso" e "Lontana", ambedue "Versi e musica di Giuseppe Tusiani", di sua mano datati "1952" e marcati con dedica che suona: "ex iuventutis cinere".

Ma fra in casi in cui l'opera di Tusiani si incrocia con la musica vanno ricordati anche scampoli come questi: un "dramma sacro in due tempi per soli coro e orchestra", *Alba di gloria*, rappresentato a Londra nel 1960: Tusiani ne scrisse i versi, mentre la musica fu composta da un suo conterraneo e compaesano, il sacerdote Michele Bonfitto, residente a Londra, autore fra altre cose di una messa, *Sei grande nell'amore*, ben nota fino a pochi anni fa e forse ancora oggi in uso nella liturgia cattolica.

Quando alcune rime di Michelangelo furono messe in musica per baritono e piano da Ezra Laderman e rappresentate nel 1973 a New York, i testi usati furono quelli della traduzione michelangiolesca di Tusiani. In occasione della giornata di studi a lui dedicata dal Comune di San Marco in Lamis, nel 1999, i musicisti della scuola di composizione del Conservatorio "Tito Schipa" di Lecce, sotto la guida del Maestro M. Gianfreda, misero in musica moderna ardita e suggestiva alcune poesie latine di Tusiani e ne produssero un CD. E in musica sono state messe anche sue liriche dialettali, ad opera di un altro compaesano, Peppino Coco, anche in questo caso affidate a un CD intitolato *Lu frustere*. Attivo anche come fruitore, abitando a Manhattan, sulla 72esima, non molto distante dal Lincoln Center, Tusiani era regolare frequentatore del Metropolitan, il teatro dell'opera che ha sede in quel comprensorio per le arti dello spettacolo.

Di musica Tusiani parla particolarmente in un saggio autobiografico intitolato "Providential Humiliations", che fu la relazione di apertura di un convegno italoamericano organizzato dalla NIAF (National Italian American Foundation), dall'Italian Cultural Institute di Washington, D.C., e dalla Georgetown University, della stessa città, nel 1995. Qui Tusiani riporta un episodio che ha a che fare con musica e musicisti, e su cui è tornato ripetutamente: uno scontro verbale fra il noto violinista Mischa Elman, che denigrava Toscanini, e Frances Winwar, accompagnatrice e guida di Tusiani negli anni '50-'60, che si erse a difesa del maestro italiano e di tutti gli italiani.

Un'altra delle "umiliazioni formative" che Tusiani racconta è appunto di natura musicale. Nella stessa occasione in cui ebbe luogo l'incidente sopra riportato, a metà anni '50, il musicista Vergil Thompson interrogò come uno scolaretto il giovane professore su cose musicali italiane, e lui non seppe rispondere (in dettaglio: chi aveva musicato il canto "Roma divina, a te sul Campidoglio", divenuto popolare in epoca fascista: *i.e.* Puccini).

Ricordando, Tusiani commenta: "…non solo dovevo imparare più cose su Puccini ma, se volevo entrare in conversazione con gli intellettuali americani, dovevo arrivare a conoscere tutto ciò che il mondo già conosceva e che io avrei dovuto già sapere. Grazie a Dio, amavo la Musica… Perciò non fu difficile mettermi al lavoro, con dilapidazione dei miei stipendi mensili per l'acquisto di dischi su dischi. Mi accingevo alla traduzione delle poesie di Michelangelo: non era forse mio compito sapere quanti dei suoi madrigali fossero stati messi in musica dopo Arcadelt, e quali e da chi? E più tardi, quando cominciai la traduzione della *Gerusalemme liberata* del Tasso, non ci si aspettava da me anche una totale familiarità con l'enorme numero di opere e poemi sinfonici ispirati ad Armida, Erminia, Clorinda, e allo stesso Tasso? [...] Potete immaginare la mia gioia [...] quando finalmente ebbi fra le mani un'opera intitolata *Torquato Tasso* nientemeno che di Gaetano Donizetti".

Su quest'ultima opera Tusiani scrisse un saggio inedito e non datato (ma risalente agli anni Settanta), ora leggibile nella rivista *Frontiere*, dicembre 2003, del Centro Emigrazione di San Marco in Lamis. Saggio che è più letterario che musicale. Si può essere o no d'accordo sulla tesi sostenuta, che il fallimento dell'opera donizettiana sia in buona parte dovuto all'infelicità del libretto; agli esperti e specialisti la sentenza. Ma forse anche a questi ultimi gioveranno le annotazioni letterarie di un lettore-ascoltatore in special modo sensibile allo spessore poetico del testo.

IL GIOVANE NARRATORE

Tusiani si trovava in America da meno di un anno, e non aveva ancora un posto fisso di docenza, quando prese a comporre un lungo romanzo in prosa italiana, largamente autobiografico, ambientato a San Marco in Lamis e Foggia nel 1943. Ne dà notizia lui stesso in una delle numerose lettere scritte quei primi tempi all'intimo amico foggiano Matteo Vigilante.

In data 6 agosto 1948 dice infatti: "Ho cominciato un romanzo dallo sfondo meramente sammarchese, pieno di umanità. La trama di esso prende le mosse dal tragico bombardamento che subì Foggia il 22 luglio 1943. Ho scritto già le prime cento pagine [...] penso di pubblicarlo coi tipi delle Edizioni Universitarie di New York". E il 1 ottobre 1949: "Il romanzo è alla conclusione. Un'altra decina di pagine, e mi darò da fare per la pubblicazione".

Il dattiloscritto del romanzo è datato "New York, 18 ottobre 1949", e rimase inedito nonostante le intenzioni dell'autore. Appare a stampa soltanto oggi, in un volume di 350 pagine: *Quando la Daunia bruciava. Romanzo* (A cura di Antonio Motta e Cosma Siani,

San Marco in Lamis, Centro Documentazione Leonardo Sciascia/ Archivio del Novecento, 2020).

La trama vede l'ufficiale tedesco Arrigo Strauss innamorarsi della fanciulla sammarchese Luisa e giungere a sposarla. Questo semplice filo conduttore è intrecciato di avvenimenti nati da fantasia multiforme e sorprendente. Ci imbattiamo in scenari quali il bombardamento di Foggia nel 1943, l'epopea degli sfollati verso il Gargano, le vicende di singoli personaggi fra incontri, scontri, ammazzamenti; e poi la realtà del paese con tipi ed episodi che rimandano agli anni Quaranta.

Il romanzo in effetti è cangiante e sfocia in registri molteplici. È romanzo storico perché si fonda sull'occupazione tedesca in Daunia; psicologico per il tormento intimo di vari personaggi; amoroso, con grande trasporto e molta passionalità; memoriale, per il ricordo continuo della terra d'origine pulsante nell'animo del giovane emigrato. Il tutto elaborato con un po' di giovanile ingenuità (gli scontati pensieri e parole fra innamorati, ad esempio) che tuttavia giunge ad essere accettata nell'intrecciarsi della narrazione.

Ciò che colpisce è il trapelante impegno sociale del giovane autore, che fa pensare a certi suoi scritti dimenticati, in particolare gli articoli nella rivista dei comboniani *Nigrizia*, vertenti sulla figura di Lincoln, la guerra civile americana, la segregazione razziale, Martin Luther King.

Nell'anno intercorso fra il suo arrivo in America e questo romanzo, Tusiani non scriveva ancora in inglese. Nella lettera del 3 maggio 1949 all'amico Vigilante dice: "Si vorrebbe che io scrivessi in inglese, ma ne ho poca voglia". Invece, sicuramente egli già si riversava nello studio della nuova lingua con la foga e la febbrilità che metteva in tutto.

Infatti, pur redatto in italiano, il romanzo presenta influenze e calchi tipici della lingua inglese: gli aggettivi di nazionalità con l'iniziale maiuscola (Tedeschi, Italiani, Foggiani), secondo l'uso anglosassone; l'espressione "*pensoso* soltanto *delle* ampie gugliate del suo refe", dove *pensoso delle* è calco dell'inglese *thoughtful of*; l'ordine delle parole nella locuzione "burrone cinquanta metri profondo", che ricalca lo schema inglese ("50 metres deep"), mentre all'italiano viene più naturale anteporre *profondo* a *cinquanta*. E altri esempi ancora che sarebbe troppo lungo elencare.

Secondo la volontà dell'autore stesso, che ha riletto il proprio testo dopo settanta anni, questi tratti dell'originale sono stati per la maggior parte "normalizzati" dai curatori in base all'italiano corrente; e insieme a questi varie altre caratteristiche.

I curatori hanno ritoccato non solo tratti materiali quali refusi vari e la totale assenza di accenti, che com'è noto mancano nelle tastiere americane, ma anche — sempre secondo volontà dell'autore — il tipo di lingua, fortemente improntato a usi letterari o desueti: "in sul vespero", "leggiera", "per isvegliarsi"/"per ispiegare", "indarno", gli innumerevoli "sì" per "così", e molte altre forme, derivate in gran parte da letture dannunziane.

Con tutto questo, il romanzo del giovane Tusiani si fa leggere, e arriva perfino ad avvincere. Non solo. Ma va ricordato come primo esempio di scrittura letteraria sul bombardamento di Foggia, molto prima dei volumi scritti dai conterranei Luca Cicolella, *...e la morte venne dal cielo* (1973), e Maria Marcone, *Le pietre si muovono* (1989).

Infine, non si può tacere l'afflato lirico sgorgante dal Tusiani poeta che abbiamo imparato a conoscere in seguito: "Il cielo era tra azzurro e biancastro; soltanto ad occidente era un residuo assai tenue di porpora, quasi drappo funerario disteso da una ignota amante del sole, dolente di sua morte. Espero luceva languida, e un'altra stella le si appressava timidetta, forse innamorata della bellezza di lei, perdutamente. La campana della Chiesa Madre lentamente sonava la preghiera della sera".

YOU CAN'T GO HOME AGAIN!
Retro-Reading 'Exile' and 'Return' in the *Oeuvre* of Joseph Tusiani

Ryan Calabretta-Sajder

Thomas Wolfe's proverbial declaration, "You can't go home again!" distinctly highlights the impossibility of the return, which I would argue, for Wolfe, but more importantly for this contribution, home here refers to homeland, as I intend to clarify later. Although home may be where the heart is, one's home never remains static. Wolfe's quotation, one which exists in many translations with diverse cadences over the years, underscores two significant aspects: the *desire* to return, and unfortunately, the *inability* to integrate back into the world you left behind. The *desire* to return to the homeland, to return to one's past, is an innate feeling, which stresses a longing for the comfort of both a time and place, retroactively unattainable aspects. The *inability to go* back to one's homeland proves challenging, and although exile can be voluntary or involuntary, the process of leaving one's nation is challenging and creates both internal and external tensions. The situation of Joseph Tusiani from San Marco in Lamis (Gargano, Italy) is no exception; in fact, it is quite the ironic case, as the poet indubitably struggles with this tension his entire poetic life. Through "retro-reading" Tusiani's *oeuvre*, I argue that the Poet Laureate Emeritus of New York remains forever exiled from his homeland, being forced to set up house in the United States.

Known by many as "The Poet of Two Lands," Joseph Tusiani (1924-2020) was a noted poet, translator, novelist, teacher, mentor, scholar, and the first recipient of the AATI's Distinguished Service Award in 1986. Even though "Two Lands" only begins to define the celebrated New York State Poet Laureate Emeritus, Tusiani's poetic repertoire spans a period from 1943 in Italian and 1954 in English until his recent death in 2020. Moreover, his lyric voice extends four languages — his native Gargano, Italian, Latin, and English — the latter coloring his most plentiful collection. Although Tusiani split his life physically between "two lands," Italy and the U.S., the concepts of home, homeland, and return have been foundational tropes the poet has dealt with since his first poem of international success, "The Return" (1954), which won the coveted Greenwood Prize of the Poetry Society of England. Moreover, Tusiani's concept of "home" had been challenged early on, as his father left Gargano for the U.S. five months before his birth. It was not until 1947 when Tusiani, after graduating from the University of Naples, took his mother and migrated to New York City, the Bronx, to be precise, reunites with his father. To a certain extent, Tusiani began his life 'chasing' the concepts of "father," "family," and even distinguishing between the concepts of "home" and "homeland" being "forced" into exile in the process. In fact, these images are present in all four poetic tongues and cycle through most of his works, functioning in and of itself as an internal memorial monologue or stream of consciousness aimed at better understanding his true identity, one that may never be fully grasped, especially for someone who has never experienced exile. As Hamid Naficy suggests in his "Introduction: Framing Exile from Homeland to Homepage," to *Home, Exile, Homeland: Film, Media, and the Politics of Place*,

> ...exile appears to have become a postmodern condition. But exile must not be thought of as a generalized condition of alienation and difference, or as one of the items on the diversity-chic menu. All displaced people do not experience exile equally or uniformly. Exile discourse thrives on detail, specificity, and locality. There is a there *there* in exile. (4)

By exploring the concepts of "home," "homeland," and "exile," through a post-colonial and psychoanalytic lens, this contribution will demonstrate that as much as the poet attempts to integrate as an American, part of him will always remain in Gargano.

Because of the nature of this contribution, which considers topics of exile and psychoanalysis, it is necessary to examine a few poems in his native tongue, Gargano. Although language is an intrinsic conceptualization any migrant must address, whether poetically or physically, Tusiani, the avid poet-scholar-teacher-translator, had a particular relationship with each language and linguistics at large.[1] Additionally, I would be remiss if I did not initiate this piece with his most noteworthy poem, "The Return" (1954), as it represents the impossibility to go back to the motherland. Moreover, "Song of the Bicentennial" (1978) portrays the continued conflictual nature the poet displays in solidifying a new home/relationship concerning his homeland. A deep sense of earnest difficulty still demonstrated over 25 years after his initial arrival. His dialectal poetry offers an extreme personal sentiment, as it is expressed through mother-tongue.

Although examined elsewhere, it is critical to initiate this essay by re-exploring Tusiani's foundational piece, "The Return" (1954).[2] In this masterpiece of 11 stanzas, Joseph Tusiani assumes a reflective, figurative tone in which the narrator dialogues with himself through nature, a trope regularly cited in the poet's lyric voice. Born out of a trip to his homeland of Gargano in 1954 with noted novelist and poet Frances Winwar, the piece addresses his loyalty to both his homeland and the land of his newly adopted home. Winwar, a friend and fellow Italian American (Francesca Vinciguerra), encouraged Tusiani to write "The Return" in English; in turn, she entered it into the Greenwood Poetry Prize competition. In 1956, Tusiani won the prize and became the first winner to date to have been in the U.S. for only nine years. This prize launched Tusiani's literary career, affording the poet-scholar international fame.

Tusiani's inaugural, prize-winning poem overtly begins with a rhetorical question, "My cradle-land, who suffered? I did not, / Nor did I ever miss your wonderbreeze" (1-2), which establishes the various tones present throughout not only this foundational poem but also much of his work. His rhetorical question of the first line introduces a tone of uncertainty, or ambivalence, as most of the poem proposes additional questions, similar in nature, revolving

---

[1] See Luigi Fontanella's *Migrating Words: Italian Writers in the United States*.
[2] See Ryan Calabretta-Sajder, "Rediscovering Joseph Tusiani. From "Return" to *Il ritorno*: A Psychoanalytic Approach." In this contribution I have decided to focus on his English and dialectal poetry as my original piece focused on his Italian poetry.

around the concepts of home versus homeland and the narrator's relationship with both worlds. In his introduction to the poet in *Poets of the Italian Diaspora*, poet-scholar Peter Caravetta argues that "Tusiani's work is eminent proof of the psyche split that emigration brings at all levels, from the familial to the social, from the professional to the cultural" (1073-1074). Caravetta's observation is spot-on as the poem never offers the narrator closure. Instead, "The Return" demonstrates the difficult journey the migrant undertakes in his exile, one which often never leads to closure. As Naficy notes, "It is possible to go into exile voluntarily and then return, yet still not fully arrive;" this exemplifies the struggle Tusiani, the poet, reinforces throughout his lyric (3).

The suffering manifest in the opening lines permeates Tusiani's works; thus, it is critical to understanding his lyric from a psychoanalytic interpretation. Although the opening lines might suggest the narrator is not suffering, the reader is later confronted with a contradictory tone. Linguistically speaking, the narrator's announcement of the question in itself, not to mention its place — the opening line of the poem — declares a conflictual sentiment, though it is still unclear in the beginning if this emotion is one of guilt or nostalgia. Concluding the first stanza with a metaphor regarding boyhood versus manhood, the narrator states, "and the man / Has not outgrown the child. / The child, my land, was here; then here am I" (9-11). In these lines, the narrator mixes emotions related to both maturing and his relationship to place, i.e., through a psychoanalytic reading thus the man who resides in the U.S. can never lose the boy within who was raised in Puglia — one can never outgrow his homeland. In this vein, what remains "Real" for the narrator? Is his return to Gargano a "true" return or just a continuation of the "Real?" Is Puglia a *home*, *house*, or *homeland*? As Naficy argues, "Exile is inexorably tied to homeland and to the possibility of return. However, the frustrating elusiveness of return makes it magically potent." (3). The magical potential of return, as Naficy offers, presents itself in diverse manifestations in Tusiani, from the dream to the imagination.

Noted French psychoanalyst and psychiatrist Jacques Lacan studied various aspects and moments of child development. At the

Fourteenth International Psychoanalytical Congress hosted at Marienbad in 1936, Lacan pitched his concept of the mirror stage. On that topic, he stated:

> The mirror stage is a phenomenon to which I assign a twofold value. In the first place, it has historical value as it marks a decisive turning-point in the mental development of the child. In the second place, it typifies an essential libidinal relationship with the body image. (*Some Reflections on the Ego*, 1953)

Lacan's use of the term "historical value" refers to the development process of the mind within the confines of the child, while structural value deals with the libido and its expression of body politics. Later in his career, Lacan tries to clarify the process of the mirror stage, claiming that the reflection in the mirror, the individual can differentiate the Imaginary from the Real; self-identification of the Ego, thus, occurs in this stage of development.

Circling back to Tusiani's award-winning poem, the narrator's boyhood and manhood intertwine metaphorically in this return to his homeland. When exploring *homeland* in this piece, I refer to the poet's homeland of Gargano and his dialect. *Home,* on the other hand, "is anyplace; it is temporary, and it is moveable; it can be built, rebuilt, and carred in memory and by acts of imagination" (Naficy, 5-6). As seen in both line 6 and later in 52, the poet's persona, which drifts and explores his homeland, is only present in a thought. Even if the poem lacks any concrete conclusion in the first part, the poet's return can be read through the Lacanian mirror stage. Although there is no mention of a mirror, the narrator's dialogue with his homeland indeed replaces the actual reflection of glass, particularly since it is through pondering his homeland that he arrives at exploring his past. At this moment, the narrator experiences both the Imaginary and the Real, according to Lacanian psychoanalysis, and he initiates his quest to reach the *I*. Moreover, as Naficy argues, "it now appears that one's relation to 'home' and 'homeland' is based as much on actual material access as on the symbolic imaginings and national longings that produce and reproduce them" (5). As we will continue to see with Tusiani's opus, the concept of memory and return, whether physical or solely emotional, is inescapable.

As "The Return" progresses, the poet reexamines his thoughts, "And are you, land of love, / Still watching over my thought that is aching?" (51-52). The use of the present participle "aching," describing the poet's thought again highlights his negative inner emotions, more precisely the grief he feels when pondering his *paese materno*. In this vein, the reader can infer from his choice of adjective, both on a philosophical level and an emotional one, that he invokes a sense of conflict and anguish for the narrator, a pain that triggers tears in the subsequent two lines. As the narrator weeps, his philosophical pain manifests itself into the physical realm.

Later, the narrator proposes another rhetorical question: "Now which / Of us knows more, or which is happier, / I cannot tell" (86-88). Through this literary device, the narrator deliberates his decision to migrate, balancing how happy he feels. This uncertainty is first underscored by "I cannot tell," referring to the narrator's amount of happiness. It is doubly evidenced by line 92 when he states, "I do not know," in relation to other people's tales with his homeland. The uneasiness the narrator applies to this thought process, and eventual voluntary exile illustrates the difficulty inherent in leaving his homeland, one which circles back in his consciousness without producing any clear-cut answers. As John Durham Peters reminds us, "'Exile' suggests a painful or punitive banishment from one's homeland. Though it can be either voluntary or involuntary, internal or external, exile generally implies a fact of trauma, an imminent danger, usually political, that makes the home no longer safely habitable" (19). It seems impossible then that the poet could even fully integrate back into a society from which he was forced to leave.

Underscoring his uneasiness with his homeland again, the narrator proposes yet another rhetorical question, "My land, do you still hear me?" (103). With this query proposed as a rhetorical question, the narrator emphasizes both a longing and worry about being heard. Without any confirmation from his homeland, the poet continues his dialogue with Italy, later affirming, "I know you hear me still." (115). Calling out his "land" through apostrophe — the assumption of being heard — demonstrates the narrator's sentimental distress, but more so, it is shared with the reader. The narrator's desire that Italy not only listens but additionally responds is foundational for sustaining his relationship with his homeland because the reader later learns that "[he is] here reborn, and sing / To the air of the mountain and the plain." (129-130). Rebirth is indispensable for the narrator and his *bildungsroman*, and its manifestation in Italy proves even more substantial. Even if he struggles to separate himself from his feelings associated with his homeland, it is noteworthy that his rebirth still transpires in Italy. Although his rebirth is celebratory and significant, nonetheless the poem ends with a slightly more negative tone:

> Ah, too late, it's too late:
> What was gold is not crocus, and the sheen
> That was morning is life
> To be felt, no more seen.
> Into this sea
> Of loveliness the night is lost and gained,
> And all my cares are drowned. (150-156)

The use of the negative, "not" and "no" and the descriptions pertaining to the semiotic field of darkness, "too late," "night," "lost," and "drowned" paired with the concept of time fleeting into the nighttime sea, an image that sombers any hope the reader or the narrator may be fully accumulated.

As the reader experiences the passing of time through a series of images, one discerns that what prevailed as delightful and glorious has lost its luster: first noted through the shifting color imagery — from gold to crocus — and later referring to time — morning to night. The poetic adoption of enjambment is striking and serves not only as a device to create anticipation with the reader but also to accentuate an emotional break — "is life / to be felt, no more seen"

— change from morning to night, from birth to death, and from past to present. Another example of this sentimental adoption of enjambment is "Into this sea / Of loveliness the night." From both a linguistic and emotional level, the line leaves the reader hanging with the word "sea" as its metaphoric possibilities are immense. In a psychoanalytic reading, water recalls the womb, and as such, rebirth; however, once the reader continues to "Of loveliness," the tone transforms the mood of the poem negatively through the imagery of the sea, implying that it has engulfed the night. Therefore, the opposition between past — represented by positive images — and present, described with a sense of loss, perpetuates the internal conflict evident in the poet's persona. In fact, the narrator invokes an oppositional approach to the negative concepts, "life," "gold," "sheen," "morning," "loveliness," which attempts to contradict, or at the very least parallel the negative concepts.

The final image of the poem is striking as it concludes with a negative sentiment, offering semi-closure as the last line of the poem suggests, "And all my cares are drowned." This negative image of drowning, especially in the "late night" water, acts here as an oxymoron, which ends the poem negatively and is in direct opposition to the early morning water of rebirth earlier in the poem. The concept of drowning, obviously a negative symbol, recalls the "sea"; however, "cares are drowned" offers a sense of relief, interpreted positively. Thus, time serves as the narrator's grandest nemesis and can be read as the architect of his internal conflict. Accordingly, the narrator must *drown* his sense of identity, the Lacanian *I*, ensuing the narrator's desire to be complete. As Anthony Julian Tamburri points out in his "Un rimpatrio linguistico ovvero un recupero culturale? *Il ritorno* di Joseph Tusiani," Tusiani's use of nature reminds at least the Italianist of Giacomo Leopardi's pessimism in relationship to nature, "l'unica possibilità che ci offre il nostro io narrante per scansare il pessimismo leopardiano di cui è intrisa la poesia tusianea" (47). Although Tamburri was addressing a poem from *Il ritorno*, Tusiani's drowning recall's Leopardi's famous "L'infinito," "e il naufragar m'è dolce in questo mare. This trope of self-denial and "psyche split," noted by Carravetta, is echoed throughout the poet's *oeuvre*. Not to be forgotten either is the narrator's use of personification of his homeland with whom he maintains a one-sided conversation.

Originally published in 1978 in his collection *Gente Mia and Other Poems* and later included in a subsequent collection, *Ethnicity: Selected Poems* (2012), Joseph Tusiani's "Song of the Bicentennial" is a clear example of the poet's conflicted exilic nature, the confrontation "with two realities, 'old world' and 'new world,' and feeling that he does not belong to either" (Giordano 84). As already noted in "The Return," our poet favors rhetorical questions in his lyric voice. In the six-part poem, the narrator engages in another conversation with himself in which he reflects on the series of events in his life and what would have happened if he had stayed in Southern Italy. As in "The Return," he initiates the long poem with questions:

> What would my life have been
> had I remained where I was born? What dreams
> would I be dreaming now? I cannot even
> compare my human state
> with that of a plant plucked
> from its salubrious ground
> and placed elsewhere under a roof for heaven. (1-7)

The opening lines introduce the reader to the internal monologue of possibility, confusion, and most apparently, the uncertainty that the narrator embodies as a quotidian nature. As the narrator questions his past, he directly connects the concept of the past with the possibility of the future — the dreaming occurs in the present tense — underscoring the ongoing, conflictual nature he currently endures. His use, however, of the past conditional tense suggests an unreal situation in the past, one which is unattainable, one which is often regrettable. When considering the poet's relationship with Dante and the author's importance both professionally, as scholar, and personally, as author, one can connect the metaphorical significance of the spiritual, along with dreaming and attention to woods and forests, as denoted in Dante's *Divine Comedy*.

In line three, the narrator begins a comparison, although he prefaces it with the inability to do so, with a plant "plucked" and replanted somewhere else. This "non-comparison" composed by the narrator, which is both romantic and poetic, lightens the tone of the poem and, as such, the migratory experience. However, the image of a plant is a noteworthy and rather common one to represent exile, used simplistically yet purposefully. Like the plant, the migrant often has little to no choice in migrating. In her chapter entitled "Home: Smell, Taste, Posture, Gleam," Margaret Morse argues that "'home' is not a real place, (though it always was once upon a time), feeling at home, in essence, a personal and culturally specific link to the imaginary" (64). Morse's theoretical framework connects the sociological with the psychoanalytical, demonstrating the intense history "home" creates for the individual. She continues:

> Feelings and memories linked to home are highly charged, if not with meaning, then with sense memories that began in childhood before the mastery of language. A fortuitous and fleeting smell, a spidery touch, a motion, a bitter taste — almost beyond our conscious ability to bid or concoct or recreate—home is thus an evocation that is of this sensory world, ephemeral and potential in the least familiar. (63)

Although sensory and only imagined through literature, these images can be effectively utilized to instill in the reader an affect. According to Dan Sperber, although difficult to describe, the perfume of flowers can attach an image to the imagined thought (117). Thus, "the invocation of an imaginary realm tied to early childhood nourishes the capacity for emotional investment in the body and the world, and, culturally speaking, the management of sympathy, the ability to identify with others" (Morse 65). Simultaneously, however, the narrator's use of the flower replicates the concepts revolving around migration: movement and resettling.

The floral imaginary does not cease there, however. Before returning to the concept of the plant, the narrator discusses how his question(s) will forever remain "incomprehensible" to eternity, which is partnered with a series of naturistic wonders — mountains and rocks, ocean and waves, clouds and sky, sun and light. His use of nature functions twofold: first and foremost, the poet uses nature as a means of communicating with God/Fate/the spiritual world beyond. Additionally, he uses nature as a means to recall his homeland. His metaphoric use of nature creates a tone in which he expresses his exilic relationship with home and homeland, sharing psychoanalytic undertones of his struggle with identity.

As such, the metaphor of the plant continues throughout the entire first section of the poem:

> Yet I have ceased to be
> the man I was; the roots wherefrom I sprung
> are somewhere else instead. Deracinated —
> is this the word that somewhat hides the grief
> of one uprooted and no longer young?
>
> What would my life be now
> if I were still with my familiar trees? (16-22)

The plant metaphor continues here with one significant enjambment, "to be / the man I was," elaborating on his voluntary exile marked by his upheaval. Stressing this concept of past and present conditional, what could, or should be, the narrator breaks the lines, forcing the reader to pause before learning the second aspect of the "if" clause. This tactic, which often appears in the poem, breaks the line and timeframe, underscoring the split "psyche" of the narrator and his exilic distress.

Scientifically we know that moving a plant even from one pot to another can cause shock and damage to it; the plant may grow in incorrect directions due to the new pot or even die. If the transplant proves successful, which is likely, it finds a new home and grows, at times, into something new and more elaborate. Moreover, plants bud, flourish, bloom, and die; there is a passage of time that follows the life cycle. If planted correctly, perennials experience a rebirth the following season. Therefore, Tusiani's symbolism of the plant evidences this constant inner strife present, within both narrator and poet, a struggle to come to terms with home and homeland, as well as one's identity. On a higher level, particularly for Tusiani, plants are rooted in the earth, bringing the reader back to the spiritual aspect omnipresent in his opus; none of this is by chance, but by some sort of blessing from the divine.

The narrator asks if "deracinated" is the most appropriate word to describe his situation, therefore playing with language. Although the narrator focuses on the roots of the plant — the upheaval and chaos it causes — he omits the positive imagery the plant might represent — growth and rebirth. As Paolo Giordano has already argued, "These three powerful words [sunder, deracination, and uprooted] evoke lucid images of the bitterness, violent separation and displacement that for many is the final *resolution* of the emigration experience" (Giordano 75).[3] Yet, Giordano omits the concept of shame in his analysis, even though we similarly read the poem; the narrator focuses on his uncertainty. In these final lines of the section, the narrator assumes a sense of shame. When the narrator defines "deracination" as "hides the grief of one," there are all the emotions positively mentioned by Giordano — bitterness, violent separation, and displacement — but also a sense of guilt; otherwise, there would be nothing to hide. As the narrator seriously reflects on his situation, he expresses a sense of stigma for losing his youth away from the homeland, highlighted by the question, which concludes the section. Using the conditional tense, "would," the narrator employs a stronger image, the tree, a plant with enormous, powerful roots, and asks how his life would have been had he not been uprooted. Once again, the tree in this situation is hardly summoned by chance as forty percent of Italy's olive oil comes from the poet's native homeland, celebrating a plethora of ancient trees. Thus, the

---

[3] Giordano continues his justification by citing the historical/political/social implications plaguing *la questione meridionale* in Italy and its endless repercussions to Italy.

poet conveys his long-standing relationship with his homeland and his remorse for the current state-of-affairs.

In the first section, the narrator presents two recurring and significant symbols: dreams and the sky/heavens, which later become even more pertinent to understanding the poem. In the second section, the poem focuses on the stars. The stars, as Giordano suggests, chart a storytelling narrative for the emigrant as he, too, embarks on a similar voyage:

> The shape — let me be wondering about
> the shape of stars that glow,
> for something tells me that I too was born
> under the sign of one
> formed like an ocean liner going far,
> crowded with silent men called emigrants—
> my ethnic star. (31-37)

Giordano refers to the stars as a reminder of the vast Southern Italian sky. To expand his reading, the stars, I argue, additionally offer hope for those migrants, some who voluntarily choose exile, others who did not choose, but really had no other financial possibilities in their homeland and "must" leave. Either way, within the narrative of the poem, the stars, particularly "my ethnic star," offer direction to the emigrant as the narrator is born under one. Moreover, the first two stanzas of the second section connect the stars in the sky with the divine, again highlighting the interconnectedness of the migrant's journey.

Section three of the poem transitions the narration to the arrival to the new land where the poet finds a "home" and replants his roots. In *Home, Exile, Homeland*, Naficy explores the following:

> house, home, and homeland — a framing that moves from the literal to the abstract. *House* is the literal object, the material place in which one lives, and it involves legal categories of rights, property, and possession and their opposites. *Home* is anyplace; it is temporary and it is moveable; it can be built, rebuilt, and carried in me-

mory and by acts of imagination. Exiles locate themselves vis-à-vis their house and homes synesthetically and synecdochically. (5-6)

Thus, "home" can never actually replace "homeland," and as Naficy implies, offers an aspect of more control, i.e., one can move, build, and rebuild one's home; irreplaceable, however, it is not.

Repeating previous literary devices, the narrator once again initiates with questions concerning language, another trope the poet not only plays with, as he has published in English, Gargano, Italian, and Latin, but also considers deeply since it is such a present aspect of his personal and professional identity. These questions reiterate the narrator's sense of shame as he finds himself in a quandary — which language to speak? These lines illustrate the duality of identity provided the migrant experience, one of "I" vs. language:

> Do I regret my origin by speaking
> this language I acquired? Do I renounce,
> by talking now in terms of only dreams,
> the sogni of my childhood? What has changed
> that I thought unchangeable in me? (38-42)

Yet language is at the core of this selection. The narrator adopts a series of action verbs: regret, acquire, renounce, think; these verbs work in pairs to question the poet's own identity through language, only to end with a "rhetorical" question, which indeed has no subject, underscoring its involuntary nature.

Moreover, directly attached to the concept of development through Lacanian psychoanalysis is the ability to speak, referring again to the mirror stage. The mirror stage of development occurs when the child sees him/her/themself in the mirror and recognizes the mother's separation, and can pronounce the concept of *I*. According to Lacan, it is at this moment when the infant becomes a child. In this manner, the pronunciation of the *I* is critical for the growth of the individual. When the narrator arrives at his/her/their new home and questions the language of communication, this moment ruins the development and forces the individual to reconsider his/her/

their identity. In fact, the narrator does just that, questioning if he must keep his childhood memories, the Italian and Gargano languages, within his dreams. As a scholar of Dante himself, Tusiani's reference here could easily be read as death, i.e., must he kill his native tongue completely, or, at the very best, leave that tongue only while dreaming, returning to the happy moments of childhood in the homeland?[4]

To underscore the significance of language, the narrator (and poet equally) purposely, or "by chance," slips into Italian when discussing his dreams. The mixing of languages, in general, demonstrates in "real time" the confusion and conflicted nature present within the individual. The narrator believed that his native tongue would be something not changeable; his language would forever be a part of him, yet he acknowledges that this is no longer the situation upon arriving at his new home and "something's changed — and what, I do not know" (6). His uncertainty returns in this third stanza and only intensifies:

> Yet something's changed — and what, I do not know.
> Now every thought I think, each word I say
> detaches me a little more from all
> I used to love — your faces, ancient friends,
> and all our phrases of so much delight
> as needed no translation in my mind. (44-49)

Until this moment, the third section of the poem consists of a series of reflective, internal questions without any sort of answers. Line six offers the first "half" declarative statement: "Yet something's changed," followed by more ambivalence — i.e., he does not understand what has actually changed. The narrator's inability to understand the change suggests that he is stuck in the Lacanian cycle of development. Moreover, he cannot accept his new home because

---

[4] Luigi Fontanella notes Tusiani's allusion to Dante in his use of hendecasyllable in *Il Ritorno*. This return to Italian also evidences a psycho-analytic reading. See Calabretta-Sajder. See *Migrating Words*, 91-92.

he has no closure with his homeland. Line six splits the first two halves of the third section of the poem. The second half is one continuous sentence, which underscores the detached nature the narrator endeavors presently. The fluidity of the lines along with enjambment heightens this sentiment as the reader has to keep reading until we arrive at the period, which is the most important phrase of the sentence, "as needed no translation in my mind."

Language's role assumes a major aspect of this section. Considering his new home with its English tongue, each word he says further removes the narrator from his homeland, his childhood, everything he used to know and love. Although an awkward syntax, the phrase is completely understandable, reflecting on his bilingual nature and how beautiful it is to need no translation. Distress is noted in this first section of the three-parts of the poem; yet, a glimmer of positive energy is shared, the "delightfulness" of being multilingual.

This glimmer of positive energy, however, does not remain. Instead, it escalates beginning in line 49 when he addresses his mother:

> Mother, I even wonder if I am
> the child I was, the little child you knew,
> for you did not expect your little son
> to grow apart from all that was your world,
> the world that he saw first with your own eyes—
> simple and untranslatable, composed
> of one unclouded clarity of light. (49-55)

By addressing his mother, the narrator returns to his past, his own development in his homeland, questioning his own identity more deeply, wondering if his mother would be capable of identifying him. There is an emphasis on his youthfulness in Italy, with the repetition of "little" in two consecutive lines, underscoring the narrator's innocence present in his *bildungsroman*. Moreover, the repetition of the word "world" also suggests a variety of interpretations. Initially, it highlights the differentiating worlds: Italy vs. the U.S., but subconsciously notes Old World vs. New World[5] while simultaneously discussing a difference in language.

In this section of the poem, the narrator switches subjects, which is additionally significant, moving from "I" in the series of rhetorical questions to "the child," clearly creating distance from the personal. Moreover, as Giordano generally suggests, this distance serves on a higher level to remove the personal experience and replace it with the general emigrant adventure. Although Giordano highlights the Southern Italian aspect in his piece, and Tusiani, the poet, often utilizes Southern Italian imagery, here the narrator speaks for every migrant, all who are in exile, whether Italian or not. In this address to the mother, the narrator demonstrates that at first, they had a shared vision, a shared language — a sentiment of comfort as evidenced by:

> the world that he saw first with your own eyes —
> simple and untranslatable, composed
> of one unclouded clarity of light. (53-55)

Yet upon his arrival, what was known and learned was removed:

> Yet of a sudden he was taught to say
> 'Mother' for Mamma, and for cielo 'sky'.
> That very day, we lost each other. Now
> I know you look at me as though I were
> a little more and yet a little less
> than what a son — your child — should be. (56-61)

Reading childhood through a Lacanian lens demonstrates an urge to return to a past, to a homeland lost but not forgotten, yet the narrator's passage is intercepted as this new language establishes distance from Mother and Son.

---

[5] See Paolo Giordano's "From Southern Italian Emigrant to Reluctant American: Joseph Tusiani's *Gente Mia and Other Poems*" for a short, but poignant exploration of the topic in Tusiani's lyric. For an expansion exploration of Old World vs. New World, see Anthony Julian Tamburri (2018).

As noted by the interweaving of singular personal pronouns, the migrant experience at this point of the poem is both personal and universal. By swapping these pronouns, the narrator creates empathy for the reader while maintaining a tone of nostalgia and remorse. As the narrator continues, however, the tone worsens:

> Oh, they have taught me to translate all things —
> even my very self — into some new and old infinity of roots and boughs,
> so that I wonder whether I am old
> or whether I am new beneath the sky,
> beneath the cielo of my long-lost land. (62-66)

The tone intensifies in this last part of section three due to the change of the subject again; this final experience with language is both the narrator's and the poet's. The narrator's change of language acquires more than just a communicative mode; it solidifies his identity and his place in the world as he questions the concepts of Old World vs. New World and his role in those societies. By recalling the sky, the narrator illustrates his longing for his homeland — not only its nature but everything it represents — language, family, beauty, and comfort.

These concepts are further illustrated in section four, as the narrator repeats, "My long-lost land was one that / when snows enveloped it ...'" (68-69). This section is organized as almost a comparison of the two worlds through Christmas imagery. In his homeland, the narrator celebrates with "presepe, full of / tu scendi dalle stelle — / the only song and rule of / intime cose belle." (84-87) It is unclear what the subject of "scendere" is in line 85; however, it seems to refer to the heavens, again, which references God for the poet. Thus, God becomes the only "song and rule of" intimate, beautiful things. Those four lines are full of positive imagery and tone, associating a sense of longing for what the narrator appreciated in life. Moreover, in his homeland, the narrator had a voice, one he used to sing with while in the "new-found land...where men like me and your, / called immigrants, are silent / when Silent

Night is sung..." (88-93). This section closes once again on the communal experience:

>...like me,
>and you, uprooted friend,
>who think of Italy—
>our lost presepe land. (96-99)

Although communal, the narrator returns to the image of the tree/plant and "roots." The image creates the sense of a new community, which, to a certain extent, offers a positive sentiment, yet together they reflect on their lost homeland, that of the *presepe*.

Like his other symbols, Tusiani's use of the *presepe* marks him in various ways. On the surface, the *presepe* is a reminder of his religious/spiritual roots and the celebrations that occur during Christmas. The *presepe* simultaneously presents Mary and Jesus as "outsiders," people forced from their own homeland and not allowed to return, forced into an exilic state to save their child. Thus, the narrator finds direct comfort in the representation of the *presepe* and the new-found land of the U.S., only thinking back to his own roots and experience longing for that comfort that is forever gone. On a more spiritual note, Christmas marks a time of birth and newness in the calendar of the Catholic church; it celebrates the birth of the Savior. In this manner, the *presepe* notes the concept of birth on a certain level and, as such, rebirth for the narrator. Moreover, Christmas is a time to surround oneself with family and celebrate. Although the *presepe* is present throughout Italy, its presence is heavily pronounced in the South and adds to Giordano's thesis regarding the unique Southern migrant experience.

Section five extends the divided nature of the narrator's identity again with a query: "Two languages, two lands, perhaps two souls?" (100). This gradualism, first speaking as an adult using the plant metaphor, later as a child with his mother, then as a baby in this crib, now we return to the basics — questions around languages, land, and souls. This opening question furthers the argument and repeats the opening nature of each section. Yet, the narrator worries about the repercussions of his question because he

> dare[s] not ask these flowers I know well
> ...
> Nor can I question that forbidding oak:
> though low and long, its roots
> cease at the hindrance of the nearest brook
> as if abhorring alienness of ground. (101-107)

The poet's use of nature here illustrates his relationship to his homeland, Puglia, with the strong-rooted trees throughout the countryside; however, the roots cease, metaphorically, returning to the poet and his difficulty in moving from homeland to home, solidifying his own new roots and allowing him to continue to flourish.

Serving as a transition, the narrator proposes another challenge, "Then, who will solve the riddle of my day?" and repeats the opening question of section five, this time, however, phrased as a statement rather than a formal inquiry, ending the line with an ellipsis that leads into a second question, "Am I a man or two strange halves of one?" (110). This rhetorical device reminds the reader of section four and the *presepe*, as his question recall's the Catholic Church's conceptualization of Christ being fully human yet fully divine. I am not arguing the poet is defining himself as divine; yet, he is drawing a comparison from the identity politics he himself has encountered and that which the Christ-child faced; the plight is similar.

After pondering the question, the narrator concludes that

> because there is no answer to my plight
> I find some solace only in this thought—
> that maybe, just as this revolving earth
> must not proclaim your triumph all at once,
> I too must be, while waiting for my dawn,
> the night of my own self.
> Or maybe, just as your unbridled flame

would, undivided, scald this hemisphere
and turn it into ashes, I fulfill
my human fate by giving you, O sun,
a chance of mercy on my helpless life. (113-123)

The narrator admits that his situation is unsurmountable, and he can only receive a certain level of happiness and contention as he awaits a new day for blessings. As the sun revisits daily to replenish the earth, so, too, does the sun bring hope to our narrator, acting as a symbol for rebirth.

The final section of the poem, section six, begins with a pledge in Latin, "Civis Americanus Sum," one he expressed in allegiance to the U.S. Ironically, the poem boasts a celebratory, upbeat tone, underscoring both physically and emotionally the poet's conflicted nature, the two halves of the whole mentioned earlier in the poem. Additionally, this section retains aspects of a sonnet; even though it is 22 lines, the rhythm scene is ABA, CDC, DED, EFE, FGF, GHG, HIH, I. The poet plays with this conventional structure. The first two stanzas (six lines) focus on his allegiance to the U.S.; the last six stanzas focus on the narrator's identity, which are philosophically intertwined.

At the end of the third stanza, the narrator arrives at a self-realization, "do I discover who I am at last — / the multitudinous Italian throng" (131-132). The rhythm helps to synthesize and connect the narrator's various persons into one. Next, he discusses the various persons who make up his identity. The fourth stanza addresses time and how the narrator is the present for his past and the future of those to come, yet he is still an outcast. Ending the stanza and rhythm on "outcast," rhyming with "past" two lines earlier returns the analysis to the concepts of home vs. homeland and how the poet, although having pledged allegiance to the U.S., still cannot and does not feel 'at home.' Moreover, the narrator does not speak for himself but all migrants; thus, the collective is noteworthy for the poet as he is willing to fight for others similar to him. The fifth stanza focuses on dreams, both his and those of other migrants:

> the dream they dreamed in the mines bereft of light—
> I am their darkness and their only ray,"
>
> their silence and their voice: I speak and write
> because they dreamed that I would write and speak
> about their unrecorded death and night. (137-141)

These few lines illustrate the importance the poet has for his entire community; the word "because" serves as a conjunction, as well as a reminder of the narrator (and poet) for those without a voice or pen. Not only is he a ray of light in the darkness of exile, but also the voice, both written and spoken, for the unheard. Following the rhythm words, the poet is the "light" in the "night," if we do a reading in that manner. Likewise, the poet "speak[s]" to "seek" the "peak" of the doom created earlier in the poem.

The end of the poem attempts to change the tone from somber to hopeful, as the narrator becomes almost a "savior" figure, to return to the metaphor of Christ and the *presepe*. The second to last stanza reads

> O glory! I'm the bread they came to seek,
> the vine they planted to outvanquish doom,
> their most majestic and enduring peak. (142-145)

The narrator is being sought after to help the community, and as he returns to the metaphor of the plant/roots, he is being placed exactly where he needs to be, in this new home, where he can fight for others. He will become the object that "outvanquishes doom." Although not necessarily by choice, this role serves a significant function for the community and society in which he lives.

The poem "Song of the Bicentennial" approaches the notion of exile and migration from unique and various perspectives. The poet's use of symbolism accompanied by the assorted levels of interpretation testifies to the multi-layered nature of the poet's psyche. Although he aspires to be "American," integrating into the newfound society and home created in New York, he is incapable of effectively distancing himself from his beloved homeland of Gargano. Moreover, Gargano lives within him, as he expressed throughout this and other poems.

Another intense, yet beautifully emotional and heart-wrenching poem that masterfully demonstrates Tusiani's conflicted character, is "La letta ma'mpustata" ("The Letter Never Sent," 1991).[6] The letter is addressed to his dear Gargano, mentioned both overtly and covertly, as "Mutagna," always with a capital "M," personifying the mountain. The letter highlights a sentiment from the poet as being a "deserter" of his homeland. Although he has never left his homeland in his dreams, he simultaneously feels as if he is an imposter as his dreams are contemporary. The power of dreams presents itself again in the poet's corpus, and early on in this poem:

> dallu iurne
> che ss' partute, me vi sempe'nzonne
> come ve'nzonne allu site la zita,
> come vè'nzonne allu figghie la mamma.
> Me sònne che mme trove, come pprima,
> ammeze la Padula e, sse me cride (2-7)
>
> from the day I left,
> you never fail to come into my dreams,
> as the beloved comes to a lover's dreams.
> I dream I'm there — down in the Marsh again—
> as long ago, and if you can believe me

The repeated use of the present tense in his dreams highlights how active his thoughts concerning Gargano are, comparing his dreams of his homeland to that of a partner coming into a lover's dreams or as a mother is thought of by her son; this double-edged metaphor for the same original image is autobiographical as the poet was both

---

[6] I am referencing the version published in *Poets of the Italian Diaspora*, 1084-1089. The English translation is by Luigi Bonaffini.

married and was a son. His relationship with his mother has already been explored and shows how this experience of exile proves significant in relation to his mother. He also shares about his dreams of being in the Marsh of the homeland. Additionally, he describes in his letter how he can hear the bells of his church of St. Anthony, intensifying his psyche to believe it can truly be one divided soul in two places.

On the theme of the "psyche" as seen through childhood feelings and memories, Margaret Morse, in her chapter "Home: Smell, Taste, Posture, Gleam," argues,

> Since "home" is not a real place, (though it always was once upon a time), feeling as home is, in essence, a personal and culturally specific link to the imaginary. Feelings and memories linked to home are highlight charged, if not with meaning, then with sense memories that began in childhood before the mastery of language. A fortuitous and fleeting smell, a spidery touch, a motion, a bitter taste — almost beyond our conscious ability to bid or concoct or recreate — home is thus an evocation that is of this sensory world, ephemeral and potential in the least familiar…Thinking about "home" is like being given a hunting license for anamnesis, or reflection on those things "which enthrall me without my knowing why." (Barthes in Morse) (63-64)

Thus, the bells of St. Anthony function as much as a symbol of his own childhood as language, or maybe even more. This aspect of the psychoanalytic reading brings the interpretation to another level, a sensual one that can equally be explored through affect theory.

After the poet reflects on missing his beloved Gargano and an internal question which he poses to himself, "La lettera ma'mpustata" drifts in tone from being nostalgic to embarrassing, as the narrator shares, "tegne nu nùdeche'ncanna / che sule chi è emigrante pò capì. (An emigrant alone / can know the lump that rises in my throat)" (11-12). In this manner, the narrator speaks in general terms, removing himself from the narrative as subject and replacing it with "an emigrant," suggesting his feelings are part of the common experience, a similar strategy utilized in "Song of the Bicentennial Man," used to build an emotional bond between the narrator and reader, many who are exiles themselves. This bond frees the narrator emotionally while simultaneously revealing to the reader an underexplored world.

The narrator's embarrassment heightens in the next lines when addressing how he actively writes letters to the Mountain/Gargano but never mails them for two reasons: they weigh too much, "Te scrive sempe, ma tutte li lettere / non te li'mposte ché pésene assà," (13-14) and also the mailman would laugh at him, "e llu pasture ce mettesse a rrire" (15). Thus, integrating into U.S. culture takes priority for the narrator in these lines as he worries about how others will conceive of him and his longing for his homeland. In fact, the narrator has become so integrated into the society of his new home that he asks forgiveness and understanding for the mailman, "L'ha'cumpatì: iè mmerecane nate / e non capisce che ssi'mmegghie tu / de tutte quiddi ch'ànne studijate." (18-20), as he defends his newfound culture and society, demonstrating again how only a migrant could completely comprehend those feelings.

The poem continues to praise Gargano and discusses how much he still thinks about and misses his homeland. He attempts to trick Gargano into believing his original trip "me pare che non zo'mache partute / e cche ddu bastemente l'ej sunnate" (25-26) but later he confesses stating,

> Ma po' ce penze e ma'accorge che face
> peccate se tte diche na buscia:
> sope ddu bastemente ce so'state,
> inte sta terra so pure sbarcate
> e tre quarte de vita so ppassate. (28-32)
>
> But then I reconsider, and realize
> it would be a sin for me to tell you a lie:
> Indeed, I did sail once upon that ship,
> And I did come ashore upon this land

After his jubilant tone recalling his Gargano and emphasizing his relationship with his homeland through dreams, the narrator reiterates the facts of his life, again from a moralistic and embarrassing point of view, especially when highlighting that "three quarters of my life are gone." The tone change, which swithes to the somber action of passing 40 years in the U.S. attempting to create a home, yet being unable to completely do so, still dreaming of his homeland and never leaving, longing to make things right with Gargano. In fact, the narrator's application of personification illustrates the difficulty Tusiani maintains with his homeland. Even though he is a volenatary exile, he struggles in the happiness of building a new home in the U.S.

Later in the poem, the narrator elaborates on his longing, how much he thinks of and misses Gargano, moving into a description of his day:

> Fatije come ttutte quante l'ati,
> ma l'ati ce repòsene cuntente;
> invece i'me face sti dumanne:
> 'Pecché so nnate? pecché so partute?
> pecché non zo'rrumaste pure i'
> sope ddu belle Monte risciurute?'
> Gargane mia, iàvete che durmi! (38-44)

> but other people go to sleep content;
> instead, I ask myself these selfsame questions:
> "Why was I born? Why did I ever leave?
> Why didn't I stay behind with all the others
> on that beautiful Mountain in full bloom?"
> My dear Gargano, there is no sleep for me.

The fact that the narrator cannot sleep and restlessly tosses and turns thinking about his beloved Gargano demonstrates the torment he lives with daily; moreover, because this anguish occurs at night in his private bed, the narrator pretends his life is 'normal,' that this way of life is acceptable.

As he sleeps and dreams, he recounts what he sees, which returns him to his past and the action of leaving: "de povere emigrante come me ... / Lu vi', lu vi', che mmo me vè lu chiante / comme ddu iurne allu pórte de Nàpele? (48-50). Although he claims that he should not continue to address his town, he does, fondly and emotionally, attempting to salute everything he misses with love and grace; the lines demonstrate a shared part of his soul that remains, a part that can never forget and survives internally. In fact, his concern with "Non mi prolunghe..." (52; I won't go on) even though he does, suggests an embarrassment for leaving behind what he understood to be his homeland. However, through embracing his town, he fights the temptation merely to forget it; embodying his love for his homeland pains the narrator but illustrates the difficulty of exile.

To that end, the poetic letters also concludes:

Cara Muntagna mia, sti duje uuasce,
iune è ppe' gghiessa, l'atu jè ppe' tte.
Cu ttant'affette e amore,
    Tusijane. (60-63)

Of these two kisses; my dear Mountain, one
is meant for her, the other one for you.
With all my everlasting lo e,
    Tusiani.

Tusiani sends two kisses back to his homeland, one to his aunt, buried there, and the other to his dear mountain, a visual and metaphoric image for his hometown, which can only be a symbol, as Mount Gargano exists in his memory alone. His two kisses go back to family and homeland, two pieces of his soul that remain conflicted for the poet.

This poem is critical for understanding Tusiani's opus for diverse reasons. First and foremost, he offers this letter as almost an apology, written in his dialect (it was translated into English and Standard Italian), revealing its very personal nature, i.e., through his first language. The poet and narrator are the same since the letter is signed Tusijane, again using his last name's dialectal spelling. Thinking back to psychoanalysis and the importance of language, the child pronounces his first words when he realizes the separation of self from the mother, a huge step in development. Yet his sense of language and intimacy persists audibly by consciously choosing to write this piece in dialect; this choice highlights the essential relationship his homeland maintains, even if only in his dreams. Returning to the concept of homeland and native tongue, Tusijane's Mount Gargano can only understand the author's dearest and most profound emotions in that shared, early language.

Similarly, Tusiani uses his dialect once again in "Ce sta nu cante/There is a Song" (1991).[7] In this sonnet, he speaks about the song that brings him back to his past, which happens to be in dialect, a trope the poet uses to return to his childhood. Employing the medium of a song once again, the poet reverts to his childhood as well as the struggles related to grasping his identity, both American and Pugliese, as noted in line 8: "me dà tremente ma m'è ssempe amica." Yet this conflict opens the poem, as the song itself, "che m'unneja 'mpette (surges deep inside)" (1). The fact that the narrator cannot remove the song from himself underscores how integrated these two aspects exist for the speaker. In this first stanza, the poet once again utilizes nature to explore his feelings figuratively. The narrator's thoughts have "movement," i.e., they come and go like the tides of the sea. The employment of the sea underscores a return to Lacanian psychoanalysis again as water reminds the reader of rebirth; however, the metaphor brings the symbolism again to a more profound level of discourse. Even though the tide represents rebirth, especially from the movement of the seawater, the tide still leaves remnants on the shoreline. The remnants left for the narrator are his memories of his homeland, which still lives inside him:

---

[7] I am referencing the version published in *Poets of the Italian* Diaspora, 1090-1091. The English translation is by Luigi Bonaffini.

e quistu cante iè lu' ndijalette
de dda Muntagna (Ddì la bbenedica)
che mme dà pace e no mme dà recette,
me dà tremente ma m'è ssempe amica. (5-8)

This song's the dialect spoken on the side
of the blessed Mountain, forever a godsend,
that gives me peace, yet leaves me unsatisfied,
that makes me suffer, but is still a friend.

His relationship with the mountain, his homeland, is critical not only metaphorically but also physically. In fact, it is the song that provides tranquility for the narrator and again functions as a means to return to the "feeling at home" that Morse argues, an "invocation of an imaginary realm tied to early childhood [that] nourishes the capacity for emotional investment in the body and in the world" (63; 65). Moreover, it is the dialect here that takes the stage. In the seventh and eighth lines of the poem, the narrator creates four clauses, two per line; each line presents two contradictory sentiments, emphasizing the paradoxical nature present within the poet's psyche: the dialect, which offers peace and serenity, leaves the narrator unfulfilled and suffering, yet is a friend. Thus, in the end, the narrator remains an estranged friend to his dialect, which represents his homeland. Although difficult for the narrator, a positive, even though strained, relationship does remain intact.

The poem ends with another trope exhibited throughout his overture, drowning. The narrator puns on the concept of physically drowning by mentioning the surges of the ocean and metaphoric suffocation with words, drawing attention to language and particularly his dialect. It is the words, not the sea, that floods the narrator and his mind. The concepts of "foreign" and "alien" shadows which are forever a part of the narrator: "ce scròzzene fulìmmije frustere, / ce annetta cullu core ogni penzere" come and go and even if his thoughts are "cleansed" and his "heart is pure," the experience returns like the tide (9-10). Thus, even though the narrator has matured, he cannot leave these "other" shadows which lurk within his inner soul. As such, the poem concludes with the image of drowning.

Light and darkness in the final couplet of the sonnet prove critical for understanding the lyric. In these final lines, although the narrator is faced with drowning in the sea, the night is eventually flooded with the dawn of light, thus repeating the mercy afforded by dawn as in the second poem. The narrator's ability to look forward to the new day, loving both the U.S. and Italy, still brings hope to his distressed state. Even though he refuses to let go of the past completely, he is willing to go through this process of drowning and rebirth.

In one of Tusiani's earliest collections, *The Fifth Season* (1964), in which one can find the beloved "The Return," the poet had already demonstrated, as Sante Matteo suggests, "the tension between the centrifugal impulse to leave one's home and seek other lands of opportunity and the countervailing centripetal impulse to remain home-bound or to return homeward" (xvi). Here again, the narrator longs for his homeland and remains blocked, recreating memories to suffice in his newfound home of NYC/the U.S.

In "Italian Serenade," the narrator again explores his split feelings of being both American and Italian through song. The organizational structure of the poem is complex as the poet uses a combination of anaphora and epistrophe, resulting in symploce, which not only adds emphasis to certain concepts and themes presented throughout the poem but also often creates rhythm, allowing the "serenade" aspect to thrive when read/performed. Structured into four stanzas of six lines, each with repetition present in the first (anaphora), third (anaphora), and final half of the sixth lines of each stanza (epistrophe): "Window, guitar and mandolin, and what" (1,7, 13, 19 with a small replacement of 'and what' with 'and let'); "On the Gargano Mount" (3, 9, 15, 21); and "and that is that" (6, 12, 18, 24). The poem's organization visually is noteworthy as the repetition immediately brings the reader to see the divided narrator through the image of instruments: the guitar representing America and the mandolin personifying Italy. From an audible perspective, the use of symploce renders the poem alive to the ear. Additionally, each stanza's second line also contains the repetition of the narrator's "darling," which is never defined directly in the lyric but seems to refer to his homeland. When we arrive at the final stanza, the line changes, and the repetition is broken, signaling a change in tone and action for the narrator.

In this poem, the first three stanzas aim to create a lush and intensely positive image of the narrator's lost Gargano as he uses song to communicate once again with his homeland playing on the narrator's memories, especially noted in the fourth line of each stanza. Morse's theory of "sense memories" once again proves significant in this piece through both the musical instruments and the Gargano Mount's sound and image. Yet, with each stanza, the sense of separation anxiety does, in fact, increase. Due to the second line of each stanza, the poem underscores the narrator's slipping relationship with his homeland, which remains an image of a forgotten home at this stage in the poet's life. In the second line of the first stanza, the narrator questions the impact of music if the darling is still asleep, while in the second stanza, the inability to hear heightens to a certain level of deafness, and in the third stanza, the speaker worries about the darling still being his. In this manner, the narrator spirals the difficulty of maintaining a long-distance relationship and demonstrates how it deteriorates.

The first stanza is constructed through a type of antithesis, opposing the luscious aroma of thyme on the mount with the reality that his hand does not carry its perfume. In the second stanza, the same rhetorical structure is followed, but the image is the friendly Gargano Mount with its lack of protection offered. The third stanza still describes the dry brook to its potential for drowning; this final image creates a clear antithesis and completes the image of the internal conflict.

In the fourth stanza, however, the poem draws to a more surprising end. The repetition of the first line of the stanza remains while the second line drastically changes from a longing for the narrator's darling, "and let / me think of my America and stay." (19-20). The line demonstrates his possession of America, taking ownership of his new home, as well as declaring that he will stay there.

This attestation solidifies his commitment to his new life in the U.S. Even though the tone is instructive and suggests a positive nature, the poem does not end with the image of the U.S., rather with Gargano and the sacrifices the narrator must endure.

As previously mentioned, Gargano Mount is less idyllic in stanza four in comparison with the other stanzas. Here, we find parallelism, a cemetery where the narrator would like to pray but is unable; yet mourns his youth. Unlike numerous other poems where the narrator encounters a rebirth, often in water, it does not occur in this piece. In fact, he does not even have the capability to pray, to appeal to a higher power, his needs, and desires. The entire serenade brings the narrator back to his youth. The cemetery image underscores the exilic sacrifice the narrator encounters in rebuilding his life in the U.S.

Although the narrator will always maintain memories of his youth, filled with bucolic recollections and emotions, he will never be allowed true reentry to his homeland. Those picturesque thoughts from childhood drive the narrator into mourning, evidenced by the bleak tone that concludes the poem. The narrator is left to construe the leftover memories of his homeland as an "imaginary home."

To return to Thomas Woolfe's opening citation, "You can't go home again!", one absolutely can, but what does that return look like? Physically, one can even return to his homeland; however, will the homeland be waiting with open arms? Or will the migrant be forced to forever live in the home of one's mind? As demonstrated through the *oeuvre* of Joseph Tusiani, not to mention his own resigning of his poetry, once Giuseppe and later Joseph,[8] the concepts of "home" and "homeland" are ever-present. Additionally, Giuseppe/Joseph continuously struggled with his own identity — Italian, American, or Italian-American — as underscored by my psychoanalytic reading. His own use of language and poetic rhetoric, as well versed in numerous languages and poetic traditions, only blur the lines of understanding Tusiani's lyric genius. Even

---

[8] See Luigi Fontanella, *Migrating Words*, 90. See Anthony Julian Tamburri, *Un biculturalismo negato* and *Re-Reading Italian Americana*.

though Tusiani did go back to his beloved homeland, Gargano, various times during his lifetime, he was never truly able to return. And although he eventually built a happy home in NYC, his painful love for Gargano persisted in words, thoughts, and sounds. As Margaret Atwood states in *The Blind Assassin*, "Farewells can be shattering, but returns are surely worse," as the struggle to balance home and homeland only intensify with each visit. (76).

These poems offer a somewhat chronological reading of Tusiani's internal conflict, which presents as personal and poetic, and vice versa. "Returning" to the *homeland* manifests itself in numerous facets for Tusiani, including thematic, structurally, and linguistically, to underscore only three major areas. His trajectory is constant, his struggle real. Yet, he remains blocked in the imaginary — "Two languages, two lands, perhaps…" two homes, one in which he is fully American and the other in which he is fully Gargano.

In *L'eloquenza,* scholar Alfredo Galletti states,

> without wanting to reduce poetry to an exclamation or to a hiccup, or, as certain aesthetes would like, to an *ineffable* intuition (and because ineffable, completely inexpressible) — poetry and eloquence are inseparable like the body and soul. When they are separated, the body dies and the spirit enters the realm of shadows. Tusiani's eloquence is entirely permeated with enthusiasm and passion; lyricism circulates in it like generous lifeblood in a robust body, and thus his eloquence is poetry (trans. Luigi Fontanella, 86)

Although understudied in this piece, Tusiani's classical training becomes abundantly evident through his allusions, thematically and structurally, to the leading Italian and American poets of the canon. As an exilic author, he purposefully and programmatically plays with his predecessors while solidifying his voice as part of the current and future poetic traditions.

WORKS CITED

Atwood, Margaret. 2000. *The Blind Assassin*. New York: Anchor Books.

Bonaffini, Luigi and Joseph Perricone, eds. 2014. *Poets of the Italian Diaspora: A Bilingual Edition*. New York: Fordham UP.

Calabretta-Sajder, Ryan. 2016. "Rediscovering Joseph Tusiani. From 'Return' to *Il ritorno*: A Psychoanalytic Approach." *Italica* 93.2 (Summer): 358-369.

Carravetta, Peter. 2014. "Introduction" in *Poets of the Italian Diaspora: A Bilingual Edition*. Luigi Bonaffini and Joseph Perricone, eds. New York: Fordham UP.

Fontanella, Luigi. 2012. *Migrating Words: Italian Writers in the United States*. New York: Bordighera Press.

Giordano, Paolo. 2012. "From Southern Emigrant to Reluctant American" in *Ethnicity: Selected Poems*. New York: Bordighera Press.

Matteo, Sante. 2014. "Italian Roots in Global Soil" in *Poets of the Italian Diaspora: A Bilingual Edition*. Luigi Bonaffini and Joseph Perricone, eds. New York: Fordham UP.

Morse, Margaret. 1999. "Home: Smell, Taste, Posture, Gleam." In *Home, Exile, Homeland: Film, Media, and the Politics of Place*. Hamid Naficy, ed. New York: Routledge.

Naficy, Hamid, ed. 1999. *Home, Exile, Homeland: Film, Media, and the Politics of Place*. New York: Routledge.

_____. 1999. "Introduction: Framing Exile: From Homeland to Homepage." In *Home, Exile, Homeland: Film, Media, and the Politics of Place*. New York: Routledge.

Tamburri, Anthony Julian. 2018. *Un biculturalismo negato. La letteratura "italiana" negli Stati Uniti*. Firenze: Franco Cesati Editore.

_____. 2016. "Un rimpatrio linguistico ovvero un recupero culturale? *Il ritorno* di Joseph Tusiani," *Italica* 93.2 (2016): 338-57.

_____. 2014. *Re-reading Italian Americana: Generalities and Specificities on Literature and Criticism*. Madison, NJ: Fairleigh Dickinson UP.

Tusiani, Joseph. 1964. *The Fifth Season*. New York: Ivan Obolensky, Inc.

_____. 1978. *Gente Mia and Other Poems*. Stone Park, IL: Italian Cultural Center.

_____. 2012 *Ethnicity: Selected Poems*. New York: Bordighera Press.

JOSEPH TUSIANI
A Contemporary American Poet[1]

Maria C. Pastore Passaro

In 1962, Joseph Tusiani entered the American Literary scene with his first collection of poems, *Rind and All*.[2] While in his native Gargano, the young poet had already published different books of poetry in Italian, and in the U.S. he had contributed poems in English to the *Catholic World*, the *New York Herald Tribune*, and *Sign*. In 1956, the *New York Times* had already announced him as the winner of the "Greenwood Prize," conferred to him by the Poetry Society of England. Tusiani had also already translated into English the *Complete Poems of Michelangelo* (1960) and was preparing for publication *Tasso's Jerusalemn Delivered*. In *Rind and All*, a collection of fifty poems, the reader can immediately see Tusiani's discovery of his realistic journeys in his new daily life as a New Yorker: "Fellow Passenger," "Elegy Written in a Subway Station," "Saint Francis in

---

[1] I first met Joseph Tusiani at Lehman College (CUNY) in 1968, one afternoon when he lectured on Dante's *Divine Comedy*. That day I discovered what I wanted to do with my life, I too would someday become a professor of Italian Language and Literature. Entering College as a matriculated student was not an easy task. When I first came with my family to the USA, I had already attended High School and a year of professional school in Italy. Therefore, when I enrolled at Columbus HS in the Bronx, I was quickly advised to graduate and go into the work force. "But I would like to go to College," I told my advisor." She replied that I should get a job and help my family. I took her advice and went to work in Manhattan in a bank, in an insurance company and later in the airline industry. Meanwhile, I also got married and became mother of two daughters. But now I had met Prof. Tusiani and with the help of my mother who watched my young daughters, I took all the necessary steps to enter College. I attended many of Prof. Tusiani's classes as an undergraduate student at Lehman College, and also some graduate courses at Fordham University. In the 80's, after I graduated Hunter College with a Master in Italian, I attended The Graduate School and University Center (CUNY) that led me to graduate in 1987, with a Ph.D. in Comparative Literature. Meanwhile, I was teaching as an adjunct both at Lehman College (CUNY), and at Fordham University. I achieved my goal, first inspired by Prof. Tusiani, of becoming a professor of Italian Language and Literature at Central Connecticut State University, in 1989.
[2] Joseph Tusiani, *Rind and All* (Fifty Poems) (New York: The Monastine Press, 1962).

Times Square," "Commuter Train," and other poems with themes common to city dwellers. This is the America that the poet discovers after a decade of nostalgic memories of his native town. Often the remembrance of his rural Gargano becomes a comparison for the vibrant city that never sleeps (i.e., "Post card: New York under Snow") or as he sees the wealth of Fifth Avenue and recalls the poverty of his village (i.e. "Thirteen Each Day"). But the collection includes also poems like "Lovers," "The Book of Love," "Music of the Thunder," "Gregorian Chant on the Hi-Fi," "Concert in Death Minor," "Concert in Death Major," "A Sequence of Inner Sonnets," and it is through internal and external music that the poet discovers a pure and ideal humanity.

Tusiani's English poetry has the supreme quality of being timeless and universal. In 1964, when the second book of poems came out, *The Fifth Season*,[3] *The Philadelpha Inquirer* wrote:

> In an age in which creativity seems aimed at quite different goals and the art of poetry seems in decline, Joseph Tusiani, Italian born, emerges as an English poet of supreme quality.

Along these lines, the *Indianapolis Star* commented that we are "... in the presence of the great poetry," and the *Library Journal of New York* wrote that: "...the one of Tusiani is moderate irony... all of his poems celebrate a distinctive and immediate identity with nature and life. For the readers who react with hostility to the dry bones of the Pound-Eliot tradition, here is a garland that we recommend to all lovers of modern poetry." The poem, "The Fifth Season," that gives the name to the collection of the second book of poetry, refers to a season that goes beyond the four seasons, casting us out of time and in a contest of time. *The Fifth Season* is an even more difficult text. The Irish poet Padraic Colum says that Tusiani's is: "Poetry that comes out of the tradition of Christian Mysticism. I thought that there was only one poet today who wrote such poetry — Kathleen Raine. But here is another poet whose work comes out

---

[3] Joseph Tusiani, *The Fifth Season* (New York: Ivan Obolensky, 1964).

of that tradition — Joseph Tusiani. His poetry is set against another tradition, for he is Latin and knows

> the empire of the oak, the Sybil's word,
> the omen of the thunder.

He is one who has

> lost Jerusalem and Rome,
> and emperor and slave meet in my soul.[4]

About *Rind and All*, Padraic Colum goes on to say that the collection is "about the finding of grace and keeping of it. That grace cannot be indefinitely held. The postcard from New York under the snow shows him skyscrapers resembling

> mountains, mountains columns of some archaic temple
> become a frozen prayer,

and makes him realize:

> tomorrow terminates borne by the sun, effacing
> what I painted and carved — my yesterday's grace.

The Fifth Season includes a collection of 80 poems: 40 in Part One and 40 in Part Two.[5] Some of the titles of Part One are "Minima Theologica," "Aesopiana," "Symphonie Fantastique," "Sketch of a Tree," "Dilemma in the Morning," "Italian Serenede," "Beauty Perished," and other titles.

Some of the titles of Part Two include: "Homage to Carl Jung," "If I say wine," "Definition of a Poem for a Child," "Thanksgiving," "Standstill," "The Return," and others. The last two poems had a special meaning for Tusiani. Whereas "The Return" was the poem

---

[4] The opinion of Padraic Colum appears in the rear cover of *The Fifth Season*.
[5] The two collections, "*The Fifth Season* and *Rind and All* consecrate Tusiani as an American poet," says Cosma Siani, the first top scholar of Joseph Tusiani, in *Le lingue dell'altrove. Storia testi e bibliografia di Joseph Tusiani* (Rome: Confine, 2004) 81.

that awarded Tusiani the Greenwood Prize of London, "Standstill," became part of the volume *Poetry in Crystal*, a show sponsored by the Steuben Co. of America where poetry and sculpture came together.[6] And here are Tusiani's verses of:

Standstill

Something is standing still
around or in me,
soothing that is or could be
the world with its last heaven
or even the end of my will
or my soul.

For the first time, if ever at all,
my mind now follows my body asleep
and knows the name
of the water deep
now that all water is still
and seems no more to be water
just as my will unafraid of tears
is not my will — is not my birth.

And I can see the worth
of things, the size
and purpose of each star
and of man's earth
in the skies,
and my own will

a useful, useless speck apart
and very far.
I cannot tell
what all this is and what I am—
heartbeat or sham
life of another or will of my own.
Something, I feel, if not lost yet,
is standing still.

Tusiani's third collection of verse is *Gente Mia and Other Poems*.[7] The first part of the title, *Gente Mia*, the ethnic content that is, has received

---

[6] Interpretation in Crystal of thirty-one new poems by Contemporary American Poets. New York: Steuben Glass, 1963. The poem "Standstill" was interpreted by George Thompson, a sculptor whose work in crystal are in many museums, among these, the Metropolitan Museum of Art of New York, the Palais du Louvre of Paris and the National Gallery of Modern Art in New Delhi.

[7] Joseph Tusiani, *Gente Mia and Other Poems* (Stone Park, IL: Italian Cultural Center, 1978). When the book first came out and I read the first lines of "Song of the Bicentennial," I felt that Tusiani was, indeed, expressing in poetry what I, as an immigrant, was feeling. As I read the ethnic poems, I was translating them in Italian in my mind. At that time, I used to write articles for an Italian magazine, *La Follia di New York*. For the October issue, I wanted to contribute the translation of the poem, "Columbus Day in New York," from *Gente Mia and Other Poems*. One day, I went to visit Prof. Tusiani with my father (who also lived in the same area of the Bronx

so much attention that the poet has, perhaps, unjustly suffered a sort of *diminution capitis*.[8] Published at the peak of our Italian-American self-awareness and subsequent self-esteemed, *Gente Mia* was hailed as "a landmark in the literature of a people" (Pastore, 100) and the poet, Joseph Tusiani, became the Homeric voice that lyrically revitalized the immigrant experience. But in Part Two of the book, "And Other Poems," we find no trace of the immigrant experience — The simple conjunction "and" becomes the key that opens the door to the less explored poetry of Joseph Tusiani as a unique contemporary American poet. In the first part (the ethnic portion) of *Gente Mia*, we find very few instances that link Tusiani to his two earlier poetic works. He is recognizable in verses such as:

> Let me tonight be wondering about
> the shape of every star —
> not the unbounded magna that confounds
> my human thinking that at best is doubt...

Or if we remember the title of several lyrics from *Rind and All* and *The Fifth Season*, we may re-experience the typical aura of Tusiani's poetry in a lyrical sentence from "Song of the Bicentennial." But, while in "Song of the Bicentennial," we see the immigrant as a passenger on a ship, in the opening poem of *Rind and All*, "Fellow Passenger" becomes a metaphor — it is a passenger on a train that travels to his destination being his home on Mother Earth or his last destination in Heaven. To find the supreme quality that permeates the pages of *Rind and All* and especially *The Fifth Season*, we must now

---

and enjoyed speaking to his mother) and asked him. The editor of *La Follia* wanted a written permission from the poet. In his immense generosity, Prof. Tusiani wrote: "Professor Passaro has my permission to translate into Italian all my English books of poetry." This is when I embarked on translating the three books of Tusiani's English poetry. *Gente Mia e Altre Poesie* (San Marco in Lamis (FG): Gruppo Cittadella Est, 1982). For the translation of *The Fifth Season* and *Rind and All*, see *Mallo e Gheriglio e La Quinta Stagione*. Roma: Bulzoni, 1987.

[8] See my essay: Giordano, Paolo, ed. "*Gente Mia*, Part Two: An Indispensable Reading" in *Joseph Tusiani Poet Translator Humanist an International Homage* (West Lafayette, IN: Bordighera Press, 1994). 100-112.

turn to Part Two of *Gente Mia*. We must shift our attention from the "ethnic" to the "metaphysical" writer or — to interpret the spirit of a recent important anthology — from a "marginal" to a "central" totally American poet.[9] Ample credit must be given to the poet Luigi Fontanella, who affirms that Part Two of *Gente Mia* is "the highest moment of Tusiani's entire poetic production," and he further mentions "the fervid accent of sincerity that literally move and cannot but involve the reader." In his essay, Fontanella goes on to mention Tusiani's suggestive "Nocturnes," full of grace and lightness, "Ornithology: Footnotes One and Two," where the poet touches points of a "sacralità visionaria" (visionary sacrality). With these two words, "sacralità visionaria," perhaps unknowingly, Fontanella links Part Two of *Gente Mia* to *The Fifth Season*.[10] We are suddenly reminded of John Duffy's often quoted analysis of *The Fifth Season*: "Most of the poems demand and deserve a patient second reading. Phrase by phrase they come alive. Even at a first reading the poems which one fails to penetrate have the urgent suggestiveness of all beautiful things only dimly understood, like the suggestiveness of half-heard words in a distant hymn. Are there other ways to say what Tusiani says? Yes, but one would miss the restraint, the superior detachment. This is not the kind of poetry which floats on every easy wind; it blows cold and very serious. I said 'grave' very serious. I said 'grave' somewhere above; I come back to as the best one-word summary."[11]

Indeed, Duffy's "gravity of vision," is what Fontanella calls "visionary sacrality," the word that best captures and defines Part Two's entire tone and empathy. One has but to read the opening

---

[9] Paolo Giordano. "*Gente Mia*, Part Two: An Indispensable Reading" in *Joseph Tusiani Poet Translator Humanist an International Homage* (West Lafayette, IN: Bordighera Press, 1994). 104.

[10] *La Letteratura dell'Emigrazione*, a cura di Jean-Jacques Marchand (Torino: Edizioni della Fondazione Giovanni Agnelli, 1991) 459-466. This volume contains also my presentation at the University of Lausanne (Switzerland), on the first volume of Tusiani's trilogy, *La parola difficile* (Fasano, Bari: Schena, 1988).

[11] Paolo Giordano, ed. "*Gente Mia*, Part Two: An Indispensable Reading" in *Joseph Tusiani Poet Translator Humanist an International Homage* (West Lafayette, IN: Bordighera Press, 1994). 105.

poem, "Two moments at Patmos," to witness, and be part of, a vision in the highest incandescence of its occurrence:

> Not that which lapses between dream and dreamer,
> not that which passes between thought and sound
> have you been made to know, but that which throbs
> as life between a never-ending sun
> and a ray ended, between lips that drink
> and water being drunk...

Here Patnos, the Greek island where Saint John the Apostle allegedly wrote the *Apocalypse*, stands for the ultimate source of theological enlightenment — the very theme, that is, that opens The Fifth Season in the poem "Minima Theologica":

> How simple is the dogma of the sun
> when no theology of cloud makes your earth doubt.
> Suddenly luminescence, life and heat
> turn unity around you, who begin to wonder
> why you have been until this moment wondering
> about unfathomed trinity of light.

"It is in such a climate of pure metaphysics that *The Fifth Season* begins," says Lucia Petracco Sovran in her book, *Joseph Tusiani, Poeta e traduttore*.[12] Whether steeped in metaphysics or Mysticism, Tusiani's idea, as Cosma Siani suggests, "fully penetrates and almost dissolves all things remembered."[13]

Metaphysical flights and lyrical paradoxes are Tusiani's natural habitat. Both elements are firmly sustained by a basic musicality, to which the poet's familiarity with Latin prosody gives a dimension rare to find in other contemporary poets. It is a classical music that gives a sense of 'sacrality' to all things touched by it.

---

[12] Paolo Giordano, ed. "*Gente Mia,* Part Two: An Indispensable Reading" in *Joseph Tusiani Poet Translator Humanist an International Homage*. 106.
[13] Ibid.

At times, Tusiani's musicality makes itself manifest in the complex score of a *quinta rima*, as in "Analysis in Late November," in which the juxtaposition of pentameters and diameters creates its own reverberating reply:

> In the effusion of this earthly grace
> made of a golden pardon of the sun,
>
> I must now trace,
> and boldly face,
> the elements whereby this beauty is undone.
> But that's the play of light, as old and new
>
> as children run-
> ning in fun
> away from fancied foes that charge out of the blue.

Or, as in "Moment in the Snow," all tercets are linked to one another by no more than two rhymes recurring throughout, thus creating a sort of hypnosis that, given the particular theme of wintry revelation (the number of nests on bare branches), compels the reader to observe and listen:

> Now I adore the Essance on my knees,
> now that bare branches tell the deeds of God
> through all this white simplicity of snow.
>
> Oh, now for the first time I know, I know
> what love it takes to dress in green the trees,
> what tenderness to color every bud.

Throughout Part Two of *Gente Mia*, Joseph Tusiani faithfully obeys the precepts of his own *ars poetica*, facetiously yet solemnly stated in *The Fifth Season*:[14]

---

[14] "Definition of a Poem for a Child Who Does Not Know What It Is, Yet Would Like to Write One," in Joseph Tusiani, *The Fifth Season*, 50. In 1988, when the first

> You see, the poem is in you
> before you watch it in the blue ...
> A poem, then, in you must sound
> before you hear it all around ...
> A poem, then, is you in you,
> and you again outside of you,
> reflection of both gray and blue,
> and anticipation, too.
> Now listen: as far as the writing goes,
> just copy the bee and copy the rose.

As far as the metaphysical flight, I would like to mention "For a definition of Mathematics,"[15] a poem that balances itself on seemingly unintelligible, and therefore baffling, terms of reference, only to descend and finally rest on an incontrovertible truth:

> It is not even the unknown
> embraces, multiplied in dream
> by all the mouths that joined my own,
> can be the parallelogram
> I need to close the curving graph
> Of my predestined epitaph.

Of the same amplitude is "Footnote to Vivaldi," in which Fall, "fool's errand of the sun/sweetened intimacy of leaf and light," is only a pretext for a sudden Pindaric flight to Grecian skies, to the land of Eunomia sleeping in Dike's arms, utterly oblivious of Phidias and his hand." A poem of a totally different tone is "The Confession of Prince Empirion," a collection of thirteen irregular sonnets in which the poet re-handles, re-shapes and finally altogether changes, the myth of Narcissus. In his lengthy soliloquy Empirion — the "empirical" man, that is — tells the gradual, exasperating

---

volume of Tusiani's trilogy, *La parola difficile* came out, I had some of my students present a short musical about it, on the stage of Westchester Community College.
[15] Joseph Tusiani, *Gente Mia and other Poems*, Part Two. 67.

conflict between himself, man of action, and Narcissus, his brother, man of dream. The two cannot understand each other, as there can be no place for both of them on the same earth. So one day, Empirion pushed Narcissus into the pool and watched him drown.

Listen now to the conclusion of the soliloquy:[16]

> They even tell me now, to make
> my murder seem a myth,
> Narcissus was myself, the dream
> of beauty I was born with.
>
> They tell me that my mourning
> Narcissus meek and mild
> means I should be ashamed
> of what in me is still a child.
>
> And there is no court on earth
> would dare pronounce sentence on me.
> Murder the flesh and you must die,
> murder the soul and you are free.
>
> But since mankind now bears my name
> I am accustomed to my shame.

A probative example where the music is more researched and refined in Part Two of *Gente Mia*, is the lyric "Aubade in Gray":

> Gray was the color of all timelessness
> when timelessness and color were all one.
> There was no fire yet, there was no sun,
> there was God dreaming of a light, called man.
>
> And then time trembled out of timelessness,
> victory rising from no battle won.

---

[16] This poem, "The Confession of Prince Empirion," in Part Two of *Gente Mia*, originally appeared in *The Kansas Quarterly* 1.5, 1973.

> There was no music yet, no crying done,
> there was God dreaming of a voice called man.
>
> Now look and listen. In this timelessness
> the first bird twitter, the first shadows run,
> heaven and earth and dusk and dawn are one,
> and I am dreaming of a God called man.

As for the astonishing paradoxes that, as in *Rind and All* and in *The Fifth Season* appear and predominate, in *Gente Mia*'s Part Two, this is, I believe, the distic that best exemplifies the poet's penchant for unorthodox axioms:

> I can kill you with a rose,
> I can heal you with a thorn.

Only at a second reading — to go back to Duffy's warning[17] — do we understand, in this particular case, that flatteries kill, and truth heals. But we have here the key to the penetration to Tusiani's Nocturnes — the genre that is, in which our poet can express himself at his best not only in English but also in Italian, and especially, in Latin.

Gente Mia's ten "Nocturnes" range from the theme of the inutility of speech ("I wonder what my word has ever meant "to that of the unreliability of sight) "the last and easy languor of the night / lest all I see grow suddenly less bright"); from the painful realization of the importance of human thought ("I only know I thought / I could control the dark") to the joyous acknowledgement of this world as it is ("I cherish all of you that's now my earth"); from the common image of daily events ("imagine your mortality surpassed / and think that death can be as beautiful / as all this transmigration of new love") to considerations of no immediately discernible impact at all ("the rain I always knew could not perform;") from meditations of redeeming value ("I held your finger pointed to a

---

[17] For Duffy's quote see note 12 of the present study.

star, / who could not hold your marvel in my soul") to primordial doubts ("And was not chaos essential to Thy plan / before thy order made the first sea rise / and the last land obediently yield?") and reassuring victories of faith ("the triumph of the morning in my soul).

This, of course, only gives a cursory glimpse of the ten "Nocturnes" I have mentioned; but it is not the readers task to discover the beauty, and especially, the music that enwraps all of Tusiani's poetry. (Incidentally, it might be noteworthy to remember Tusiani's acknowledged indebtedness to music — from *The Fifth Season*'s "Symphony Fantastique" (Berlioz) to the "Brahms" of the *Exilio Rerum* and "Ad Verlaine Poetam" of the same collection.) One, at this point, may be tempted, after all that has been said of metaphysical flights and paradoxes, to think of Joseph Tusiani as a poet blissfully unmindful of what we call the crudeness of reality. But one lyric alone from Part Two of *Gente Mia*, "Wishing for a Wrong Number," (one of the best poems of 1965)[18] is sufficient to prove our poet's awareness of the *lacrime rerum* around us:

> Call me, whoever you are, and tell me
> whatever you please. Speak even
> of wind and heaven to
> a wounded eagle in the grass, of bread and fire
> to a famished beggar in the snow.
> Be cruel and be rude
> but talk to me and let me know
> that I am not alone
> in this my human solitude.

Tusiani's concept of "human solitude" is a theme that recurs quite often in his poetic production. It has nothing to do with the ordinary feeling of "loneliness" which is part of our human condition. It is born out of man's aching sense of his "*quotidie morior,*" to be

---

[18] See, *The Best Poems of 1965,* an *Anthology of Poetry* (Boreston Mountain Awards, 1965).

sure; but, suddenly shifting to a loftier vision of the human existence it becomes tantamount to an awareness of a "solitude" of cosmic proportions and laws. Man's Earth itself is seen as "alone" in the midst of the miriads of galaxies floating around it, with everything in it equally and forever "alone":

> And I have even lost my human right
> to die with you or call your sadness mine,
> for all things born seem to be now alone:
> alone the firefly and alone the wind,
> alone the ocean and alone the sky.
> And in so vast a loneliness, O love,
> O last illusion of my daylight done,
> how dark this very world, how small this I.[19][20]

This is the Solitudo that Tusiani extends, to the infinitesimal celestial speck called Earth. In the most celebrated of all his poems, "Standstill" — the lyric that placed Joseph Tusiani in the company of the most famous American poets of the Twentieth Century, the poet makes such cosmic solitude synonymous with total absence of purposeness in human as well as planetary life:

> I cannot tell
> what all this is
> and what I am—
> heartbeat or sham,
> life of another or will
> of my own.
> Something, I feel, if not lost yet,
> is standing still.[20]

"If not lost yet"! There is a poem in Part Two of *Gente Mia* ("End of the Game") in which "loss" seems to equal "solitude," or vice versa:

---

[19] From "Solitudo," in Joseph Tusiani, *The Fifth Season*. 71.
[20] From "Standstill," in Joseph Tusiani, *The Fifth Season*. 63.

> After some time of severance and search,
> an inner ache, a sudden loneliness,
> a feeling of inexplicable loss
>
> Will tell me it is time to learn the worst:
> I shall remove my blindfold then, and know
> by some less obvious omens in the light
> that you are gone forever from my life.[21]

We would be tempted at this point to detect a morbidity of temperament or *forma mentis* if we were not still lucidly cognizant that Tusiani sings the breathtaking immensity of the universe as well as man's need of belonging to, and in, it. Similarly, we easily understand that, the more they seem to plunge into total darkness, the more clearly his "Nocturnes" celebrate the apotheosis of the desperately awaited morning.

Part Two of *Gente Mia*, is indispensable for the comprehension of what may be Tusiani's highest and purest poetry, which is in Latin.[22] Numerous are his *Nocturna*, from "Oratio Nocturna," "Nox Serena," "Nocturnum" of *In Exilio Rerum* to "Nocturnum,: "Melos Nocturnum" of Confinia Lucis at Umbrae, "Nocturna (quattuor)" of the Classical Outlook (May-June, 1989), and "Nocturnum Neo-Eborancense" which obtained the publica laus in the Certamen Capitolinum XLIII of 1992. Even more than his English Nocturnes, Tusiani's Latin *Nocturna* leave the reader with a pervasive sense of triumphant faith. It seems to me (but this will be better said and demonstrated by authoritative Latin scholars) that the spirit as well

---

[21] Joseph Tusiani, *Gente Mia and Other Poems*. 66.

[22] Joseph Tusiani's four collection of Latin verse are *Melos Cordis* (New York: Venetian, 1950), *Rosa Rosarum* (Oxford, OH: American Classical League, 1984), *In Exilio Rerum* (Avignon: Aubanel, 1985) and *Confina Lucis et Umbrae* (Louvain: Peeters, 1989). A complete bibliography of Tusiani's Latin lyrics published in the U.S., England, Belgium, France, Germany, Switzerland, and Italy has been compiled by Dirk Sacrè of the University of Antwerp, and appears as an appendix to *Confinia Lucis et Umbrae*, an Anthology of Poems Selected and Introduced by Dirk Sacrè. 111.

as the music of *Gente Mia*'s entire Part Two can easily be summarized by the untarnishable luster of this Sapphic stanza:[23]

> Quot rosae in longa periere nocte
> quotque nascuntur refovente sole!
> Nostra sic aetas renovatur in te,
>   vita futura.

> (How many roses have perished in the long night,
> how many have burgeoned to the nurturing sun!
> In the same guise our day's renewed in thee,
>   O life to come.)

Talking about Tusiani as an American Poet, Furio Colombo, the well-known Italian journalist and former editor-in-chief of *l'Unità*, says:

> Tusiani appartiene all'America perchè la lingua inglese è stata per lui uno strumento prezioso e unico per entrare nella poesia con una grandiosa facilità che sarebbe stata pascoliana (il Pascoli della maturità, sempre più lontano dal *fanciullino*) se non avesse, anche, risposto al tratto collettivo e pubblico della poesia americana, che non è mai un viaggio nell'intimo alla ricerca di se stessi, ma unmuoversi insieme per scoprire e descrivere il mondo. Questo spiega Tusiani poeta americano e rende ragione del passaggio, insolito e forse unico attraverso il latino, dove risponde a un bisogno di rigore classico. In quelle poesie la parola è trattata come il marmo, ogni colpo deve essere unico e perfetto perché non esistono correzioni.[24]

> (Tusiani belongs to America because the English language was for him a precious and singular instrument to enter poetry with a

---

[23] Published in *Nuovo Confronto* (Bari, December, 1992) with an Italian translation by Emilio Bandiera. It is the last of the four "Nocturna" published in the May-June 1989 issue of The *Classical Outlook*.

[24] Furio Colombo. *Il fatto quotidiano*, November 2, 2016.

grand facility which was *pascoliana* (the Pascoli of his mature age, always more distant from the *fanciullino* (the innocent child) if he had not also answered to the collective and public feature of the American poetry, which is never a journey in the innermost to the search within oneself but moving together to discover and describe the world. This explains Tusiani as an American poet and gives the reason for the unusual and perhaps sole crossing through Latin, where he returns to a need of classical rigour. In those poems the word is handled like marble, each stroke must be unique and perfect because there are no corrections.)

As I have done in other studies,[25] I would like to conclude by suggesting that if we are to look for Tusiani's DNA, we must read and read again Part Two of *Gente Mia*, along with *The Fifth Season*, *Rind and All* and particularly his vast Latin production. With his twenty thousand and more published verses, Joseph Tusiani, a Contemporary American Poet, is also the most prolific neo-Latin poet of the Twentieth Century.

"Serietà dolorante" (Aching seriousness). With these two words, Cesare Foligno, Tusiani's Professor at the University of Naples, defined the content of his booklet of verse, *Peccato e Luce*, of the twenty-year old poet Joseph (then, Giuseppe). And "aching seriousness," seems to characterize, at a distance of seventy-six years, the mature and multilingual poetic activity of the man that we commemorate today with immense admiration.

---

[25] I have contributed to the *Journal of Italian Translation* (Summer 2020), "La poesia inesplorata di Joseph Tusiani" (The unexplored poetry of Joseph Tusiani). I presented this study at the Symposium held in honor of Joseph Tusiani, at Hunter College (CUNY), on September 29, 2012, organized by the John D. Calandra Italian American Institute (Queens College, CUNY) and co-sponsored by Hunter College.

UN RIMPATRIO LINGUISTICO OVVERO UN RECUPERO CULTURALE?
Il ritorno di Joseph Tusiani[*]

Anthony Julian Tamburri

La raccolta lirica in italiano di Joseph Tusiani *Il ritorno* (1992) si figura indubbiamente come un testo importante nella sua traiettoria poetica. È un libro di poesia italiana pubblicato quarantacinque anni dopo il suo arrivo negli States e apparso dopo diversi volumi di poesia sia in inglese sia in latino, accompagnato poi da qualche volume di versi in dialetto. In un certo modo, *Il ritorno* è una specie di rimpatrio linguistico, un recupero se si vuole, e al tempo stesso una riacquisizione culturale delle radici: ovvero un desiderio di ritornare perlomeno all'ambiente linguistico del Bel Paese che lo scrittore, insieme a sua madre, aveva deciso di lasciare tanto tempo addietro[1]. Ne aveva parlato nel 2003 Luigi Fontanella, che vede in questo suo *nuovo* italiano "[...] un colpo d'ala davvero straordinario, [un ulteriore] alleggerirsi [...]". Tusiani compose l'opera in un periodo di circa tre anni, dal 1988 al 1991[2]. Le sfide di tale impresa si articolano lungo tutta questa breve raccolta; ma sono diverse e di varia intensità emotiva e significativa[3].

---

[*] Questo saggio apparve per la prima volta su *Italica* 93.2 (2016). Viene ripubblicato qui in una versione leggermente alterata.
[1] Ricordiamoci che Tusiani e la madre decisero di lasciare l'Italia con lo scopo di riportare in Italia il padre emigrato ventitré anni prima. Invece rimasero negli States anch'essi, trasformandosi a loro volta in "americani italiani". Su questo loro viaggio nel 1947, si veda Cosma Siani (1999: 7 e segg.). Invece, per l'uso del binomio "americano italiano" anziché "italoamericano", rimando il lettore innanzitutto al primo capitolo Tamburri (2010: 17-20), che ha le sue radici in Tamburri (1991).
[2] Si veda Fontanella (2003: 94-95), adesso rielaborato in inglese (2012).
[3] È pure vero che Tusiani aveva pubblicato altre opere in italiano in questo periodo. Ma sono i tre volumi in prosa della sua autobiografia, *La parola difficile* (1988), *La parola nuova* (1991), *La parola antica* (1992), i quali, comunque, trattano gli stessi temi di questa raccolta. Altri libri di poesie in italiano, invece, risalgono ad anni addietro, dal 1943 al 1957, firmati col nome Giuseppe anziché Joseph, quest'ultimo poi adoperato per tutti gli scritti salvo quelli in latino.

A. J. Tamburri • "Un rimpatrio linguistico o un recupero culturale?"

C'è innanzitutto il fatto che qui parliamo di uno scrittore — italiano di nascita e, fino a un punto considerevole, di costumi — che, dopo quarant'anni di attività letteraria, in italiano all'inizio della sua carriera, successivamente in latino e infine in inglese, torna a pubblicare poesie in italiano. Non è un compito per nulla facile, in quanto qualsiasi poeta con tali esperienze deve, in primo luogo, ritrovare un vocabolario lirico italiano. In secondo luogo, la poesia italiana nel 1992 non è più quella di metà secolo che Tusiani aveva conosciuto prima di emigrare verso gli Stati Uniti. Mentre prima si poteva parlare di poesia piuttosto formale con una certa pratica estetica di rime e versi tradizionali, dopo l'esperienza del Gruppo 63 si era cominciato a fare i conti con una poesia di versi liberi, versi non tradizionali, e pure forse con una crisi di identità[4]. È inoltre una poesia che cerca di rispondere ai cambiamenti del ventesimo secolo, alle frammentazioni sia estetiche che emotivo-filosofiche. Nel caso di Tusiani le tematiche sono analoghe, anche se articolate a volte in modi diversi.

Il primo componimento della raccolta mette in moto una serie di considerazioni nei confronti dell'esperienza migratoria. Innanzitutto, va segnalata l'inevitabile sfida comunicativa del linguaggio. Infatti, non ritengo assolutamente strano che Tusiani apra questa raccolta con un immediato sguardo verso il passato, e cioè verso la sua lingua nativa che si palesa già nel titolo della poesia "Lingua materna", se non addirittura nel titolo stesso del volume, *Il ritorno*. Ma non è soltanto uno sguardo indietro. Anzi, si potrebbe piuttosto dire che invece di una svolta verso il passato, è il passato che si fa presente: un fenomeno semiotico, direi, che fa capire che nonostante miriadi di esperienze nel mondo nuovo — come si suol dire, ma forse potremmo dire anche "diverso" — il nostro passato e le nostre radici non spariscono mai in modo definitivo[5].

---

[4] Tale crisi d'identità risulta evidente anche nella poesia di Alfredo de Palchi, altro italiano trapiantatosi negli Stati Uniti, nel caso suo negli anni 1950, e che ha continuato a scrivere i suoi versi in italiano. A proposito della questione identitaria si veda Tamburri (2011: 269-89). Si veda anche Tamburri (2018).
[5] Di questa specie di circolarità parla Fontanella (2003: 96), legando il "ritorno" di questa raccolta al "ritorno" della famosa e premiata poesia in inglese "The Return".

Sono invece sempre presenti in noi in qualche forma, seppur soppressi — addirittura nascosti e pronti a spuntare al momento propizio — ovvero in un momento o l'altro vengono a galla, come infatti si legge qui (il soggetto, si badi, è la lingua italiana): "Non io a te, sei tu che a me ritorni / come da cupa grotta"; "E mi giungi così, piana e perenne". E quando queste esperienze ci raggiungono dopo tanto tempo, sono sempre legate, come anticipa lo stesso titolo della poesia, alla lingua materna e, in modo ancor più significativo, arrivano in veste quanto mai emotiva anziché razionale:

> Forse più pura e semplice risuoni,
> all'orecchio non più ma solo al cuore,
> per il contrasto che ti fa più dolce
> e per l'incontro che ti fa più buona.

"Pura" e "semplice" sono i due aggettivi che segnano l'aspetto primordiale della lingua materna. Questi poi vengono accompagnati da altri aggettivi che sottolineano diverse caratteristiche positive del nostro modo primario di comunicazione di essere umani. Significativo è che si tratti di una lingua *materna*, un aspetto determinante, specialmente oggigiorno, di questo mondo più migratorio che mai. Nonostante gli anni che possano separare il momento di arrivo da quello attuale, la lingua materna si fa sempre presente in qualche maniera; e quando lo fa, essa risulta sempre "dolce" e "buona".

Ma non è senza "contrasto", come dice l'io narrante, giacché si legge a metà componimento, nella seconda delle tre stanze, che il "fruscio di foresta un dì sentito" che accompagna questa lingua così "piana e perenne" si contrappone a quegli "accenti di favella strana" che l'io narrante vorrebbe "scordare". E forse non è da scartare l'ipotesi di una volontaria ambiguità da parte dell'io narrante in quanto questa sua lingua materna rimane senz'altro la "parola indispensabile / a rivelare il [suo] complice fato". È proprio l'aggettivo

---

Dice lo studioso: "Ecco allora se 'ritorno' ctonio alla propria terra era la poesia eponima del '56, sei lustri dopo il medesimo sta a significare il ritorno alla propria lingua natia: insomma una koiné tusianea che procede avanti e indietro, circolarmente, da Giuseppe — a Joseph — a Giuseppe, ovvero da Tusiani a Tusiani".

"complice", a mio avviso, che problematizza la situazione *significativa* — quale sia cioè l'origine del significato. La domanda che ci possiamo porre allora è la seguente: "Questo aggettivo "complice" possiede un valore positivo o negativo nei confronti della situazione attuale dell'io narrante?" Vale a dire, si attribuisce all'aggettivo una valenza positiva, intendendo che questa lingua materna sia in connivenza con l'atto migratorio e che la lingua materna non ci lascia mai? Che essa sia in amichevole rapporto con uno stato di vita extra-italiano? Oppure, è possibile vedere nel suddetto aggettivo una valenza meno positiva nei confronti dell'emigrazione per cui il "complice fato" potrebbe esser inteso come metafora dell'azione migratoria che, sempre in termini di valore semantico, figurerebbe a tal proposito come il commettere una specie di reato? Queste sono alcune domande che possono porsi in situazioni semantiche di questo genere. Sono anche tali costrutti lessicali, in questo loro stato di potenziale semiotica plurima, che rendono più pertinenti composizioni liriche che mettono in risalto la questione migratoria e tutti i suoi benefici e/o svantaggi.

Tale caratteristica linguistica nei confronti della migrazione dell'individuo si era già manifestata nel passato lungo la traiettoria dell'*oeuvre* tusianea. Basti pensare al famosissimo poemetto "Song of the Bicentennial", del lontano 1976, in cui l'io narrante mette in rilievo le differenze tra l'uso di una lingua e un'altra, tra quella "materna" e quella "acquisita", sottolineando contemporaneamente ciò che ho discusso altrove come manifestazione di *coincidentia oppositorum*[6]. La differenza si denota anche tramite parole come "sky" messa accanto a "cielo" nella voce dell'io-narrante, e facendo così, la lingua, che qui possiede un valore primario, si colloca in una posizione di importanza uguale a quella della soggettività dell'immigrante[7]. La sua nuova lingua, "acquired" ("acquisita"), lo rende una persona "nuova"; lo disaggrega dal suo vecchio mondo in quanto "detaches [him] ... from all/ he used to love..." ("[lo] distacca/ da tutto quello che soleva amare"). La lingua chiaramente trasmuta

---

[6] Rimando il lettore Tamburri (2014: 75-88).
[7] Si veda a tal proposito il saggio di Giordano (2000: 73-86).

tutto, pure ciò che si pensava "thought unchangeable" ("pensiero immutabile"); e di conseguenza il proverbiale "Cogito ergo sum" perde il suo valore originario e viene adesso sostituito da ciò che si potrebbe considerare un motto proto-decostruttivo, secondo ciò che si è suggerito sopra, "Loquor ergo sum" ovvero "Parlo, dunque sono". Alla fine, quindi, la lingua diventa quello strumento indispensabile per l'identità, in quanto l'uso dell'inglese si figura come segno che comunica la *de*-italianizzazione dell'individuo in relazione a una sua possibile americanizzazione.

Posto l'interrogativo a proposito dell'emigrazione in "Lingua materna", si noti che la seconda poesia della raccolta, "Vetrina natalizia sulla Fifth Avenue", sottolinea il contrasto fra *adesso* e *allora*, fra lo stato attuale del migrante negli States e quello invece di chi non sarebbe emigrato, che abbiamo appena visto. Questo secondo componimento si apre così:

> Nonno emigrato, vedi?
> Non sei più minatore, anche se tutto
> fuligginoso hai il viso:
> sei il fanciullo della tua montagna
> con grandi occhi sgranati
> innanzi a tante stelle in terra scese
> a posarsi ammalianti e colorate
> su vetri e verde. Su finestre e porte—
> un vero paradiso.

Pure qui c'è il contrasto tra il nuovo mondo e quello vecchio che aveva lasciato decenni fa il nostro "nonno emigrato" il cui stato migratorio adesso viene subito sottolineato all'apertura della poesia. E anche qui, come nella prima poesia, c'è una specie di rientro sentimentale nel vecchio mondo italiano. Il "nonno" ormai "emigrato" — che avrà lavorato tutta la sua vita nelle miniere negli States, che ha ancora la faccia annerita dal duro e faticoso lavoro da minatore — si trasforma qui in quel "fanciullo della tua montagna", italiana si capisce. È un recupero emotivo di uno stato di innocenza, del ragazzino dai "grandi occhi sgranati" il quale si trova sedotto dalle "tante stelle in terra scese" che vengono "a posarsi ammalianti e colorate / su vetri e verde". Il ragazzino si trova, seppur momentaneamente, in "un vero paradiso". E questo "ritorno", va notato, viene articolato più dalla prospettiva dell'italiano che non da quella dell'americano, altrimenti non si potrebbe spiegare la scelta dell'aggettivo "emigrato" anziché "immigrato". È proprio la scelta deliberata del lessico che risulta una delle caratteristiche significative della poesia tusianea; è un lessico indubbiamente ponderato come pochi: è frequente per il lettore intuire nelle varie parole chiave della poesia di Tusiani più di un significato. La polivalenza del vocabolo è, a mio avviso, uno dei doni maggiori di questo poeta, una delle componenti che rende la sua poesia ancora più efficace e, dal punto di vista estetico, più bella.

Come diversi immigranti del periodo storico all'inizio del ventesimo secolo, il nonno è analfabeta; gli serve qualcuno che scriva la lettera che vorrebbe mandare alla defunta moglie:

> A Nonna Carolina che ora dorme,
> laggiù nel tuo paese,
> come la narrerai tanta bellezza?
> Come vorresti saper scrivere, ora
> Che miri tante cose ch'ella ignora!
> A chi domani scriverà la lettera
> (sia benedetto il dollaro che paghi)
> una per una detterai le forme

L'analfabetismo del nonno ci conduce poi a due altri punti importanti a proposito dell'estetica generale del narrare, verbo appunto adoperato in questo stesso componimento, giacché la poesia possiede anche una funzione narrativa seppur in forma alterata. E mentre è vero che il verso "come la narrerai tanta bellezza" si riferisce al fatto che il nonno non sappia scrivere, non sarà per nulla esagerato percepire in questa frase, e specialmente nel verbo "narrare", un riferimento all'atto di scrivere. Cioè, davanti a tante cose così belle, "ammalianti e colorate", come si fa a descrivere in modo adeguato tale ben di Dio che è un "vero paradiso"? Si può dipendere da questa nostra lingua per descrivere in maniera congrua e sufficiente le cose che uno non conosce ("ch'ella ignora")? Questo secondo potenziale significato ci rammenta l'inizio del *Paradiso*, dove Dante spiega perché non sarà in grado di raccontare in modo adeguato ciò che si troverà davanti nell'ultima tappa del suo pellegrinaggio:

> La gloria di colui che tutto move
> per l'universo penetra, e risplende
> in una parte più e meno altrove
>
> Nel ciel che più de la sua luce prende
> fu' io, e vidi cose che ridire
> né sa né può chi di là sù discende;
>
> perché appressando sé al suo disire,
> nostro intelletto si profonda tanto,
> che dietro la memoria non può ire.
> *Paradiso*, 1-9

Qui Dante si lamenta in primo luogo della sua incapacità di ricordare le cose, perché dal momento in cui vediamo ciò che desideriamo, in questo caso Dio, ci dimentichiamo di tutto ciò che conoscevamo prima ("che dietro la memoria non può ire"); vale a dire, dopo l'incontro col divino il nostro intelletto non è in grado di ritenere in mente cose passate. Ma anche se avessimo la capacità di richiamare certe cose di fronte a tale fenomeno, la lingua non sarebbe abbastanza adeguata per poterci permettere di comunicarle: "vidi cose che *ridire / né sa né può* chi di là sù discende" (corsivi miei).

L'altro aspetto significativo di questi versi tusianei è il riferimento alla differenza tra lo scritto e l'orale. "A chi domani *scriverà* la lettera / [...] / una per una *detterai* le forme" (corsivi miei). Si manifesta così la differenza, di classe innanzitutto: quelli che sanno leggere e scrivere vis-à-vis gli altri che sono analfabeti. E in questo caso si richiama anche il fatto che l'emigrato di un certo ceto sociale — e cioè il manovale, il cosiddetto proletario — rimarrà continuamente vittima di un sistema di classe che, specialmente se non sa né leggere né scrivere, lo terrà sempre soppresso, e quindi lo collocherà in uno stato di interstizio in cui non sarà né più italiano né mai americano[8]. Infine, oltre alla marginalizzazione dell'immigrato, viene anche scartata qualsiasi valenza socio-culturale caratteristica della sua società orale. Come infatti dice Walter Ong (29): "molti dei contrasti spesso avvenuti tra punto di vista 'occidentale' e altri punti di vista sembrano riducibili a contrasti tra alfabetizzazione profondamente interiorizzata e più o meno stati orali residuali della coscienza". E cioè, l'oralità si trova in una posizione narrativa inferiore allo scritto anche se, come si è suggerito sopra, l'oralità rappresenta una mente più attiva in quanto chi ascolta può subito reagire a ciò che viene oralmente articolato, mentre lo scritto rimane per quello che è: statico, fermo, e non responsivo a qualunque reazione spontanea.

Ma bisogna anche tener presente che l'aspetto orale del linguaggio è pure quello stadio preliminare che non è soltanto mancanza di capacità performativa e tecnologica dello scritto. Anzi, l'oralità è in fin dei conti la base non solo per l'alfabetismo ma addirittura per lo scambio di idee: infatti lo scritto rimane quello che è, mentre l'orale è subito soggetto a reazioni di chi ascolta e di conseguenza offre la possibilità di cambiamento e, aspetto più significativo, sviluppo di idee e concetti, proprio perché le dichiarazioni preliminari vengono contestate (Ong, 78-79).

Tutto ciò che abbiamo detto finora si riferisce in modo chiaro e distinto alla questione dell'auto-referenzialità del testo creativo, e

---

[8] L'idea che l'italiano rimanga in uno stato di interstizio non è per niente nuova. Già nel lontano 1915, Alberto Tarchiani ne aveva parlato in un suo saggio: "Gli italiani d'America non possono (per ragioni sentimentali superiori a qualunque controllo) che naturalizzarsi a metà: e di questa metà si debbono contentare i nativi. Per la medesima ragione che gli italiani d'Italia si contentano della seminazionalizzazione degli stranieri che acquistano la cittadinanza sperando e a ragione (e con magnifici risultati) che le nostre scuole e il nostro ambiente facciano degli ardenti e generosi patrioti dei loro figliuoli. Così, è inutile illudersi, nonostante che l'ambiente, le scuole, il carattere anglo-sassone che qui impera, non abbiano un'influenza così diretta e decisiva, pure i figli di italiani che nascono e crescono negli Stati Uniti, sono fatalmente destinati a divenire degli americani, e purtroppo [...], in molti casi, non degli americani modello" (1915: 73).

del testo lirico in questo caso. E tale discorso continua quando l'io narrante dice al nonno emigrato, "A chi domani scriverà la lettera / (sia benedetto il dollaro che paghi) / una per una detterai le forme", nei primi tre degli ultimi dodici versi della poesia. L'insistenza sullo scrivere continua qui, a mio avviso, con due altre frasi pertinenti. Innanzitutto, il messaggio, mentre si continua con la lettura, è "vangelo", qualche cosa da prendere sul serio, in cui credere, e che ha quindi un valore comunicativo: e tale valenza significativa dell'atto comunicativo rimane in vigore tramite la scrittura. Non è allora per nulla esagerato nemmeno in questo caso, e a questo punto di chiusura della poesia, che l'azione del nonno emigrato passi dal dettare allo scrivere ("e sì, lo crederà, tutta incantata, / se glielo scrivi, Nonna Carolina".). Lo scritto a questo punto rimane l'atto comunicativo più efficace in quanto Nonna Carolina, leggendo ciò che avrà scritto il nonno emigrato ("vangelo"), lo "crederà" fino in fondo, "se glielo scriv[e]". Ci ricorda in termini proverbiali il vecchio detto latino, "verba volant, scripta manent"[9].

Tale auto-referenzialità ci riporta in questa raccolta anche alla questione della musa lirica che sta alla base di alcune poesie se non pure al fenomeno semantico della significabilità della parola. Due sono le poesie che contengono dei riferimenti ambigui, se non proprio polivalenti, nei confronti dei possibili valori e significati delle parole adoperate. Nella poesia "Quale fragranza esotica" si vede che lo stimolo della poesia è un fenomeno insolito:

> Quale fragranza esotica,
> da te sola avvertita,
> tutto il mio amore ti giunga;

---

[9] E ci rammenta pure un più recente episodio filmico in cui, al contrario, l'oralità viene messa in prima posizione. Ho in mente la conversazione fra Rosa e Fortunata nel film di Emanuele Crialese, *Nuovomondo* (2006). Quando Rosa, una delle due giovani donne destinate a partire per l'America, porta alla madre di Salvatore una busta contenente delle cartoline, Fortunata risponde: "No, no, io non mi fido a leggere parole di carta", cui la giovane donna ribatte: "No, no, queste non sono parole di carta, queste sono cose vere". Vengono, aggiunge quindi, dalla "terra nuova". Una volta esaminate le cartoline, Fortunata dice al nipote Pietro di bruciarle, gesto alquanto palese della diffidenza da parte di lei nella scrittura.

A. J. Tamburri • "Un rimpatrio linguistico o un recupero culturale?"

> quale essenza di vita
> che un'altra vita distilli.
> È quanto a me a volte
> accade lungo la solita via:
> piú non m'arriva qual luce
> la luce del sole
> ma come la prima di tutte le parole,
> l'unica mia poesia.

Il paragone tra la natura del presunto amore per una donna e il meccanismo dell'origine della poesia dimostra che le loro rispettive radici provengono da un qualcosa di insolito se non addirittura di stravagante: "Quale fragranza esotica".... / È quanto a me". Come l'amore dell'io narrante non sarà per tutte ("da te sola avvertita") e si figura come base sostanziale della vita ("quale essenza di vita"), così la poesia non è una semplice costruzione di parole in versi. Piuttosto, è un fenomeno non sovente ("a volte / accade lungo la *solita* via"; corsivi miei), addirittura è al di sopra del linguaggio non lirico ("la prima di tutte le parole") essendo addirittura "la prima", e cioè occupa una posizione preminente, *primaria* diciamo pure, rispetto all'articolazione usuale; dopo tutto, la frase "l'unica mia poesia" in questo caso si potrebbe anche leggere con l'enfasi sulla parola "unica" per cui sarà unica la poesia rispetto ad altri tipi di linguaggio, ovvero "tutte le parole".

In questa poesia appena letta, come pure in quella che segue, "Ai confini del senso", si riprende il discorso dell'adeguatezza dell'espressività della lingua. In primo luogo, si nota la ripresa del vocabolo "fragranza" come *trait d'union* che riallaccia questa poesia a quella precedente. E la fragranza di questa seconda poesia è altrettanto insolita quanto quella della poesia precedente; questa "fragranza / d'ogni soave ardente primavera / [...] senza odoroso fiore", si legge, riesce ad emettere un aroma anche se le manca quella caratteristica necessaria, quell'"odoroso fiore". E come nella prima poesia, dove le radici dei fenomeni amore / lingua erano un qualche cosa di unico, così pure qua l'espressione di un potenziale messaggio della poesia dipende da un

> estraneo sussurro [che] rammenti
> giorni remoti...
> ... giorni di parola
> non ancor fusi in parola silente
> ch'è piú del giorno e finalmente è questa
> felicità che ferve
> e, per sussistere allo stato puro,
> non deve piú descrivere
> sé a se stessa o sé fuori di sé
> per farsi immagine in aliena mente.

In primo luogo, il binomio "estraneo sussurro" sottolinea il particolare ed unico aspetto della comunicazione che, come nella poesia precedente, è altrettanto incentrato soltanto fra i due interlocutori; e questo viene subito rivelato all'inizio della poesia, nel primo verso: "Or certo comprendiamo, tu ed io". E pure qui la lingua rimane inadeguata ad esprimere ciò che dovrebbe. Giacché sono "giorni remoti [...] /giorni di parole" che eventualmente arrivano al loro stato della "parola silente" la quale, seppur "silente", porta eventualmente allo "stato puro" di quello che si desidera comunicare ("questa / felicità che ferve"). È qualche cosa al di sopra del linguaggio ("non deve piú descrivere / sé a se stessa o sé fuori di sé") che riesce a creare le condizioni per arrivare al summenzionato "stato puro", quel qualcosa diverso dal solito che pensiamo sia in grado di comunicare: "per farsi *immagine* in *aliena* mente" (corsivi miei). Tale verso è una classica descrizione del processo semiotico e/o ermeneutico che si sperimenta quotidianamente nell'atto comunicativo in cui il destinatario ("aliena mente") crea per se stesso un'"immagine" mentale di ciò che riesce a comprendere da chi gli ha inviato il messaggio[10]. E a sua volta, in fin dei

---

[10] Senza dover scendere troppo in un discorso di differenza tra Charles Sanders Peirce and Ferdinand de Saussure, faccio presente che ambedue parlano in termini di immagini mentali. Peirce, infatti, dice (2005: 124): "Consideriamo lo stato mentale del concetto. E un concetto perché ha un significato, una comprensione logica; se lo si può applicare a un oggetto è a causa del fatto che quell'oggetto ha dei caratteri che sono contenuti nella comprensione di questo concetto". In modo simile, De

conti, nella chiusura della poesia, l'io narrante mette in rilievo la particolarità del linguaggio che, una volta raggiunta, rende poi inesplicabilmente "inutile" tutto quello che non è affatto efficace per comunicare:

> E allora parla tu, inesprimibile
> facile luce, in cui s'abbaglia e liquefa
> ogni vocabolo inutile e oscuro.

Nell'esortare che parli l'"inesprimibile / facile luce", sembra alquanto palese che il messaggio ("facile luce") rimanga al di sopra del veicolo tramite il quale deve passare (la lingua), giacché essa si disfa di ogni cosa non necessaria, cioè "ogni vocabolo inutile e oscuro", proprio perché la lingua, come si è visto sopra ("parola silente"), non è all'altezza del messaggio. Questo potenziale significato che presento qui e, ritengo, un lettore potrebbe non difficilmente trovare per conto proprio, viene poi sottolineato dall'ossimoro che è fra l'altro diviso dai due versi in cui appare ("*inesprimibile / facile* luce" [corsivi miei]), mettendo in rilievo appunto i due aggettivi contrastanti: "facile" nonché "inesprimibile"; oppure "inesprimibile" eppur "facile". In ambedue i modi, l'ossimoro regge; e in maniera analoga un secondo paio di contrasti vi si presenta nelle parole "luce" e "vocabolo" per cui, anche qui, la lingua è in una posizione secondaria date le sue inutilità ("inutile") e inadeguatezza ("oscuro") nel comunicare ciò che si dovrebbe comunicare.

Sia in questa che nella poesia precedente, ci si riferisce alla capacità comunicativa della lingua e, in questo caso specifico, della poesia come canale valido tramite il quale inviare un messaggio. Detto questo, allora, l'unicità della "poesia" di Tusiani rispecchia dunque un'analoga unicità del sentimento d'affetto articolato appunto con la parola "amore". Il sentimento dell'amore viene di conseguenza messo allo stesso livello, ovvero visto nello stesso modo

---

Saussure offre una nozione analoga (1968: 21): "Supponiamo che un dato concetto faccia scattare nel cervello una corrispondente immagine acustica: e un fenomeno interamente psichico, seguito a sua volta da un processo fisiologico: il cervello trasmette agli organi della fonazione un impulso correlato alla imagine…"

in cui vien vista la capacità di parlarne, al di sopra ("allo stato puro") di qualsiasi aspetto del solito linguaggio quotidiano ("ogni vocabolo inutile e oscuro").

Il tema del valore significativo di un segno appare nella poesia "Pioggerella" in cui si articola fin dall'inizio una specie di diffidenza nella valenza definitoria del lessico:

> Sei piú che scherzo di nuvola, ennesima
> pioggia che cadi e canti.
> Sembri quella di ieri,
> quella di sempre; eppure
> l'ultimo boccio ti sente novella
> e di me stesso io qui mi meraviglio
> se osano i miei pensieri
> candidi interrogarti.

Ci sono innanzitutto delle parole da notare all'inizio della nostra lettura: "scherzo", "canti", "Sembri", "di ieri", "di sempre" sono dei termini che si riferiscono alla comunicazione ('canti') e, al tempo stesso, ad un attimo di dubbio nei confronti del loro valore semantico ("scherzo", "Sembri", "di ieri", "di sempre"): non sono ma "sembra[no]," e non necessariamente di oggi, ma pure "di ieri", se non "di sempre". Ma l'io narrante non ci casca; mette in dubbio il loro carattere significativo: "... *osano i miei pensieri / candidi interrogarsi*". Audace a dir poco è che l'io narrante abbia il bel coraggio ("osano i miei pensieri") di metterne in dubbio il valore semantico. Altrettanto audace è la scelta dell'aggettivo "candidi" e dell'infinito "interrogarsi". Nel contesto di una raccolta di poesie che parla di un ritorno di qualsiasi specie — vero o metaforico che sia — al paese natio dopo tanti anni all'estero, la decisione di adoperare sia l'aggettivo che l'infinito già menzionati risulta significativa proprio perché questi due termini hanno delle valenze definitorie più che rilevanti per quanto riguarda la tematica della poesia. "Candido" comunica una serie di qualità che possono in qualche modo figurare importanti per il contesto in questione: innocente, puro, e/o ingenuo proprio perché l'io narrante non ha altri fini se non quello di trovare, come dirà poco più in avanti, "quel numero esatto", ovvero il valore semantico del comunicato. "Interrogarsi", in modo analogo, ci riporta alla scoperta di una riposta, di un accertamento, che ci permetta in qualche modo di valutare la situazione attuale.

E l'incertezza che apre la poesia continua in questa prima lunga strofa suddivisa in tre da due capoversi, ognuno che inizia con un referente di sembianza e non di certezza: "A me parete"; "Vi crede oggi sorelle". La seconda suddivisione pertanto continua così:

> A me parete
> tutte uniformi, gocce
> che, l'una dopo l'altra e sopra l'altra,
> caste cadete a calme,
> ma, disuguali tutte, vi sospinge
> un ordine o un amore
> di cui non colgo senso.
> Immenso, chiamo immenso (altro non posso)
> il numero che siete; ma Qualcuno
> certo quel numero esatto conosce,
> e di voi tutte, ed anzi di ciascuna,
> sa veemenza e multiplo valore.

Vediamo, infatti, che anche se le "gocce" paiono ("A me parete") "tutte uniformi", sono invece "disuguali tutte", spinte da "un ordine o un amore / di cui non colgo senso". E cioè l'io narrante non riesce a comprendere fino in fondo la vera natura (leggasi pure, significato) delle gocce. E a metà suddivisione, prima che egli passi ad ammettere che ci sia "Qualcuno", mette di nuovo in dubbio la capacità della lingua di arrivare a ben descrivere la situazione — fisica o emotiva che sia — in cui si trova. Non potendo capire l'essenza delle gocce ("un ordine o un amore / di cui non colgo senso"), il nostro io narrante attribuisce loro l'unico aggettivo possibile: "Immenso, chiamo immenso (*altro non posso*)" (corsivi miei). Perché solo quel "Qualcuno" con la "q" maiuscola "conosce" di "certo" fino in fondo la natura di "tutte" le "gocce". Quella loro natura che sa di "veemenza e [di un] multiplo valore".

E qui con l'incapacità linguistica di parlare in modo approfondito sia di "un ordine" che di "un amore", non solo torniamo al tema dantesco della inadeguatezza della lingua, ma si rientra pure in un discorso diretto anche sul mistero dell'esistenza, se non proprio del creato, ovvero del mondo in cui si vive. Quanto alla lingua, si ricordi ciò che si è visto sopra con il riferimento alla *Divina Comedia*, che la lingua, secondo Dante, non è sufficientemente adeguata a permetterci di articolare certe cose intorno al mistero, nel suo caso del Paradiso, e, nel caso del nostro io narrante, del creato[11]. Infatti, la terza suddivisione di questa prima strofa ci riporta proprio a quel mondo umano pieno dei tanti misteri e "segreti", come si leggerà verso la fine della poesia, che l'essere umano è incapace di intendere:

> Vi crede oggi sorelle
> alla sua pena questa mente mia
> se, accomunandovi alle umane ambasce,
> vi immagina capaci
> di chiedervi perché, fra mille e mille,
> una debba finire in allegria
> su cespo e ramo per bel fiore e frutta,
> uno in tristezza sotto impuro piede
> e un'altra inutilmente (a me sí pare)
> su straripante mare
> e non su labbro arroventato ed arso
> di viandante in deserto lontano.

---

[11] Rimando il lettore di nuovo al saggio di Fontanella per una lettura acuta dove, fra l'altro, si parla anche di un'eco dantesca: "In questo movimento magmatico assistiamo a un certo punto anche a un'immersione dei sensi: una sensualità calda e genuina qui individuabile in un personaggio femminile celato ch'è fonte di fantasie e fantasmi, di improvvisi accensioni, come pure subitanei ripensamenti. *Ama se stessa, amando, giovinezza,* recita un vibrante endecasillabo tusianeo via Dante; sorta di cartiglio memorabile e universale. [...] Tusiani non cessa di interrogarsi su tutto e sul nulla della vita, sui suoi affetti e diletti, sulle sue speranze e delusioni, ben sapendo che questi interrogativi sono destinati a restare senza risposta..." (2003: 97-98; corsivi testuali).

Vediamo sopra che l'io narrante continua il suo interrogatorio sull'esistenza delle cose e sul perché certi fenomeni accadono in certi modi. E si capisce nel contempo che l'io narrante soffre dell'assenza di certezza ("alla sua pena questa mente mia") sperando pertanto che le stesse gocce siano in grado, se non proprio di risolvere l'enigma o di svelare il "segreto", almeno di porsi il dilemma della irrazionalità dei fenomeni naturali, come si legge in questa suddivisione della strofa. Sono gli ultimi versi a mettere in risalto questa contraddittorietà della natura: che la goccia d'acqua vada a finire in un alto ("straripante") mare, dove non avrà nessun valore positivo, anziché capitare "su labbro arroventato ed arso / di viandante in deserto lontano", dove invece avrebbe un risultato sicuramente positivo. E non perdiamo di vista l'ironia nell'accoppiamento di "viandante" con "lontano" in questo contesto oltre oceano: una poesia scritta da un italiano che vive da tanti anni all'estero, per cui il passaggio semiotico da un essere universale ad uno più particolare non è affatto eccessivo.

Siamo indubbiamente in un ambito di negatività nei confronti della natura, onnipotente figura del tutto indifferente all'essere umano, come si desume da questi versi sopra citati. È chiaramente un richiamo a un leopardismo pessimista per cui la natura risulta totalmente misteriosa e, come appena detto, indifferente — un aggettivo appositamente leopardiano in questo contesto — nei confronti dell'esistenza umana, la quale, secondo il poeta di Recanati, non è altro che uno delle tante componenti dell'universo. Riporto qui a tal proposito due brani dallo *Zibaldone* di Giacomo Leopardi: "Non si può meglio spiegare l'orribile mistero delle cose e dell'esistenza universale (vedi il mio *Dialogo della Natura e di un Islandese*, massime in fine) che dicendo essere insufficienti ed anche falsi, non solo la estensione, la portata e le forze, ma i principii stessi fondamentali della nostra ragione. Per esempio, quel principio, estirpato il quale cade ogni nostro discorso e ragionamento ed ogni nostra proposizione, e la facoltà istessa di poterne fare a concepire dei veri, dico quel principio, *Non può una cosa insieme essere e non essere*, pare assolutamente falso quando si considerino le contraddizioni palpabili che sono in natura" (4098, 3 giugno 1824). E quasi un anno dopo, Leopardi stende la nota seguente (1972): "Anzi il fine della natura universale è la vita dell'universo, la quale consiste ugualmente in produzione, conservazione e distruzione dei suoi componenti, e quindi la distruzione di ogni animale entra nel fine della detta natura almen tanto quanto la conservazione di esso, ma anche assai più che la conservazione, in quanto si vede che sono più assai quelle cose che cospirano alla distruzione di ciascuno animale che non quelle che favoriscono la sua conversazione; in quanto naturalmente nella vita dell'animale occupa maggior spazio la declinazione e consumazione ossia invecchiamento (il quale incomincia nell'uomo anche prima dei trent'anni) che tutte le altre età insieme (vedi *Dialogo della Natura e di un Islandese*, e *Cantico del Gallo Silvestre*)..." (5-6 aprile 1825).

Tornando adesso alla chiusura della suddetta poesia, si veda come l'unica possibilità che ci offre il nostro io narrante per scansare il pessimismo leopardiano sia di

accoglier[e le gocce come] appa[iono],
giovevoli, gioconde,
incapaci (mi cullo in questo sogno)
di subissare il mondo.

Cioè, l'unico modo da poter superare questo pessimismo leopardiano di cui è intrisa la poesia tusianea è quello di ricorrere alle illusioni che ci si creano intorno. Questo è il "sogno" dell'io narrante, di poter credere che le gocce siano "incapaci ... di subissare il mondo".

Chiudendosi in tale modo, "Pioggerella" si presenta inoltre come un esempio delle "grandi figurazioni cosmiche" che, secondo Pietro Magno (1992: 12-13), attraggono Tusiani, "come in 'Notturno', uno dei culmini di questa raccolta [*Il ritorno*] e forse dell'intera sua produzione pure in lingua inglese. C'è un senso arcano che ricorda il Leopardi del 'Canto notturno' e de 'La ginestra'...." Infatti, nella poesia "Notturno" si compie il pensiero leopardiano della totale indifferenza da parte della natura nei confronti dell'essere umano e di altre creature, analogamente alle riflessioni sopra menzionate secondo cui "il fine della natura universale è la vita dell'universo, la quale consiste ugualmente in produzione, conservazione e distruzione dei suoi componenti, e quindi la distruzione di ogni animale entra nel fine della detta natura". L'essere umano a tal proposito non è altro che uno delle tante "componenti" dell'universo, per cui non ci dovrebbe sorprendere, come suggeriscono le parole di Magno, che il nostro io narrante dica le seguenti parole in riferimento a se stesso:

... E del minuscolo
granel di polvere, un giorno chiamato
sospiro d'uomo e febbre di potenza,
che rimarrà? ...

È difatti questo "minuscolo / granel di polvere", referente dell'essere umano, che vale ben poco nell'ambito dell'universo. Si legge inoltre che la stella a cui si rivolge l'io narrante è per l'appunto "serenamente ignar[a] / d'imperi e civiltà risorti e spenti"; e sottolineo qui l'uso dell'avverbio "serenamente", registro che mette in rilievo la calma e la quiete, addirittura la disattenzione nei confronti dei suddetti "imperi e civiltà risorti e spenti", null'altro che altri semplici elementi dell'universo[12].

I temi (il divino vis-à-vis il razionale e il ricordo turbante della terra d'origine) che abbiamo visto finora nelle poesie di questo volume dal nome assai suggestivo, *Il ritorno*, si ritrovano intrecciati in due poesie significative dell'*oeuvre* tusianea: "Lettera a Don Dámaso Alonso" e "Lettera a Don Fernando Pessoa". La prima poesia apre in tal modo:

Caro e illustre Don Dámaso, non vedi
come l'anima possa essere eterna

---

[12] E qui si ricordi la poesia di Leopardi, "Canto notturno di un pastore errante dell'Asia", dove si trova, al posto della stella tusianea, una luna "silenziosa" che non risponde alle domande del pastore e quindi, di non difficile lettura, ugualmente indifferente alle sorti dell'uomo.

> tra cose non eterne, essa che è cosa
> dalle altre non diversa su una terra
> che dell'eternità ha solo il sogno;

Una delle prime cose da notare è l'uso di registri che parlano di "immortalità" ("eterna", "eterne", "eternità"). Ma questa immortalità viene subito smentita perché, dato che l'essere umano non è che uno dei tanti elementi dell'universo ("dalle altre non diversa su una terra"), egli può soltanto sperare nell'eternità ("che dell'eternità ha solo il sogno"), ragion per cui la possibilità di tale "eternità" è fin dall'inizio messa in dubbio se non proprio cancellata. E tale incertezza dell'eternità viene subito comunicata con l'uso del congiuntivo nel secondo verso della poesia: "come l'anima possa essere eterna". È la speranza ("ma preghi"; "il tuo pregare") che Dio renda immortale l'anima in modo da poter ascrivere del valore al lavoro e alla vita dell'essere umano: "sí che abbia un senso il nostro terminare / dopo sí gran travaglio di ore e sangue". Tutto questo perché senza la certezza di un'immortalità la vita si figura "mendace", e di conseguenza la vita dell'individuo, anzi, proprio l'individuo, non è altro che un passar del tempo durante la sua esistenza sulla terra.

E mentre nella suddetta poesia l'io narrante parla di ciò che ho appena descritto come il passar del tempo quale metafora dell'esistenza umana, un simile pensiero riemerge nella poesia "Lettera a Don Fernando Pessoa". In questa seconda "lettera", proprio all'inizio, vediamo che la solitudine dell'essere umano è il pensiero dominante dell'io narrante: un "solitario andirivieni / che ha nome vita…." E non solo: si vede pure che l'io narrante ne soffre, non ce la fa, e i versi che seguono si rifanno a ciò che si è visto sopra nei confronti della conglomerazione degli esseri viventi come parte di un sistema più grande e più rilevante di quello dell'essere umano. L'io narrante condivide con noi il fatto che il semplice pensiero di una vita solitaria gli

> agghiaccia il pensiero
> di restar solo, orribilmente solo

> in mezzo a creature sole, alberi soli,
> in una solitudine stellare
> su questa terra, stella umana e sola.

Quel che si legge qui — "di restar solo, orribilmente solo / in mezzo a creature sole, alberi soli" — rammenta il pensiero leopardiano dell'"orribile mistero delle cose e dell'esistenza universale": davvero curiosa se non proprio significativa la presenza di una parola con la radice "orribile" in ambedue i testi. È, inoltre, una solitudine che viene ribadita costantemente dalla presenza di termini congrui; e cioè cinque volte in quattro versi si ripete l'aggettivo "solo" il quale poi viene accompagnato dall'avverbio "orribilmente", che a sua volta spiega poi la ragion d'essere dell'agghiacciamento del pensiero dell'io narrante. La solitudine "stellare" — sia come intensità di luce, e cioè in senso letterale, che in senso figurato, ovvero smisurata e al tempo stesso straordinaria — si presenta proprio come qualche cosa di esistente al di sopra delle tante componenti dell'universo e indifferente ad esse, fra cui gli esseri umani, atta soltanto alla sua durata quale universo, come si è letto sopra nella citazione dallo *Zibaldone*: "consiste ugualmente in produzione, conservazione e distruzione dei suoi componenti, e quindi la distruzione di ogni animale entra nel fine della detta natura almen tanto quanto la conservazione di esso". E in ambedue le poesie, si legge che nessuno degli dei degli esseri umani — "Iddio", "Dio" ("Lettera a Don Dámaso Alonso") o quel "Qualcuno ignoto" ("Lettera a Don Fernando Pessoa") — ha risposto alle preghiere dei poeti.

Quanto poi al tema dell'autoreferenzialità, si parte sin dall'inizio con gli stessi titoli delle due poesie, ciascuna una "lettera a" uno scrittore alquanto conosciuto per qualsiasi lettore "informato" del panorama letterario del mondo occidentale. Il fatto che sia inoltre una conversazione fra due poeti mette già in rilievo non soltanto la scrittura di per sé ma addirittura l'importanza dell'atto di scrivere, come si legge nella prima poesia:

> Forse, poeta, l'immortalità
> che noi cerchiamo è proprio questo sogno

> d'evadere dal limite intravisto
> in ogni nota o immaginata cosa:
> intravediamo, volenti o nolenti,
> noi stessi entro quel limite conclusi.

E cioè che l'"anima", e diciamo specialmente quella del poeta in questo caso, potrà diventare "eterna" attraverso la sua attività lirica.

In modo simile leggiamo che gli stessi temi dedicati alla scrittura riappaiono nella seconda poesia dove, qui in seguito, spunta fuori l'idea dell'individualità dell'io narrante:

> È opulenza di musica e luce
> che da recessi di radici e linfe,
> con pretesto di rima, mi costringe
> a ricercare rivoli e accordi
> onde allietarmi pareti senz'eco
> o senza volto che mi rassomigli.

La scrittura quale poesia si raffigura qui in forma di "rima" con la sua "opulenza di musica", la quale, si legge al tempo stesso, è indissolubilmente legata al concetto d'identità: "… mi costringe, / a ricercare rivoli e accordi / onde allietarmi pareti senz'eco / o senza volto che mi rassomigli". La scrittura, inoltre, si vede più avanti, serve anche come riparo emotivo dalla dura verità della vita dell'essere umano come semplicemente uno dei tanti elementi dell'universo. Un aiuto perché il poeta possa illudersi, secondo un registro dalle sfumature leopardiane, "lungo il [suo] andare all'ultima ventura", come si legge qui sotto:

> E che ci perdo, io che sono nato
> per perdermi o disperdermi nel nulla?
> Mi basta un gioco a illudermi e, pertanto,
> faccio con me giocare ogni sincera
> rima plausibile….

L'illusione dello scrittore di fronte ad una dura e indifferente fatalità, a cui si sente incapace di trovare qualsiasi rimedio, si può soltanto cercare nella calma, per quanto fragile sarà, della sua scrittura:

> mi lascia che, innocente quale sono,
> io, che non voglio morir solo e amaro,
> faccia rimare almeno le parole.

Questa poesia si chiude con un riferimento alla necessità dello scrivere e, al tempo stesso, con un commento curioso al valore insignificante dell'essere umano:

> Abbiam tutti bisogno di una rima:
> trovo così un amico, anzi un fratello,
> se non in te, di certo in un ruscello.

Lo scrivere è chiaramente un modo per poter trovare un'identità che distingua l'essere umano dagli altri pezzi dell'universo, tanto che, come si legge sopra, "tutti [hanno] bisogno di una rima". E se l'uomo non riesce a trovare amicizia, confidenza, ecc. in un altro essere umano — "un amico, anzi un fratello" — lo troverà in un elemento della natura — "se non in te, di certo in un ruscello".

Importanti per una serie di motivi sono questi tre versi finali. Come si è già detto sopra, lo scrivere è uno se non l'unico motivo per vivere; è messo in rilievo diverse volte lungo il libro e specialmente in queste due poesie. La necessità dell'atto dello scrivere viene anche qui, alla fine, ribadita nel terz'ultimo verso: "Abbiam tutti bisogno di una rima". E l'appagamento che l'individuo trae dalla "rima" potrà avere la sua origine o con un altro essere umano o con un elemento della natura, ragion per cui l'ultima rima della poesia è appunto "fratello" — un essere umano — con "ruscello — una componente naturale — per cui si figura come rima non soltanto estetica ma addirittura significativa e allo stesso tempo significante; cioè dà un valore semiotico più ampio ai due registri dato che si tratta di una direzione semantica a due sensi: "fratello" e "ruscello" dunque si trovano carichi di significati altrettanto uguali per quanto riguarda una potenziale importanza semantica: l'uno non è più importante dell'altro. Infine, e ancora in un senso leopardiano, gli esseri umani e gli altri elementi della natura sono tutti uguali nel più grande schema che è la vita dell'universo[13].

La raccolta chiude con la poesia "Alla mia Puglia", una specie di *addio* e non un *arrivederci*. Piena di bei ricordi di una fanciullezza "su colline di gloria" e "tra freschi / virgulti ignoti", è una poesia che parla anche dei sogni infranti in età adulta: "della stessa caligine vestita / di cui quel non più bimbo s'è incrostato, / [...] "dove s'infrange col mattino il sogno". "[P]atria perduta, / o Puglia mia" dice l'io narrante, pur cercando di resistere perché "così pensando" "perdere[bbe] [s]e stesso". Ma cede, e alla fine la sua Puglia non può che salutarla definitivamente per l'ultima volta e "in segreto", quasi incapace di accettare il destino di non poterci più tornare:

> Ecco, o Puglia mia, non oso neppure
> mandarti un bacio che ogni sguardo veda:
> triste e in segreto, o mia terra, t'invio
> questo mio bacio che sigilla il fato.

OPERE CITATE

De Saussure, Ferdinand. 1968. *Corso di linguistica generale*. Introduzione, traduzione, e commento di Tullio De Mauro. Bari: Laterza.

Fontanella, Luigi. 2003. *La parola transfuga: scrittori italiani in America*. Firenze: Cadmo.

_____. 2012. *Migrating Words: Italian Writers in the United States*. New York: Bordighera Press.

Giordano, Paolo. 2000. "From Southern Italian Immigrant to Reluctant American: Joseph Tusiani's *Gente Mia* and Other Poems" in *Ethnicity: Selected Poems*, a cura di Paolo Giordano. West Lafayette, IN: Bordighera Press.

---

[13] Fontanella (2003: 98) vuole vedere questi ultimi versi come espressione di fratellanza francescana fra il poeta portoghese e il nostro Tusiani. Sarà anche così, ma la mia lettura mi ha portato in un'altra direzione semiotica in questo caso.

Leopardi, Giacomo. 1972. *Zibladone di pensieri*. A cura di Anna Maria Moroni. Milano: Mondadori.

Magno, Pietro. 1992. "Prefazione" in Joseph Tusiani. *Il ritorno. Liriche italiane*. Fasano di Brindisi: Schena Editore.

Nuovomondo. Dir. Emanuele Crialese. 01 Distribution (2006). Film.

Ong Walter J. 2002. *Orality and Literacy, The Technologizing of the Word*. Routledge, London e New York, 2002, 2a edizione.

Peirce, Charles Sanders. 2005. *Scritti scelti*. A cura di Giovanni Maddalena. Torino: UTET.

Siani, Cosma. 1999. *L'io diviso: Joseph Tusiani fra emigrazione e letteratura*. Roma: Edizioni Cofine.

Tamburri, Anthony Julian. 2018. *Un biculturalismo negato: La letteratura "italiana" negli Stati Uniti*. Firenze: Franco Cesati Editore.

_____. 2014. *Re-reading Italian Americana: Specificities and Generalities on Literature and Criticism*. Madison, NJ: Fairleigh Dickinson UP.

_____. 2011."A Semiotics of Ambiguity: Indeterminacy in Alfredo de Palchi's *Anonymous Constellation*" in *Essays in Honor of Alfredo de Palchi*. Luigi Fontanella, ed. Stony Brook: Gradiva Publications.

_____. 2010. *Una semiotica dell'etnicità: nuove segnalature per la scrittura italiano/americana*. Firenze: Franco Cesati Editore.

_____. 1991. *To Hyphenate or Not to Hyphenate: The Italian/American Writer: Or, An Other American*. Montréal: Guernica.

Tarchiani, Alberto. 2005 [1915]. *Il Cittadino - The Citizen* (New York), 9 dicembre. adesso in Francesco Durante, a cura di, *Italoamericana*. Milano: Mondadori.

Tusiani, Joseph. 1992. *Il ritorno. Liriche italiane*, con prefazione di Pietro Magno. Fasano di Brindisi: Schena Editore.

_____. 1992. *La parola antica*. Fasano di Brindisi: Schena Editore.

_____. 1991. *La parola nuova*. Fasano di Brindisi: Schena Editore.

_____. 1988. *La parola difficile*. Fasano di Brindisi: Schena Editore.

QUESTIONS ON AN OLD MAP
Joseph Tusiani's *If Gold Should Rust*

Ilaria Serra

Why? This is the question that screams in our mind when reading Joseph Tusiani's play *If Gold Should Rust*, a *unicum* in his career of poet and writer.[1] This three-act play raises more questions than it gives answers. It is the odd man out in Tusiani's copious production: the only attempt at a theater play, a task he immediately dropped. Odd because it casts unexpected characters (the historical figures of Giuseppe Baretti and Samuel Johnson) in a strange place (London) and in a peculiar time (1769), all of which apparently have nothing to do with his own experience. Giuseppe Marc'Antonio Baretti was an Italian intellectual, quite influential in XVIII century England but almost unknown today.[2] The play chooses a peculiar event as its plot: Baretti underwent a trial for the homicide of a man who bothered him on a crowded street but was absolved thanks to the testimonies of his circle of British friends. Besides, the work belongs to a genre that is out-of-fashion: it is a "closet drama" to be read in a parlor to entertain guests, a long dialogue with almost no action, in verses, anachronistic and a little tedious. And the title too, is ever so cryptic.

This play is an exception in so many ways that reading it is like looking for clues in a mystery, especially now that the author cannot answer our questions. It resembles a search *à la* Rosebud, the unanswered life question in Orson Wells's *Citizen Kane*. It also proves the truth of Paolo Giordano and Anthony Tamburri's claim that Tusiani is too complicated to be read only in Italian-American light: the trajectory of his literary hyphen has not a bilateral direction, but turns 360 degrees like the hand of a watch![3] Such oddity may also explains

---

[1] "If Gold Should Rust" in Paolo A. Giordano (ed.), *Joseph Tusiani*, 271-338.
[2] In the last decade, Francesca Savoia renewed critical interest for Baretti with the publication of his unpublished letters (*Il Baretti Vostro.*).
[3] See Paolo A. Giordano (2016).

why no critic has ventured to consider this theater play, except for Italian critic Cosma Siani, family friend and author of an insightful essay, and poet Felix Stefanile who wrote a short introduction.

The Italian American Joseph Tusiani has always been defined as a man divided in two halves: "two languages, two worlds, perhaps two souls," as his most quoted, never trite, verse recites.[4] His entire life trajectory oscillated in difficult balance between his home in the Bronx and his home in San Marco in Lamis, his "two affective poles" (Magno 127).[5] Every year, since his migration as a young man, he would fly back to Gargano in May, and dwell in via Palude, the road where his old house stood, for two months, "with Anglo-Saxon punctuality" (Motta 5). His prolific work develops on the regular exchange between these two geographical extremes. So, why does *If the Gold Should Rust* shoot out like an erratic planet, in Tusiani's binary universe? Why this deviation to gloomy 1769 London?

There are some apparent similarities between the two Giuseppe turned Joseph, Tusiani and Baretti. Cosma Siani demonstrates that this play is in fact a mirror of Tusiani's experiences and titles his essay collection on Tusiani, *Baretti in London* (2013). Siani points out that Baretti who is a scholar and an immigrant in London, is a reflection of the scholar and New York immigrant Tusiani. It is true that Tusiani himself points to his identification, during his acceptance speech at the Poetry Society of America the night he received the Alice Fay di Castagnola Prize for the first act of *If Gold Should Rust*, then a work in progress. It was April 11, 1968. Remembering that night in his memoir, Tusiani writes: "In Giuseppe Baretti, the protagonist of the play honored that night, I had seen myself, I had analyzed my disquiet, my nostalgia for Italy and the

---

[4] "Two languages, two lands, perhaps two souls… / am I a man or two strange halves of one?" ["Due lingue, due terre, forse due anime… / sono un uomo o due estranee metà d'uomo?"], "Song of the Bicentennial" in *Gente Mia and Other Poems* (1978). Tusiani knows these are his "most famous verses in America… everyone quotes them" (*Gargano mio* 45-6).

[5] "Arrivava in Italia con puntualità anglosassone il 4-5 maggio (in tempo per vedere la partenza della 'Cumpagnia' di San Michele Arcangelo per Monte Sant'Angelo, a cui era molto legato) e ripartiva due mesi dopo."

tremendous desperation of feeling neither Italian nor American" (*Parola nuova*, 174).⁶ Even the prize he accepted brought him closer to Baretti: "That check reminded me the 80-pound annual pension that King George gave the Turin intellectual after his full absolution" (*Parola nuova*, 175).⁷

Furthermore, Tusiani is like Baretti because he is an intellectual and translator. Both were victims of stereotyping, but both were embraced by literary admirers and friends. Siani affirms that Tusiani is not new to this kind of *transfer*: he often operates a process of appropriation and identification towards his characters and the writers he translates (when he translates a poet, he becomes the poet). However, the similarities between Tusiani and Baretti stop there. The play remains puzzling, and Siani himself has to admit defeat when stumbling on one more "why": why on earth would Tusiani be interested in the murder Baretti committed in London and for which he was acquitted? Siani raises his arms: "It is impossible for me to find out why the theme of lethal violence, – the deep motif of this work – may germinate from Tusiani's experience" (61).⁸

I will attempt here to consider this odd play through a different optic. My exploration leaves the printed pages and hunts for clues in an old map of London. It is obvious that in this play, the places become metaphors for its drama. I would call them geo-metaphors, a hybrid literary figure that locates real places of the geographical map of earth and fills them with metaphorical, cultural and literary

---

⁶ "In Giuseppe Baretti, il protagonista del dramma premiato quella sera, avevo visto me stesso, avevo analizzato la mia irrequietudine, la mia nostalgia d'Italia, e la tremenda disperazione per non sentirmi più né italiano né americano."

⁷ "Finanche quell'assegno mi ricordò la pensione annua di ottanta sterline che Re Giorgio III fece assegnare al letterato torinese dopo la sua piena assoluzione"

⁸ "Non mi è possibile rintracciare come il tema della violenza letale – motivo di fondo in quest'opera – germini nell'esperienza di Tusiani." Siani proposes that Tusiani is transferring the violence of the drama of immigration onto the violent episode that marred Baretti's immigration. The homicide becomes therefore an example of "the violent reality that the immigrant experiences in the new world." ("Sembra che questo dramma in versi incentrato sul tema dell'omicidio nasca in effetti dallo scontro con una realtà violenta che l'emigrato si trova ad esperire nel nuovo mondo. Nel taglio intellettuale qui dato, la crisi di coscienza attribuita a Baretti è una proiezione operata da Tusiani sul proprio personaggio" (2013, 61-62).

meanings. Similar to a Bakthinian chronotope, but more specific. In the case of this strange play, the locations existed in the past but not anymore – because all of them have been erased from London's landscape in the last two hundred years. They still maintain their aura, and I will try to exploit their metaphorical charge to consider this mysterious work of literature. These geo-metaphors are: Streatham House, a modest apartment, the old London Bridge, and dark waters of the Thames River.

"Streatham House" by Edward Walfard (1880)
Source: http://www.thrale.com/streatham_park

Act I opens in "London. The Streatham House. The Year 1769." We are in the country house owned by Baretti's friend and patron, Henry Thrale, a wealthy brewer who loved literary company. His villa was six mile from town, but in the play, Tusiani brings it much closer to the center of London, so that Baretti can walk home and find himself in a dangerous alley, where he is assaulted. Streatham Park was demolished in 1863 and replaced by a residential area of housing with the same name. Today it is one of the busiest areas of

London, and only the green park of Streatham Common, attests to the bucolic past of this site. At the time of Tusiani's play, the house was a mansion created by enlarging a three-story brick Georgian country building. It had an elegant pedimented front with balustrade terraces on the two sides.[9] It was a place of comfort.

The only quarter that Tusiani cares to show in the play is the parlor, with all its welcoming warmth. The hospitable space of conversation, where the owners spent evening discussing art with their guests, signifies the cordiality that introduced the foreigner Baretti into British society. Baretti was among the usual guests at the Thrales, with playwright Samuel Johnson. These comfortable chairs, the fireplace, the butler ready to serve the guests become the metaphor of Tusiani's welcome into the American society. As Cosma Siani points out, Tusiani saw himself in the cultivated immigrant Baretti, and his acceptance in the British society was a reflection of his own position in the New York society. On April 11, 1968, Tusiani was entertained with the same warmth and elegance, in the Plaza Hotel in New York, where the Poetry Society of America awarded him the "Alice Fay di Castagnola" prize for the first act of his unpublished drama work in verses. As mentioned earlier, this is recollection of the night:

> What happened to him two century before, wasn't now happening to me? Unmarried like me, he had been included in Dr. Samuel Johnson's Literary Circle as I had been included in the Poetry Society of America. He had written three works in English, and me too, if not more. (174)[10]

---

[9] For more information on this house and the phases of its building, see the website created by David Thrale to protect the family legacy.
[10] "Non stava succedendo a me quello che era successo a lui, due secoli prima? Scapolo come me, era stato accolto nel Circolo Letterario del Dr. Samuel Johnson come io ero stato accolto nella Poetry Society of America."

Joshua Reynolds, Giuseppe Baretti 1773
(Public domain)
https://snl.no/Giuseppe_Marc%27Antonio_Baretti)

The symbol of Baretti's entry in the literary British society is the portrait that Thrale ordered of him. Thrale renovated the country mansion in order to accommodate guests and created a library and a picture gallery. He collected portraits of his friends, and Baretti was among them. It was the concrete proof that the poet had gained a physical space into the British house, among the "Streatham Worthies," [11] and in a gilded frame. Baretti's portrait, now at the Tate Gallery, was commissioned to the painter Joshua Reynolds and hung in the hallway leading to the library.[12] He is represented as a myopic

---

[11] David Thrale (2009) specifies that the playful definition belongs to novelist Fanny Burney who explained that Thrale wanted "the persons he most loved to contemplate... to preside over the literature that stood highest in his estimation."
[12] Tate National Gallery. "Joshua Reynolds: The Creation of Celebrity: Room Guide: Room 4."

scholar, quietly burying his nose in a booklet, almost to show him as farther as possible from the assassin he was accused to be.

Tusiani himself earned the honor of "a frame" among peer faculty at Lehman College. When he was named New York Poet Laureate Emeritus, his home college dedicated a proud article to the poet, celebrating him as one of their retired faculty members. A smiling Tusiani appears on the article page, as he is accepting the award at the Lehman College Foundation dinner in 2015.[13] Recognition and affection surrounded Tusiani, who was welcome in every literary salon, as a marvelous conversationalist and a storyteller gifted with a deep voice.[14] Reading the remembrances of his friends and colleagues in the recent issue *Journal of Italian Translation,* published after Tusiani's passing, it becomes clear that Tusiani was the king of the parlor of his houses in New York City. His conversations have remained chiseled in the memories of those who knew him. Anthony Tamburri indeed describes in detail the place where he and Tusiani had their breakfast, with espresso and Centerbe liquor: "I mention the details of the surroundings only because they reflect still, as I think back, Joseph Tusiani in all of his elegance both as a man and as a thinker. Call it a metaphor, a metonymy, or a synecdoche, that room in all of its aesthetic glory was most befitting for Joseph's hosting," Tamburri muses with affection (381).[15]

Tusiani's play is quite effective when staging this parlor as a sample of a British society with all its small mannerism. Playwright Samuel Johnson is always "puffing and fanning himself with an enormous handkerchief" (273). The tight-mouthed British accent colors witty jokes of the guests. In this elitist, closed society, a clever question is worthy of ovation ("Your question, Boswell, merits my

---

[13] "Joseph Tusiani Named New York State Poet Laureate Emeritus." *Lehman Today.* http://wp.lehman.edu/lehman-today/joseph-tusiani-named-new-york-state-poet-laureate-emeritus/. Accessed December 1, 2020.
[14] Several videos on Youtube show his interviews and poetry readings.
[15] Not only Tamburri's memorial centers around the conversations with Tusiani, and his charming company, but also the essays by Paolo Giordano and Luigi Fontanella, while Cosma Siani retells the encounters in his family living room in San Marco in Lamis ("Da Siani a Tusiani. Storia di un'amicizia").

applause," 273), and riddles and word games are enjoyable pastimes. Here is a cunning exchange between Johnson, the playwright, and David Garrick, the self-absorbed actor:

> Johnson: ... May God
> grant him as many years as he has words.
>
> Garrick: And you as many words as you have years. (278)

And later:

> Johnson: Yes, sit beside our host, my dear Baretti,
> Lest you be caught, before our evening ends,
> Between my hammer and his anvil.
>
> Garrick: I have been called an anvil, who am thin,
> By one who, being... thick, can be no hammer. (278)

Something else in the initial conversation seems to foreshadow the tragedy about to befall Baretti. In the Streatham parlor, the guests argue over the definition of the literary critic, and Garrick compares him to an assassin:

> Garrick: There's something of the killer in a critic.
> Can you dissect a body with no knife? (281)

While in the parlor, let us face to the question of the play's style. *If Gold Should Rust* belongs to this room. It is a parlor drama, meant to be read, not recited on a stage. It is a spoken drama where the lines are poetic verses. Try reading it aloud, and it animates. It takes life. Recently, audiences have been fascinated by history played out in musical verses, as in the successful musical *Hamilton. An American Musical* (Lin-Manuel Miranda, 2015). The musicality of *If the Gold Should Rust* is extremely enjoyable. Not so much for the rhymes, that are sparse, but for the metrical rhythm of the decasyllable verses, a quantitative rhythm, like in Latin verse. Their galloping, regular pace makes music. The decasyllable remains intact even when divided in multiple characters' lines, as in this verse divided into a four-hemistich exchange:

All: Mistrust you?
Baretti: Yes, indeed.
All: Absurd.
Baretti: (firmly)   Of course.

The melody of these verses make us think of Tusiani's love for music (he had a subscription to the Metropolitan Opera). He himself admits: "It would be my innate love for music that would give vitality and echo to my syllables" (*Gargano mio* 38).[16]

It is also bizarre that this play has no action (apart from the quick knife-flashing, involuntary murder), but only dialogues and monologues. Tusiani sometimes recurred to dramatic monologues in his poems, such as in "I, Costantino Brumidi," dedicated to the frescoist of the Capitol rotunda.[17] We can also surmise that this style would fit Tusiani himself, an intellectual who enjoys the company of discussion circles. On the other hand, dialogues were didactic tools for Baretti, who earned his wages in London by teaching Italian language in British families. In particular, between 1773 and 1776, Baretti became language tutor to Hetty (Queeney), the daughter of Henry Thrale. "Queeney would choose a subject and Baretti would dash off an illustrative conversation in Italian for several speeches, then an English translation. 'Fine bubbles full of air' he called his dialogues" (Hyde, 321). For his pupil, in 1775, Baretti wrote and published a collection of discursive exchanges, *Easy Phraseology for the Use of Young Ladies*. All these reasons may explain the curious origin of this conversational theater piece.

---

[16] "Sarebbe stato il mio innato amore per la musica a dare vitalità ed eco alle mie sillabe."
[17] "I, Costantino Brumidi," in Joseph Tusiani, *Gente Mia and Other Poems*.

THE BARE APARTMENT

Act II opens in a small apartment where Baretti is found dazed, haunted by the ghost of the masked man, the aggressor he has killed in self-defense. This is a small immigrant quarter. We can imagine Baretti completing here his important works on Italy and the Italian language: *Remarks on the Italian Language and Writers*, and a bilingual collection of Italian prose and verse, *Dissertation upon the Italian Poetry*; the *Introduction to the Italian Language* and *The Italian Library,* which were short commentaries on the lives and works of well-known Italian writers. In London, Baretti published also *An Account of the Manners and Customs of Italy* (1768), a defensive reply to *Letters from Italy*, the disparaging description of Italian ways by traveler Samuel Sharp. Baretti's prolific labor brought Italy and its literary and linguistic culture to an English-speaking audience, and bridged a cultural gap, exactly like Tusiani's did two centuries later.

The most important aspect of this apartment is its bare essentiality. "A modestly furnished room" with a window and a desk. This emptiness visualizes the deep loneliness of the immigrant. The core of his soul remains unadorned and cold as the small room inhabited by ghosts. Simplicity and loneliness are other aspects that tie Baretti to Tusiani, both deprived of the warmth of a family. In the recollection of the Castagnola Prize, Tusiani mentioned that Baretti was "unmarried like me" (174). The play gives large space to the writer's mulling about his isolation.

> I am alone because I chose to be,
> or is man's loneliness life's very air?
> So here I am, admired and helpless, loved
> and lonely in my pilgrimage to death. (291)

Tusiani seems to insist on Baretti's loneliness. As soon as he leaves his friends' parlor, he is slapped in the face by the cold street air and his own solitude:

> I curse the sterile desert of my life.
> Along the mobile dunes of time I go,

and in the distance suddenly I see
A speck of green. With panting breath I then
Gather my failing strength and, unaware
Of miles, towards the great trembling speck I hasten –
But when I reach it, nothing is in sight
But the enormous emptiness of space,
And I despair of ever finding home. (285)

Another reason why both Tusiani and Baretti are metaphorically isolated in the narrow space of a room is their struggle with society's biases against Italian. Prejudice keeps them isolated. The question that Baretti was asked in court – "What do you expect from a descendent of the demon Machiavelli?" – burns twice on Tusiani's skin. In *La parola nuova*, he comments: "In similar circumstances, Americans would have said of me: 'What would you expect from a descendent of Al Capone?'" (174-5).[18] The two intellectuals both wrote in self-defense:

> He [Baretti] had felt the need, or better the duty, to defend Italy from the accusations of a British gentleman who behaved like a new Roger Ascham [a self-righteous moralist and teacher], and I too, I had to defend Italy more than once, in a country that called me *dago* and, in the higher places, a specialist of pizza and spaghetti. (174)[19]

Maybe for prejudice or for the loneliness of immigration, Baretti finds himself walking home on the damp cobblestones of London, in deep discouragement:

---

[18] "Che ti aspetti da un discendente del demonio Machiavelli?" ... In simili circostanze, di me gli americani avrebbero detto: "E che ti aspetti da un discendente di Al Capone?"

[19] "Aveva scritto tre opere in inglese, ed io altrettante, se non di piú. Aveva sentito il bisogno, anzi il dovere, di difendere l'Italia dalle accuse di un signore inglese che si atteggiava a Roger Ascham redivivo, ed anch'io, in più d'una occasione, avevo fatto altrettanto in un'America che mi chiamava *dago* o, negli ambienti più evoluti, specialista di pizza e spaghetti."

> A home
> is greater than a homage to the Muse
> I've never had a woman of my own
> waiting for me upon the end of the day.
> I've never been rewarded with a smile
> for facing a new morning on this earth.
> ...
> I'm tired of going nowhere, tired of this
> seeking a God that loves and baffles me,
> tired of these stars the call but want me not,
> tired of this godly semblance in my soul
> that makes my clay a more appalling weight,
> tired of myself. (292)

With these tempestuous thoughts in mind, Baretti crosses the dark waters of the River Thames.

THE RIVER THAMES

The darkness of the river is nothing else than a correlative of the darkness of Baretti's soul. Spiritual gloom, torment and self-pity shroud the whole play like a film of corrosive rust. The glow of the Thrale's fireplace does not last long. Johnson's description of Baretti's stormy inner personality comes early in the play: "[I] still fail to comprehend how bitter ink – / can be contained in a bejeweled well" (275). Bitter ink is his unsatisfied vision of life that turns into utmost desperation.

The character Baretti is haunted by guilt. He cannot forgive himself for the assassination, even after being acquitted in the trial. It is interesting to notice that this crisis of conscience is not found in real-life Baretti. While the fictional Baretti cannot accept forgiveness, the historical Baretti seemed

> extremely satisfied with the outcome of the trial, in particular
> with the kind demonstration of affection he received from his
> friends, so much that he felt himself even more connected

with England than before, a country which had given him justice and real friendship. He later revealed to his friend Lord Charlemont that 'those I had about me did their part so well that they have made me an Englishman forever.'[20]

In the play, this dark remorse is Tusiani's invention and it is also what makes his topic most enticing. Tusiani's Baretti is a good man. He refuses easy absolution. His moral stance is unwavering. Towards the end of the play, he confesses his ethical view of life: "Willing what is good / is the supreme reward of life to life" (332). It reminds us readers of Tusiani's declaration to his friend Antonio Motta, about the superiority of morality over art:

> More important than literature is the human goodness that literature itself inspires, or should inspire. I think now to all those poets who compared their verses to a bronze monument or to an oak tree that defies the centuries. Yes, art conquers the stronghold and survives the pettiness and misery of time. But if I also think to the millions of children that every day die of hunger, I ask myself what is the relationship between human sufferance and the victory of poetry. (*Gargano* 54)[21]

The largest part of the play is dedicated to the protagonist's coming to terms with a guilty conscience. Baretti is shown visiting the dilapidated flat of the victim's wife who shows him the lowest condition of human life, when she prostitutes her own little girl (who has a filthy yet innocent mouth). The drunk woman turns the knife in his wound when she tells him that her man was only bluffing, he would not have hurt anyone: "He couldn't hurt a fly, I'll tell you that.

---

[20] Desmond O'Connor.
[21] "Piu' importante della letteratura è la bonta umana che ispira, o che dovrebbe ispirare la stessa letteratura. Penso in questo momento, a tutti quei poeti che hanno paragonato i loro versi a un monumento di bronzo o a una quercia che sfida i secoli. Si, l'arte espugna la roccaforte e soprvvive alle piccolezze e alle miserie del tempo. Ma penso anche ai milioni di bimbiche ogni giorno muoiono di fame e mi chiedo quale sia il rapporto fra il dolore umano e la vittoria della poesia."

/ He'd rather starve than steal" (309). Not knowing that she is speaking to the man's killer, she says: "If this I-talian that he tried to rob / had told him that he was as poor as he, / he would have given him his coat instead" (310). To top the mudslide of guilt, a dismayed Baretti discovers that in fact he did have a few coins he could have given the man. This is a hint to the real Baretti, who loathed the poverty of London's streets and always brought "a pocket full of small change to give away, ill as he could afford it" (Harrold, 167).

> When I came home last night, I found I had
> some shillings in my pocket - not too many
> to save a man from famine and despair,
> but quiet enough, I still believe, to make
> a desperate hungry man go home with hope. (300)

As the drama unfolds, the darkness deepens. A nostalgia for light seeps through words that yearn for lost innocence: "Evil lays bare the good that could have been / as this dark night the image of the day" (336). The last words Baretti pronounces, while disappearing into the mist, are: "So come my conscience. Lead me to the Sun" (338).

In this yearning for light, there is no happy ending because Baretti will not be able to forgive and forget. His friend, Boswell, explains: "Why, it was easier to win the case, / than to convince Baretti he has won" (313), and later:

> Death would have pleased him more. The life he took
> has left him more despondent. He believes
> that to be that to be killed is safer than to kill
> and cannot understand why he is still free. (315)

In this passage of intense lucidity, Baretti admits the depth of his conundrum about the futility of literature in front of morality:

> Then let me leave for having killed a man,
> but let me die for having slain my soul.

He is a fraud who preaches life and love,
and then is frightened by a fleeting cloud.
Beauty is but a hollow-sounding word
if, when the hour of ugliness arrives,
it quickly turns to ugliness and dies.
It should be God and, more than sunshine, sun,
and not an artificial ray destroyed
by the least shadow passing overhead.
It should convince it's better to be grass
than tyranny of plow... (306)

The river Thames attracts Baretti with its darkness. Yes, while he looks "at the river with envy" (338), he does not heed its call. Refusing suicide, he instead accepts the company of his tormented conscience. The shame for his sin remains by his side.

The Old London Bridge (1209–1831)

The play ends on the London Bridge when Baretti meets the shadow of his victim. The man appears as his conscience. He slips an arm under his assassin's arm, and the two walk away together in the misty night, "arm in arm" (338). Baretti's last thought is a reconciliation with his own responsibility and with the darkness that surrounds his night:

... Love has one secret
The sharing of the little bread we have,
And life is easy then. We could have worked
Together, you and I; instead I was
afraid of your approaching me for help.
We could have dined together at the inn;
Instead I saw an enemy in you.
Who could have been the best of all my friends.
Come, walk with me, my conscience! Let your voice
Be the eternal company I need
                            in this incomprehensible
                                      my night. (337)

The Demolition of Old London Bridge, 1832, Guildhall Gallery, London (https://commons.wikimedia.org/wiki/File:The_Demoltion_of_Old_London_Bridge,_1832,_Guildhall_Gallery,_London.JPG)

The play's final scene takes place on the London Bridge, a bridge with a significant history. The one that Baretti traversed was the old medieval bridge, with a balustrade and benches covered by alcoves. It would be replaced in 1831, to be transformed again in an artless, asphalted highway in the 1970s.[22] All its rich history erased. This bridge was the symbol of London. The medieval bridge had a chapel in the middle, St. Thomas on the Bridge, a symbol of repentance and contrition that was slowly overtaken by stores and warehouses. The chapel was dedicated to the martyr Thomas Becket, Archbishop of Canterbury, by the guilt-ridden King Henry whose followers had murdered the bishop. For centuries, the bridge was a bustling passage of both filth and grandeur. Only a narrow passage allowed the crossing of walking crowds. Such weight caused several collapses remembered in the famous nursery rhyme, "London Bridge is Falling Down." It was also a place of punishment: by the southern gatehouse, severed heads of criminals and traitors stood

---

[22] The 1800 bridge was a landmark in T. S. Eliot's poem *The Waste Land* (1922): the shuffling commuters across the bridge were compared to souls of Dante's Inferno.

impaled on pikes. What a perfect place to have a man haunted by his conscience meet his ghosts.

Tusiani may have had no idea that the London Bridge, set of his play, would bear such symbolical weight, for its history and for other emblematic values. But the bridge location inspires further interpretations. Like Tusiani, Baretti was a bridge between Italian and English language, and their respective cultures. Paolo Bugliani comments on Baretti's role as a cultural "go-between: "What is striking in Baretti's case is the intensity with which he carried out his duties as negotiator between England and Italy" (2). The same Tusiani drew a parallel: "[Baretti] presented Italian authors that had been ignored, and I too, I had presented a neglected aspect of our Michelangelo" (*Parola nuova*, 174).[23] Finally, the bridge is a place to reflect on the crossing of identities. Tusiani's eternal question surfaces here again, his profound inner division. As he admits the day of the Castagnola Prize, Baretti symbolizes that part of himself that kept living in-between, never reaching the end of the bridge:

> It seemed to me to hear, at a distance of two centuries, the question they asked him. "Mr. Baretti, do you think in English or in Italian? If you can think in English, how can you forget to think in Italian, your maternal language? And if you still think in Italian, how can you translated in perfect English what you think in your native language?" How many times I had heard that question from people who judge you from the slightest accent that accompanies your every word!" (174)[24]

---

[23] "Aveva dato notizie su autori italiani ignorati, e avevo, anch'io, fatto conoscere un aspetto ignorato della grandezza del nostro Michelangelo."

[24] "E mi parve, anche, di udire, a distanza di due secoli, la domanda che gli rivolgevano: 'Signor Baretti, Lei pensa in inglese o in italiano? Se riesce a pensare in inglese, come fa a dimenticare di pensare in italiano, che è la Sua lingua materna? E, se pensa ancora in italiano, come fa a tradurre in perfetto inglese quello che pensa nella lingua nativa?' Quante volte quella stessa domanda me l'ero sentita rivolgere io da gente che ti giudica dal lieve accento straniero che accompagna ogni tua parola!"

Tusiani lived his entire life on this symbolical bridge. He never really crossed it but kept an uneasy balance between two worlds. Like Baretti, he never gave a definite answer to the question, "Have I betrayed my parents and my friends / for speaking languages they do not speak?" (291).

CONCLUSION

One last interrogation remains lingering in the air: what about the play's strange long title? Cosma Siani proposes that the gold be the figure of the intellectual seen as a positive hero. He who can be hurt but can never hurt someone. Even more, a being of ethical superiority, as he ties the saying to Chaucer's question in *The Canterbury Tales*, "That if gold ruste, what shal iren do?" ("That if gold rusts, what shall iron do?").[25] It is a disheartened question: if a priest or an intellectual who should be trustworthy, behaves in a bad way, how would lower type of people behave?

I would propose an alternative reading. Besides a moral interpretation, we can think of a temporal one. The rust is the rust of time, the rust that dissolves the past. Dramatic events that once burnt so strongly, scorching the life of an intellectual, have dimmed until they are gone. The qualms that disrupted the life of a meek immigrant scholar will also fade away. Today, nobody remembers the trial ("the trial that even Italians do not know," 175).[26] Nobody remembers Baretti either. That whole world is gone. No more Streatham House, no more London Bridge: it is a forgotten world. Hearing the plea of a past gone, Tusiani is the one who still raises the question: if even gold rusts, how is it possible to stop the rusting of time? How can we stop forgetting? Tusiani entrusts that drama

---

[25] Siani writes: "Il verso dei *Racconti di Canterbury* che contiene l'adagio è il 502, e nell'inglese di Chaucer suona così "That if gold ruste, what shal iren do?", cioé, "That if gold rusts, what will iron do?" / "Se arrugginisce l'oro, che farà il ferro?". Tusiani riprende questa massima inglese, ancora oggi usata in senso etico, e la applica alla propria creazione letteraria, in uno schema mentale in cui l'oro è metafora dell'intellettualità, la parte del corpo sociale – nella sua visione – dotata di naturale superiorità, e che non è ammissibile sia volta al male" (68).

[26] "Il processo di cui sanno ben poco gli stessi italiani."

of conscience to his pages. He knows that books are a safeguard from death: "Man will always feel the need to describe himself not to see or feel himself dying" (*Gargano*, 55).[27] The thought of death was never too far from Tusiani's mind. Even better, he said, mortality is the very source of poetry. To the question, "where does a poet take his images from?" Tusiani answers: "From the conscience of his mortality that the beauty of flowers and birds, the return of light and seasons, every day, every hour sharpens and soothes" (*Gargano* 23).[28] This play may well be his own act of resistance against the rust of time. Even more meaningful, now that he too, is gone.

Works Cited

Bugliani, Paolo (2019) "A Little Embroidery of His Own": Giuseppe Baretti as Cultural Mediator in Eighteenth-Century Europe", *mediAzioni* 25. http://mediazioni.sitlec.unibo.it.

Giordano, Paolo. "Joseph Tusiani: The Man and His Work" *Italica* 93.1 (Summer 2016). 318-337.

Giordano, Paolo, ed. *Joseph Tusiani Poet Translator Humanist. An International Homage*. West Lafayette: Bordighera, 1994.

Harrold, Charles Frederick. "The Italian in Streatham Place: Giuseppe Baretti (1719-1789)," *The Sewanee Review* 38.2 (Apr.-Jun., 1930): 161-175.

Hyde, Mary. "The Thrales of Streatham Park, II. The 'Family book': (ii) 1773-1774". *Harvard Library Bulletin* XXIV (3), July 1976. 306-348.

"Joseph Tusiani Named New York State Poet Laureate Emeritus." *Lehman Today*. http://wp.lehman.edu/lehman-today/joseph-tusiani-named-new-york-state-poet-laureate-emeritus/. Accessed December 1, 2020.

Magno, Pietro. "L'ultima poesia italiana e garganica di Joseph Tusani" in Paolo Giordano, ed. *Joseph Tusiani. Poet Translator Humanist. An International Homage*. West Lafayette: Bordighera, 1994. 129-141.

O'Connor, Desmond. "Baretti, Giuseppe Marc'Antonio (1719–1789). *Oxford Dictionary of National Biography*. Oxford University Press, 2004.

---

[28] "Da dove prende le immagini del poeta? Dalla coscienza della sua mortalita, che la bellezza dei fiori, degli uccelli, del ritorno della luce e delle stagioni, ogni giorno, ogni ora acuisce e lenisce."

Savoia, Francesca. *Il Baretti Vostro. Lettere inedite di Giuseppe Baretti*. Verona: QuiEdit, 2013.

Siani, Cosma. *Baretti a Londra e altri saggi su Joseph Tusiani*. Firenze: Mauro Pagliai Editore, 2013.

_____. "Da Siani a Tusiani. Storia di un'amicizia." *Journal of Italian Translation* XV. 1 (Spring 2020): 353-358.

Stefanile, Felix, "Introduction" in *Joseph Tusiani*. Paolo A. Giordano, ed. 267-29

Tamburri, Anthony Julian. "Coffee with Joseph." *Journal of Italian Translation* XV. 1 (Spring 2020): 381-3.

Tate National Gallery. "Joshua Reynolds: The Creation of Celebrity: Room Guide: Room 4" https://www.tate.org.uk/whats-on/tate-britain/exhibition/joshua-reynolds-creation-celebrity/joshua-reynolds-creation-0-3. Accessed December 1, 2020.

Thrale, David. "Streatham Park." September 26, 2009. http://www.thrale.com/streatham_park. Accessed on December 1, 2020.

_____. "The Library and Streatham Worthies." September 26, 2009. http://www.thrale.com/library_and_streatham_worthies. Accessed on December 1, 2020.

Tusiani, Joseph. *Gargano mio. Conversazione con Antonio Motta*. Fasano: Schena Editore, 2016.

_____. *Gente Mia and Other Poems*. Stone Park, Ill., Italian Cultural Center, 1978.

_____. "If Gold Should Rust" in *Joseph Tusiani Poet Translator Humanist. An International Homage*, Paolo A. Giordano (ed.). West Lafayette: Bordighera, 1994. 271-338.

_____. *La parola nuova. Autobiografia di un italo-americano (Parte II)*. Fasano: Schena, 1991.

DIVAGANDO WITH GIUSEPPE TUSIANI IN THE *SOTTOBOSCO LETTERARIO*

Mark Pietralunga

Not long after his arrival in the United States in 1947, Joseph Tusiani unexpectedly discovered a literary vitality in the Italian community of New York that appeared to be recharged by the recent war. It was the world of the Italian American artists and poets of the *sottobosco letterario*, as he defines it in his essay "The Making of an Italian American Poet," that "literary Italy best ignored" but that he willingly inherited and called his own.[1] It was through a member of the *sottobosco*, Antonio Calitri, who was one of the first teachers of Italian in New York public schools, that Tusiani was introduced to sculptor and poet Onorio Ruotolo. Tusiani soon began to frequent the "Leonardo da Vinci Art School" at 15 Union Square where Ruotolo had his sculpture studio. On Saturday afternoons, the studio would also serve as a literary and artistic circle for the Italian American poets and artists and where the official language was Italian. Ruotolo's "Circolo" provided Tusiani with the opportunity to collaborate with the major publications of the New York area. One of these publications was *Divagando*, a leading weekly magazine in the Italian language that served as an important voice for the Italian immigrant community from the 1940s to the early 1960s.

In the twelfth anniversary issue of April 27, 1955, then editor of *Divagando*, Alberto Viviani, offers a brief but informative historical overview of the magazine.[2] Viviani writes that *Divagando*'s first issue appeared on the 6th of February 1943: "Anno davvero terribile per tutta la umanità." In the midst of this "apocalyptic storm," continues Viviani, Italian American Andrè Luotto, head of a commercial service advertising company, journalist, and general manager of the Italian Radio Station WOV, and Italian Pietro Novasio, a former

---

[1] See in this volume Joseph Tusiani, "The Making of an Italian American Poet": 4-5.
[2] Alberto Viviani, "Dodicesimo Anniversario – 1943-55." *Divagando* (April 22, 1955): 5-6.

Christian Democratic member of the Italian Parliament who lived in exile in the United States because of his opposition to fascism, felt that, precisely in that year of 1943, there was a vital need to call to order and to gather together the hundreds of thousands of Italian residents in America, and to tell Italy that it had not been forgotten.[3] Viviani adds that Luotto and Novasio believed that it was important to encourage the Italian community in America, especially in that moment in which the divided, crippled, and battered "Patria" seemed like it would never be able to regain the dignity of a Nation. Viviani then highlights the guiding principle of the magazine's founders:

> E fondarono questo "Divagando" dalle cui pagine, ogni settimana, ripetettero con la fede dei puri e dei Santi, che bisognava sempre amare l'Italia; amarla per le sue sventure e per i suoi errori; amarla e non giudicarla perché i figlioli non possono mai assumersi a giudici della Mamma; aiutarla in ogni modo: con il bene e con la preghiera; aiutarla soprattutto con la fede certa nella sua risurrezione perché nè il ferro nè il fuoco nè la strage possono nè potranno mai annullare la grandezza e la civiltà millenaria di una stirpe.

Andrè Luotto, who would serve as editor and publisher of *Divagando* from its first issue in 1943 until January 1949, described to his readers in a regular column of the magazine titled "Tre me e voi" what they would find in the publication:

---

[3] In an email sent to me on September 16, 2016, actor, television personality, and chef Andy Luotto offers the following information about his grandfather: "Il nonno Andrè Luotto appartiene alla generazione di quella che ha fatto grande l'America. Ha avuto la prima radio in italiano nel nord est USA. Divenne popolarissimo e si creò anche una posizione di prestigio nella politica di New York lavorando per il sindaco Fiorello La Guardia. Qualunque personaggio italiano di rilievo passando da N.Y., doveva obbligatoriamente far visita in radio da nonno Andrea.... Caruso Pirandello Toscanini Musco e tanti altri. In tutto questo da non sottovalutare il lavoro svolto da sua moglie Ninetta Cavallaro musicista e poliglotta. Il nonno ha continuato a fare radio fino agli anni ottanta."

Mark Pietralunga • "*Divagando* with Giuseppe Tusiani"

[...] La letteratura, la poesia, la scienza e l'umorismo sono cose che troverete nelle altre pagine della rivista. Qui troverete, invece, una specie di rapporto, cordiale e franco, che io credo dovervi fare giacchè vi considero non come dei semplici lettori, ma piuttosto come parte viva ed attiva della grande famiglia di "Divagando".[4]

With the departure of Luotto as editor and publisher, Pietro Novasio, together with Associate Editor Franco Lalli, assumed the responsibility of running the magazine.[5] It was under the direction of Novasio and Lalli that Tusiani's name began to appear in the pages of *Divagando,* and it was appropriate that his "Vergil," Onorio Ruotolo, seemed to be involved in making this happen.[6] In the April 25, 1951 issue of the magazine, Ruotolo's article "Un nuovo astro sul cielo scuro della poesia" not only served as an introduction of Tusiani and his poetry to a wide Italian American readership but also appeared to be a way of indirectly recognizing the young poet as an honored member of the Italian American *sottobosco letterario*.[7] Ruotolo sets the background for his discussion of the recent publication of three booklets of poetry - *Flora, Petali sull'onda,* and *Peccato e luce* - by highlighting the hardships Tusiani experienced from his early childhood in Italy, without the guidance of his father who had emigrated to America and who for years, as a result of the war, had lost contact with his wife and child back home. Notwithstanding the heroic and miraculous efforts of his mother to nourish and educate her son, the young Tusiani remained terrorized by the barbarity of the war. As a result of this experience, Ruotolo asks: "E che altro potrebbe egli cantare, se, angosciato e senza speranza, sgomento e intenebrato, palpitò il suo cuore di poeta per tutti gli anni dell'adolescenza e per i primi della giovinezza?" (15). When turning to his

---

[4] Andrè Luotto, "Tra me e voi," *Divagando* (March 3, 1943): 3.
[5] With these editorial changes, Charles L'Episcopo became the President of the new publishing house "Divagando Corporation."
[6] Tusiani refers to Ruotolo as his "Vergil" in his essay "The Making of an Italian American Poet": 14.
[7] Onorio Ruotolo, "Un nuovo astro sul cielo scuro della poesia." *Divagando* (April 25, 1951): 15-16, 18.

analysis of the poems, Ruotolo identifies a fundamental feature of Tusiani's recent and future poetry in the collection *Peccato e luce*: "la nota, cioè che s'ispira all'umanità travagliata dai mali presenti e che va alla ricerca di Dio, che dal peccato, come suggerisce lo stesso titolo, s'innalza alla luce, tende alla pace e alla bontà" (15). For Ruotolo, Tusiani stands out among the esteemed Italian scholars and poets in America for his sensitivity to the nuances and boldness of images similar to what one finds in an Ungaretti, a Montale, a Quasimodo, and a Saba. Ruotolo's reference to an affinity between Tusiani's poetry and that of Emily Dickinson leads him to recall the former's recent monographic study on the American poet *La poesia amorosa di Emily Dickinson*, signaling his strong interest to go beyond the bounds of Italian literature and culture.[8]

Just a few months after Ruotolo's article on Tusiani appeared, the latter published a review of Frances Winwar's monograph *The Land of the Italian People* in the November 14, 1951 issue of *Divagando*.[9] In "The Making of an Italian American Poet," Tusiani recalls that Ruotolo had frantically invited him to review the book for *La Parola* of Chicago and encouraged him to do "a great job" noting that "First, it's a book about us, and second, it's by the greatest writer we Italian Americans have."[10] Tusiani would soon come to idolize Winwar with whom he would establish a deep friendship. In her role as Tusiani's "new Vergil," Winwar warned him not to remain confined to "Ruotolo's little world," otherwise he would never learn English.[11] According to Tusiani, Winwar was determined to "Americanize" her dear friend. However, Tusiani then makes clear the meaning of this "Americanization": "My 'Americanization' was not to be an end to itself. Through it, instead, I was

---

[8] Joseph Tusiani, *La poesia amorosa di Emily Dickinson* (New York: Venetian Press, 1950).
[9] Giuseppe Tusiani, "Il paese degl'Italiani," *Divagando* (November 14, 1951): 25.
[10] In "The Making of an Italian American Poet," Tusiani writes that his short review of Winwar's monograph on Italy appeared in *La Parola* of Chicago in the Spring of 1953.
[11] Tusiani refers to Winwar as his "new Vergil" in "The Making of an Italian American Poet": 25.

to return, with a fully American voice, to the Little Italy of my enlarged and more radiant vision."[12]

An eloquent sign of Tusiani's return to the world of "Little Italy" is reflected in the more visible role he would take on with *Divagando*. Under the new direction of Alberto Viviani following the death of editor Pietro Novasio in February of 1952, Tusiani would join Ruotolo, and several other members of the "Circolo," as a formal contributing editor at *Divagando*, where he would serve in various editorial roles during the remainder of the 1950s and into the early 1960s.[13] Tusiani reveals his strong ties to the Italian community and to the plight and successes of the Italian immigrants in an essay he pens for the June 23, 1954 issue of *Divagando* titled "Il primo vescovo italiano a New York."[14] In recounting the celebration of the episcopal consecration of Monsignor Giuseppe Maria Pernicone on May 5, 1954, Tusiani takes the opportunity to recall how much has been written and said in bad faith about the misfortunes of the Italian immigrants and their own inability to defend, like others have, the prestige of their land of origin. However, Tusiani quickly adds that all the "sordi rancori" and "infeconde lagnanze" surrounding the Italian immigrants came to a halt on that day of May 5th "perché una grande gloria s'è aggiunta al diadema delle nostre glorie italiche: la consacrazione del primo Vescovo italiano di New York." For Tusiani, the consecration of a native of Regalbuto, Sicily in front of his long suffering and hardworking immigrant parents and in the largest church of New York, St. Patrick's Cathedral, was something that the Italian immigrant community had never experienced before and had always dreamed of and longed for:

> lì in San Patrizio, veniva celebrato l'evento più nobile nella storia dell'Italia nomade; perché lì, in quel momento, due vecchietti nostri, della nostra terra generosa, piangevano di gioia, essi che, come

---

[12] Tusiani, "The Making of an Italian American Poet": 26.
[13] Other members of the "Circolo" who served as contribution editors at *Divagando* in these years included Antonio Calitri, Italo Stanco, and Salvatore Viola.
[14] Giuseppe Tusiani, "Il primo vescovo italiano a New York." *Divagando* (June 23, 1954): 17, 19.

noi, avevan versato lagrime di dolore per anni ed anni. Ma quel pianto compensava ogni amarezza e forse per la prima volta addolciva ogni accorata nostalgia. (17)

Later that year in the December 29, 1954 issue of *Divagando*, a recently published book by Tusiani is featured in the magazine with the title "Un libro del nostro Prof. Tusiani sui *Sonettisti Americani*."[15] Tusiani's study on the development of the sonnet in America represents an important step in the process of "Americanization" that Frances Winwar believed was crucial in order for him to discover the fullness of his potential. Winwar's words in her introduction to the volume recognizes Tusiani's willingness to go beyond the world of Little Italy and enter into a virgin territory "chè, in più di duecento anni di significative attività poetica (una notevole parte di essa proprio nel sonetto), nessun critico di America ha mai pensato di compiere un tale studio" (23). This achievement of *Divagando*'s contributing editor is viewed as a source of pride for the Italian American community: "Gli Italiani d'America sono orgogliosi del fatto che sia stato uno di loro, prima ancora degli stessi Americani, ad affrontare con competenza il vasto e delicato problema del sonetto d'America" (25).

A similar pride shared by the Italian community and his fellow contributors at *Divagando* is expressed in two subsequent short pieces published in the Italian American weekly announcing Tusiani's accomplishments as an American poet. The first appeared in the June 6, 1956 issue of *Divagando* under the title "Primo Premio Letterario a Giuseppe Tusiani." In it, as we read below, Tusiani's poem in English "Anticipation" was awarded first prize by the "Poetry Society in America." Accompanying the news of the award, the magazine included another poem by Tusiani written in Italian titled "Foglio di carta":

---

[15] Argo, "Un libro del nostro Prof. Tusiani sui Sonettisti Americani." *Divagando* (December 29, 1954): 23, 25.

Mark Pietralunga • "*Divagando* with Giuseppe Tusiani"

La "Poetry Society of America", l'accademia nazionale di Poesia di cui è presidente Robert Frost, ha assegnato il Primo Premio ad una lirica inglese del Prof. Giuseppe Tusiani dal titolo "Anticipation". E' la prima volta che un premio ufficiale di poesia americana sia toccata a un italiano e ad un collaboratore di Divagando. Ci rallegriamo vivamente col giovane e valoroso poeta al quale auguriamo di poter raccogliere sempre più fulgidi allori. Ecco intanto un'altra lirica del poeta Tusiani.

    FOGLIO DI CARTA
Resta, mio nome, sulla carta nuda,
Ov'è bianchezza ancora, e il bianco almeno,
Anche se liso un poco, sa narrarci
Favola d'alba spenta. Come il sangue
Della vena, pieghevole è tuttora
Questo mio foglio tenue e ricorda
Il primo, su cui fu l'incerta mano
D'un bimbo e la pietà d'un sole immenso.
Or se non più d'indocili acque e scapi
Silvestri tu t'intessi ma sei pietra,
O gloria, il mio nome non incidere
Nella tua forza rigida! Chè, mentre
Ravviso il biondo bimbo che apprendeva
A tracciar sulla carta un nome e un sogno,
Mi par di rammentare, intravedute
In recesso d'illimite terrore,
Marmoree lastre mute a tutti i raggi:
Ed era ognuna un'esistenza, lì
Su quell'erba di balza che tremava
Di luci che non erano le stelle,
E per tutta la notte era turbato
Di fisse croci e spettri il mio sognare.
                      GIUSEPPE TUSIANI[16]

---

[16] "Premio Letterario a Giuseppe Tusiani." *Divagando* (June 6, 1956): 10.

The second piece appeared the following year in the March 27, 1957 issue of *Divagando*, announcing that Tusiani had won the 1956 Greenwood Prize of the Poetry Society of England for his poem, "The Return," and noting that it was the first time that a fellow countryman had been awarded such a prestigious honor.

> Apprendiamo dall'Inghilterra che i giudici del Premio Letterario "Shirley Carter Greenwood" hanno deciso di assegnare a Joseph Tusiani questo ambitissimo premio di poesia inglese, per l'anno 1956. Col suo poema in lingua inglese, "The Return" (*Il Ritorno*), Joseph Tusiani, che non è altri che il nostro italianissimo Giuseppe Tusiani, entra ufficialmente e solennemente nella lista dei poeti inglesi, americani e sud-africani, e premiato con un nutrito numero di sterline, sarà pubblicato in *The Poetry Review*, la massima rivista di poesia londinese. E', questa, la prima volta, nella storia letteraria, che a un nostro connazionale tocchi un premio sì grande e un sì alto riconoscimento da parte dell'Inghilterra. Al caro Tusiani le felicitazioni più vive di Divagando per il successo letterario conseguito e per il "nutrito numero di sterline" ricevuto. (30)

In "The Making of the Italian American Poet," Tusiani writes that he owes the Greenwood Prize to Frances Winwar's almost blind belief in his poetry. However, Tusiani also notes that Winwar made sure that he would never lose sight of his ultimate goal- the Italian American heritage that had brought them together. Tusiani further reinforces this attachment to his Italian heritage a little later in the autobiographical essay when he states: "Every new step into America brought me back to, instead of detaching me from, the land I had been told to forget in order to know and love more dearly" (29). His close ties and active involvement with Italian American publications such as *Divagando* allowed Tusiani to keep this heritage vibrant and alive. In his essay celebrating the twelfth anniversary of *Divagando*, editor Alberto Viviani's words highlighting the hard work, faith and perseverance of the contributors and editorial staff of the magazine capture the spirit of Tusiani's relationship with the land of his origins:

Quanti siamo ad amarlo e a volerlo sempre migliore e più degno di quelle tradizionali immortali che furono la linfa primigenia della sua vita? Contarli non sarebbe agevole, perché attorno a questa nostra bandiera di Italianità, vedo e sento adunata senza distinzione di stato sociale la sconfinata valanga di tutti coloro che oggi lealmente operando per le fortune della grande ospitale e libera America, non hanno dimenticato le nobilissime origini del loro sangue, né la gloria e la grandezza dei Padri.[17]

---

[17] Alberto Viviani, "Dodicesimo Anniversario – 1943-55": 6.

Mark Pietralunga • "*Divagando* with Giuseppe Tusiani"

Mark Pietralunga • "*Divagando* with Giuseppe Tusiani"

UN NUOVO ASTRO SUL CIELO SCURO DELLA POESIA

Nel remoto passato in cui visse, e certamente in un periodo oscuro dei suoi tempi, l'antico poeta Coutsa invocava: "Vieni a rianimare tutto ciò che langue, Aurora-Poesia, vieni a vivificare tutto ciò ch'è morto!". Così ancor oggi implora la decimata umanità, stanca di brancolare nella tragica realtà di questa interminabile notte. E così invocano, in tutte le lingue della terra, i poeti e gli artisti, affranti, ammutoliti, delusi, accecati, disorientati dalle sataniche scienze che implacabilmente annientano lo spirito e disintegrano la materia. Oh venga l'attesa, invocata "Aurora", ed ai suoi benefici raggi d'oro risorga, dalle macerie della crollata civiltà, l'Arte-Madre, ora agonizzante.

Solo di questo anelito son fatti, oggi, gli sprazzi di quella Poesia che, decisa a non farsi uccidere, s'ostina dalle macerie sotto cui è sepolta semiviva, ad invocare l'Aurora di una nuova era di resurrezione umana e della sua nuova Gloria. Ma troppo buia è ancora la notte! Ad Oriente non v'è segno alcuno d'albore preludiante la invocata Aurora! E coloro che proteggono, nascosti nel cuore, i semi divini della Poesia per salvarli, preservarli e trasmetterli, chiedono rifugio, pace ed ispirazione alle realtà metafisiche; alle realtà fatte di Verità, ignorate, vilipese e negate dai presuntuosi dottori dei templi razionalisti; alle verità e realtà sconfinate, inesplorate ed or solamente intuite, or solamente intraviste dai pochi eletti e solo per grazia iniziati.

Ed ecco dunque gli Ermetisti, gli Esoteristi, gli Astrattisti, gli Occultisti in gara di nobili tentativi, di nuovi accenti, di nuovi accordi, talvolta limpidi e suadenti, tal'altra oscuri ed impenetrabili, ma quasi sempre, nella voce del vero poeta, lampeggianti di sensibilità nuovissime e di rivelazioni che conquidono o abbagliano.

Tentativi, accenti, intuizioni, rivelazioni, che tanto conturbano ed imbestialiscono i sopravvissuti decrepiti turiferarii di feticci ammuffiti, gli artefici contraffattori di monete devalorizzate o fuori corso, i tornitori fabbricanti di endecasillabi e di esametri ridondanti di verbosità vuota di poesia e priva di pensiero animatore.

* * *

Giuseppe Tusiani ha dato alle stampe tre interessanti volumetti di poesie in un

GIUSEPPE TUSIANI

periodo di tempo brevissimo: *"Flora"*, *"Petali sull'onda"* e *"Peccato e luce"*. Egli risiede in America solo da tre anni. Qui insegna Lettere Italiane in uno dei più importanti Collegi di New York. E' dottore in Lettere e Filosofia. Ha letto e studiato moltissimo. Ha una memoria eccezionale e una facile estrinsecazione dei suoi sentimenti in versi sonori, scorrevoli e magistralmente ritmati.

Tusiani ha sofferto, molto sofferto, fin dalla sua infanzia, privo della guida paterna, che il genitore in America, a causa della sopraggiunta guerra, per più anni non potè dare aiuti nè notizie alla moglie ed al figlio in Italia, nè potè da essi riceverne. La madre compì l'eroismo miracoloso di pensare a nutrire ed educare il figlio. Quel figlio sempre sbattuto di qua e di là, sempre terrorizzato dalle barbarie della guerra: dalle persecuzioni naziste, prima, dai bombardamenti liberatori poi. E con tutte le conseguenti miserie e brutture e torture dello spirito e della carne.

Qualcuno ha voluto insinuare ch'egli "leopardeggia", per il dolore, per il dubbio, per il pessimismo che traspare dai suoi canti. E che altro potrebbe egli cantare, se, angosciato e senza speranza, sgomento e intenebrato, palpitò il suo cuore di poeta per tutti gli anni dell'adolescenza e per i primi della giovinezza?

Se il Tusiani non fosse nato consacrato da Dio alla Poesia, se il suo poetare derivasse solo dalla sua sapienza letteraria, allora sì ch'egli potrebbe indugiarsi a seguire l'andazzo dei cantastorie suoi critici. Ma io, qui, incomincio a deviare, chè scopo di questa mia breve rassegna non è di polemizzare nè con i critici della produzione del Tusiani, nè con i tanti suoi esaltatori, che per la gioia di poterlo annoverare fra i vari e variopinti gruppetti regionali e regionalistici — Iddio vi perdoni, onesti Terroni! — potrebbero fargli più male che bene. Io non altro mi propongo che cercar di fissare gli elementi vitali ed inconfondibili della sua poesia per quindi prospettarne le possibilità di sviluppo e di individuale affermazione nel prossimo o lontano futuro.

* * *

Diamo uno sguardo sereno ed obiettivo alla poesia del Tusiani.

Credo sia in *"Peccato e luce"*, più che nei precedenti volumetti, che si debba cercar la nota fondamentale della poesia recente e di quella futura di Giuseppe Tusiani: la nota, cioè, che s'ispira all'umanità travagliata dai mali presenti e che va alla ricerca di Dio, dal peccato, come suggerisce lo stesso titolo, s'innalza alla luce, tende alla pace e alla bontà.

. . . . . *Io più non sono*
Un uomo, io son l'umanità che cerca
La luce, la gran luce della vita
E dell'amore.

La sconcertante realtà delle "lacrimae rerum" di cui è piena la vita; la visione della guerra sanguinosa, cui il giovane, come ho detto innanzi, ha assistito, gli fa esclamare:

Ma forse al mondo è bello sol quel ch'io
Non so, divino solo ciò che spero.

Ma, poichè ancor dura la tragedia, anche la sua speranza ha momenti d'esitazione sconsolata, sì che il cuore umano è, più che mai, abisso profondo e insondabile.

. . . . . *Quanto profondo*
Tu se', quanto profondo? Venticinque
Eternità silenti ho camminato,
E tanto tu se' fondo quanto il buio
Di tutte le mie spente primavere.

L'affannosa ricerca di un perchè, che spieghi il mistero della vita e della morte,

Mark Pietralunga • *"Divagando* with Giuseppe Tusiani"

vien ripresa nella breve lirica intitolata "La farfalla". La farfalla, già cantata dal Wordsworth come gentile e innocente messaggera di ricordi d'infanzia, è colta dal Tusiani nell'attimo in cui viene schiacciata dalla mano del monello che poi la metterà nelle pagine d'un libro; ed ecco l'analogia filosofica e poetica:

> *Eri uomo, ed or se' tu*
> *Pesto verme nella terra,*
> *Eri tutto e non sei' più.*

Segue un momento di apatia spirituale, forse la constatazione dell'inutilità della stessa ricerca, la sospensione tra la disperazione e la speranza. In questa crisi egli sente "il crudo bisogno di stare soli, soli con noi"; la inerzia, l'abulia, lo sconforto dell'ora che volge inutile, è in questi versi:

> *...... Più non so che sia*
> *La speranza nel mondo, la speranza*
> *In me: io vivo sol nel mio presente,*
> *Come nel suolo il seme e su nel cielo*
> *La nuvola.*

E' l'ora in cui si desidera il fior di loto che, mangiato, dà l'oblio.

> *Scordar la vita, e il mistero profondo*
> *Ch'è in me, e l'inesausta*
> *Forza ch'abbatte i tronchi e trae dal fondo*
> *Nuov'erba e fiori e tutto regge il mondo!*

Viene la Primavera, ed ecco che il Tusiani non la canta alla solita maniera, ma le dà le ali e la manda lontano, a Dio, affinchè poi essa ridiscenda a dirgli che cosa sia l'universo, l'amore, la fede, la fervida vita

> *... che nel sangue*
> *Mi brucia ad ogni roseo apparire*
> *Del tuo peplo fiorito.*

La seconda parte del volumetto canta la luce di Dio, in cui la sofferente umanità può finalmente riposare e aver pace. Parlando della lirica *"A Dio"*, Cesare Foligno, che io da gran tempo altamente ammiro e che è, come giustamente osserva Gerald G. Walsh nell'articolo su "Peccato e Luce" apparso in *Thought* (Dicembre 1949), "il più acuto e maturo dei critici letterari d'Italia e uno dei più eminenti Dantisti del mondo", scrive, tra l'altro:

"Uno spirito profondamente religioso a cui Dio parla nei fiori, nelle nubi, negli alberi e nella tempesta. Tanto religioso da effondersi, più compiutamente e perfettamente che in ogni altra lirica, negli sciolti *"A Dio"*, nei quali l'angoscia d'un'ora torbida ha accenti strazianti ed è trionfalmente superata nell'abbandono della preghiera".

Avvertiti e guidati dalle solenni parole del Foligno, i recensori americani, più che quelli italiani, hanno insistito sulla religiosità della poesia del Tusiani, a cominciare dalla summenzionata Rivista trimestrale della Fordham University fino a *Renascence*, da *Italica* a *Books Abroad*, da *The Standard Star* di New Rochelle a *El Diario de la Marina* di Cuba. Io suggerisco che non si deve perdere di vista il legame che congiunge la prima con la seconda parte di "Peccato e Luce"; soltanto così questa religiosità ha unità di pensiero e sentimento, e quindi di poesia.

Fa parte della "luce" un'altra bella poesia, la cui originalità meglio risalterebbe se sfrondata dei troppi ornamenti, una lirica che è un quadretto ove le linee pittoriche si fondono in vita d'idilio: è il canto di tre spighe, la prima delle quali vuol diventare il pane bianco sulla mensa di re, la seconda il pane scuro che sfama l'orfano digiuno, e la terza, la più umile e nascosta, l'Ostia dei cieli che dà la vita ai cuori.

Una nota minore, ma pur visibile, che si riscontra nel volumetto di versi che stiamo esaminando, è 'a nostalgia per la Italia, per la natia Puglia lontana. La nota dell'esilio, amara e disperata nel canto di Ugo Foscolo, è in quello di Tusiani accorata e nostalgica.

> *Oh se, un giorno, pas sta la gran folla*
> *Affannosa e furente, oi re le grida*
> *Frenetiche al traguardo, troverete*
> *Un petalo gentile insanguinato,*
> *Pietosi raccoglietelo e alla Madre*
> *Lontana il date! Eternamente io dorma*
> *Presso lo stelo del bel Fiore eterno,*
> *Che nel sangue de' petali divelti*
> *Affonda le radici della vita*
> *Per la gloria di tutte le sue aurore!*

* * *

Potrei continuare a lungo con altre citazioni, ma sarà bene concludere. La giovinezza del nostro poeta è evidente nell'esuberanza della descrizione, nella vivezza delle tinte e nella ricchezza delle immagini. A volte troppa esuberanza di toni e colori che appesantisce, o copre, o, meglio, distoglie dal punto focale l'essenza del concetto poetico ispiratore; una ricchezza di verso che dovrà, col tempo, snellirsi e perdere ogni accessorio per arrivare a ciò che è l'indispensabile della poesia e dell'arte. Un peccato — oh se tutti lo potessero commettere tale peccato! — di eccesso, dunque, e non di difetto. Tutti i giovani sono naturalmente eloquenti; non lo fu forse, da giovane, anche il Leopardi, che è il più parco dei nostri poeti? Esuberanza o meno, il necessario è che ci sia la poesia. In Tusiani, io credo, la poesia c'è e ci sarà.

In un articolo di Claudio Allori, pubblicato nella *Provincia* di Cremona lo scorso anno, venne ricordato l'episodio che altamente onora il nostro giovane poeta: il suo incontro con Gabriele D'Annunzio. Il Pescarese baciò in fronte il tredicenne ragazzo, che aveva osato mostrargli le sue primizie poetiche, dicendogli testualmente: "Peppinuccio, tu sarai un grande poeta". Parole di auspicio e monito che "Peppinuccio", son sicuro, non dimenticherà mai. E parole, d'altra parte, che ignorano o non vogliono ricordare certi *imbecilli superiori* di oggi, secondo i quali un giovane di venticinque anni non può scrivere una cosa di bellezza, "a thing of beauty" come direbbe il venticinquenne Keats. Non era, forse poco più che ventenne Michelangelo quando scolpì la Pietà?

Un giudizio di certo Niccolò Sigillino, apparso ne "La Fiera Letteraria" di Roma (3 dic. 1950), spaccia definitivamente il Tusiani tra coloro "per i quali l'arte resterà, assai probabilmente, un nume inaccessibile." Adagio, illustre ignoto! Non mi vorrà mica scavalcare, così ex abrupto, l'autorità di un Gabriele D'Annunzio! Ma sarebbe ora di smetterla con tutte queste ricalcate su forma tradizionale e forma moderna. In ogni scuola c'è del buono, in ogni corrente c'è del salutare, quando ci sia l'uomo, il poeta, l'artista che dia vita a detta scuola o corrente. Ogni grande poeta ha esordito, dirò col Carducci, "scudiero dei classici", e cioè legato al proprio mondo scolastico, accademico, ecc. Ognuno, poi, con la maturità del sentimento e dopo un lento processo di rinnovamento estetico, ha trovato la sua via, il suo mondo, e quindi la sua forma. Ma di questa benedetta forma non si può, non si deve parlare, quando non c'è affatto la sostanza ovvero la stoffa del poeta, in altre parole quando non si nasce tale.

Personalmente io posso dissentire, non so se a torto o a ragione, dagl'indirizzi poetici del Tusiani, i suoi pregi stilistici di rimario e musicalità, che i più ammirano in lui, a me possono fare poca o nessuna impressione. Ma l'essenza spirituale delle sue poesie, la facoltà di non negare e quindi di riconoscere il valore reale, se pur limitato e difficile a scoprirsi, dei cosiddetti poeti ermetici, futuristi, centristi, ecc., è la prova che egli saprà svincolarsi da ogni scoria accademica, e un giorno

(Continua a pagina 18)

Costruisce il suo nido. Si sceglie con cura il terreno all'ombra dei rami più fitti, degli angoli solitari dei boschi, un posticino tranquillo e sicuro. Pian piano eleva una capannetta, intreccia con cura alla base ramoscelli teneri ed altri rametti flessibili. Parrebbe già pronto il nido. Ma così nudo com'è, non piace al vanitoso sericeo.

Corre egli allora alla ricerca di variopinte piume di pappagallo per appiccicarle con finezza e buon gusto all'entrata e sul pavimento della sua casetta. Ma non basta ancora. Occorrono pietruzze, piccoli ossicini di mammiferi e persino oggetti di uso domestico, purchè di colore brillante. Bisogna procurarseli, però; anche col furto e destramente, egli corre a sottrarli ai pacifici indigeni delle vicinanze.

Ed eccolo, il fringuello canoro, è là, sulla biforcatura di un grosso ramo, quasi all'attacco del tronco a mezza altezza dall'albero ospitale. Ma dov'è il suo nido? Inutile sforzarsi a cercarlo. Esso, a somiglianza della cincia codona lo ha ben mimetizzato. La bella coppa è così ben mascherata all'esterno di muschi e di licheni dello stesso colore dell'albero, che persino l'occhio più esperto non saprebbe distinguerlo.

Accortezze per difendersi dal nemico: dal pericolo che lo sovrasta dovunque.

Soprattutto attenzione al cuculo sfruttatore. Accorti all'usurpatore dell'altrui fatica. Quest'uccello che pure ha raccolto simpatie presso altra gente quale nunzio della primavera non è degno di protezione, non desta nell'animo nostro nessun senso di poesia. Sfruttando un simpatico costume del mondo dei pennuti, quello di adottare ogni uovo trovato nel nido, egli introduce subdolamente un uovo in ogni nido dal colorito uniformantesi a quello dell'ospite ingannato.

L'intruso con innata ferocia ben presto, a colpi di dorso, si libera dei figli dell'ospite più piccoli di lui e, non pago dell'eccidio cscerando, estenua la madre adottiva con l'incessante richiesta dei cibi.

Attenzione pure alla cingallegra che è sempre in agguato. Avido di sangue, questo piccolo uccello rapace, se troverà delle uova scoperte le bucherà e le berrà. Se troverà degli implumi appena nati col forte ed acuminato becco sfonderà loro il capo. Poi se ne tornerà al proprio nido.

Può essere sufficiente l'istinto a guardarsi da tanti pericoli, a difendersi dai mille agguati con accorgimenti così logici e precisi?

Chi direbbe che il francolino di monte, non pago d'aver costruito il suo nido sicuro prima di allontanarsi, fosse solo per un istante, lo ricopre con erbe prese all'immediate vicinanze per renderlo più nascosto ed introvabile?

Pare più astuzia che istinto quella delle rondini e del passero e di tanti altri uccelli che nidificano nelle immediate vicinanze dell'uomo per attingere da questo protezione contro uccelli rapaci.

Ed ecco la gazza che ricopre il suo nido con un coperchio di spini, mentre l'usignolo arboreo vi introduce un pezzo di pelle di serpente che sarà di sicuro spavento al probabile assalitore.

Quanta scaltrezza nel tordo che per allontanare il pericolo dal nido si finge zoppo in modo da attirare su di sè ogni bramosia, e soltanto quando ha costretto il nemico a seguirlo molto distante, si alza in volo sano e forte lasciando confuso il gabbato inseguitore!

Istinto?

"Ritengo insostenibile — continua il professor Cipriani nel già citato scritto — che a guidarli basti quanto, con simplicistiche espressioni buone solo a mascherare la nostra ignoranza, chiamasi istinto, ossia una tendenza la quale costringerebbe l'animale a seguire ciecamente vie prefissate".

C'è qualcosa di più allora. Qualcosa che forse un giorno scopriremo. Ora di questi delicati abitatori del cielo, felici creature che fecero esclamare al Leopardi "... Io vorrei essere convertito in uccello per provare quella contentezza e libertà della loro vita", ci resta solo la poesia emanante dai loro garriti, dai loro gorgheggi e dai loro nidi.

Vincenzo di Guida

PREGHIERA A DIO

Resta con me poichè la sera scende
sulla mia casa
con misericordia d'ombre e di stelle.

Ch'io Ti porga il pane e l'acqua pura
della mia povertà.
Resta accanto a me, Tua serva,
e nel silenzio degli esseri il mio cuore
oda Te solo.

Ada Negri

NUOVO ASTRO DELLA POESIA

(Continuazione da pagina 16)

saprà cantarci, con tutta libertà di forma e di pensiero, i suoi canti più belli.

* * *

Ho trovato il Tusiani unico fra i più rispettabili letterati e poeti italiani di America, col quale io abbia potuto intrattenermi su certe finezze e arditezze d'immagini della poesia di un Ungaretti, di un Montale, di un Quasimodo, di un Saba. L'affinità maggiore egli l'ha, a mio parere, con Auro d'Alba, tra i moderni, per la visibile ansia di rinnovamento spirituale e un anelito di climi matafisici, e con Emily Dickinson, del secolo scorso, per la poetica necessità di raccoglimento e di sempre più intima comunione col nume che ispira e detta.

L'accenne alla Dickinson mi ricorda il recente lavoro del Tusiani. Pur assorbito da lavori improbi inerenti alla sua professione accademica, egli sa trovare il tempo di penetrare nei sacri recessi di più d'una letteratura, sì che i suoi rari conversari coi pochissimi amici sono sempre fonte fresca e ricca di conoscenze. Nel suo studio monografico sulla Dickinson (*La Poesia Amorosa di Emily Dickinson*, The Venetian Press, New York, 1950) oltre a ricostruirne in sintesi la vita, ricerca e scopre le più recondite bellezze della poesia dickinsoniana; con esso egli ha reso, un gran servigio ai poeti e letterati italiani che, per lo più, ignorano o mal conoscono la grande figura letteraria degli Stati Uniti d'America, l'alta poetessa della vita interiore e del raccoglimento mistico.

A noi fa immenso piacere apprendere che il Tusiani sia attraversando un periodo di simile raccoglimento. Egli ha, forse, già compreso che, per essere se stesso, deve rifuggire da ogni influenza di sorta, anche e specie da quella di adulatori, quasi sempre insinceri se non del tutto incompetenti. Soltanto quando egli sarà se stesso, la sua voce del vero poeta sarà canto nazionale e universale, di quella universalità, cioè, cui tende ogni vera e umana poesia.

Onorio Ruotolo

Mark Pietralunga • "*Divagando* with Giuseppe Tusiani"

Un nuovo libro di Frances Winwar:

Il Paese degl'Italiani

Degna di lode è la novità editoriale della Lippincott Company. Si tratta di una collana di monografie illustranti le varie Nazioni nei loro aspetti geografici, storici, letterari ed etnici. Ogni monografia è naturalmente affidata a un esperto in materia che, in un dato numero di pagine, sappia sintetizzare tutto ciò che è di vitale nella storia d'un popolo.

Autrice della monografia sull'Italia è Frances Winwar, la celebre scrittrice di *Poor Splendid Wings, The Romantic Rebels, The Life of the Heart, George Sand and Her Times, Whitman, Rossetti, Joan of Arc, Ruotolo—Man and Artist*, ecc. Nessun altro avrebbe potuto espletare il difficile compito meglio di Frances Winwar, che a una profonda conoscenza del Bel Paese unisce il non meno profondo amore di chi è nato in Italia.

Il volume della Winwar si divide nei seguenti capitoli: La Penisola Italiana e le sue Isole; la varietà del popolo italiano; Sicilia: nuovo mondo greco; agricoltura e industria; da Odoacre a Federico II; Rinascimento; esploratori e scopritori; letteratura italiana; arte e musica; viaggio tra le grandi città; un popolo che lavora e gioca; il sorgere della Nazione; l'Impero che fallì e il futuro d'Italia. Il titolo di ogni capitolo prova la varietà e l'ampiezza della materia trattata. E', come si vede, una policroma sintesi di ciò che fu, è e sarà l'Italia. In "questo paradiso terrestre", come il Chaucer ebbe a definire l'Italia, la Winwar c'introduce, nel primo capitolo, con una rassegna di preliminari geografici e storici, non mai pesante, ma agile e calda e piena di quella grazia che è dello stile dell'autrice. Ad invogliarvi a conoscere ed amare l'Italia, basterebbe un simile esordio:

"Nonostante la sua giovinezza politica, l'Italia costantemente ci ricorda che essa non è la bambina di un giorno. La sua civiltà è testimoniata da millenni, come vi diranno le stesse pietre delle sue città. Prendete Roma, per esempio. Poi immaginatevi a New York, nella stazione Grand Central. Vi entrate al livello della strada. Scendete a un livello inferiore, poi giù a un altro. E vi meraviglia l'ingegnosità dell'uomo che è riuscito ad aprirsi la via nella roccia di Manhattan e costruire ciò che vi sembra una piccola città sotterranea. Anche Roma ha tali livelli al di sotto delle sue antiche strade. Ma sono livelli di cultura, livelli di ere divise da secoli."

La rassegna delle diciotto province, con le loro caratteristiche d'ambiente, di folklore e d'idioma, è illustrata da opportuni rimandi storici che danno il quadro completo di ciò che fu l'Italia al tempo dei suoi aborigeni, all'aurora della Magna Grecia giù fino all'alterna vicenda delle invasioni barbariche. L'importanza della Magna Grecia è fissata in un intero capitolo sull'Isola che ispirò Goethe, Browning e Dickinson. La storia della Sicilia è condensata in otto pagine. Al lettore americano è offerto così il complesso panorama delle città sicule ricche di storia antica e moderna, gloriose di relitti archeologici greco-romani, splendide di nomi di poeti, di tiranni e di consoli, testimoni di civiltà e di dinastie regali, squassate dai terremoti e ricostrutte dalla tenacia d'un popolo laborioso e poeta.

Fu, se non erro, il Kennard ad insistere sulla "arte dell'agricoltura" del popolo italiano. E non a torto, se l'agricoltura di Italia vanta tutta una sua letteratura, in cui è Teocrito, Virgilio, Tansillo ed altri. La Winwar ne studia i prodotti e le esigenze, prima di passar ad esaminare l'industria italiana, sempre nuova e miracolosa e sempre imponente in qualità più che in estensione, come in questi giorni han potuto vedere i visitatori della esposizione di Macy's. E' strano, diran qui molti, il destino politico di questo popolo forte. Ma l'Italia, risponde la Winwar, è sempre il popolo che, nelle sue ore più dolorose, ha innalzato templi di gloria imperitura, un popolo che, quando Machiavelli deplorava la presenza di truppe mercenarie e la frode di re venduti, cantava con la voce di Lorenzo, Poliziano ed Ariosto, e s'esprimeva col pennello di Leonardo, Michelangelo e Raffaello, il popolo del Rinascimento.

Del Rinascimento la Winwar rintraccia le primissime radici in San Francesco, figlio del Medio Evo, con una audacia di pensiero che certo esclude la tradizionale distinzione dell'Umanesimo, considerato come periodo propedeutico alla Rinascenza.

In un capitolo sui viaggiatori ed esploratori italiani la Winwar presenta agli Americani le più grandi figure della nuova geografia, dal Milione di Polo all'epopea di Colombo, Vespucci, Caboto e Verrazzano. La fama di quest'ultimo, Janus Verra Zanus, scopritore di Staten Island, del Hudson River e della Baia di New York, allora Angolèmo, è stata recentemente rivendicata, grazie alla Società Storica Italiana di Staten Island, diretta da Daniel Santoro.

In un altro capitolo sulla letteratura italiana, Frances Winwar menziona i nomi più noti e rappresentativi, da Dante a Pirandello. E', qui, di capitale importanza notare che tutti i volumi di questa serie della Lippincott hanno lo stesso numero di pagine e la stessa impostazione. E' appunto per la tirannia dello spazio che la Winwar ha emesso il nome, per es., di Ugo Foscolo e, trattando dei grandi compositori d'Italia, quello di Umberto Giordano e di Francesco Cilea. Una svista, che potrebbe dispiacere e che ci auguriamo sia eliminata in una seconda edizione, è l'omissione del nome di Guglielmo Marconi tra gli uomini che hanno illustrato il genio della stirpe italica dalle molte viti.

Ma non ho ancora accennato al valore, dirò pratico, di questo libro. Ben trentadue pagine di fotografie sapientemente scelte ne accompagnano la trattazione. Si parla, per es., del folklore italiano? Eccovi la carretta siciliana, la montanara con l'ampio scialle colorato, la tipica gondola veneziana e la processione religiosa. Avete letto della suggestività dei panorami italiani? Ed eccovi il lago di Como, le Dolomiti, le Alpi, le spiagge. E così via.

Il volume si chiude con delle pagine di storia italiana moderna e contemporanea, dopo un viaggio ideale tra le più importanti città della Penisola. Un altro dei famosi "classical tours" che portarono in Italia ammiratori, artisti e poeti da ogni angolo della terra: Chaucer, Milton, Wordsworth, Byron, Keats, Shelley, Browning, Landor, Swinburne, Longfellow, Sinclair Lewis potrebbero bastare.

Moltissimi libri sono stati scritti sull'Italia, è vero; ma questo di Frances Winwar, conciso ed agile, competente e vario, dà un quadro completo ed ispirato e vien così a colmare una grave lacuna di questo dopoguerra.

GIUSEPPE TUSIANI

Mark Pietralunga • *"Divagando* with Giuseppe Tusiani"

IL PRIMO VESCOVO ITALIANO A NEW YORK

La Solenne Consacrazione di Mons. Pernicone. Un'Altra Tappa degli Immigrati Italiani. La Rievocazione di Santa Cabrini

di Giuseppe Tusiani

> *"Mi guaridi, oggi, il mio Cristo*
> *Dal veleno e dal fuoco,*
> *Dall'onda e dalla spada,*
> *Sin al giorno finale*
> *Del mio premio immortale?"*

Con questa invocazione sul labbro, anzi con tal fede nel cuore, quindici secoli or sono, un uomo di nome Patrizio, consacrato vescovo in Italia, calzava i sandali del Pellegrino alla volta dell'Irlanda. L'ultimo soldato romano aveva da poco abbandonato quella terra, ed era perciò simbolico che la croce di Roma prendesse ora il posto delle aquile di Roma e, dove era stato l'impero, continuasse l'impero. Cristo entrava con la forza dei suoi martiri a lenire la disperazione dei vinti e a pacificare, nel nome del perdono e dell'amore, il passato e l'avvenire.

Quindici secoli son trascorsi da quel viaggio eroico; ed oggi un altro Pellegrino, anch'esso partito dall'Italia, si ferma nella città di cui è patrono San Patrizio per saldare un antico debito di lealtà e di cooperazione. I tempi sono mutati, è vero, e forse più non è il caso di parlare di bordone e sacco e pericoli dell'onda e della spada, ma immutata è la fede, e sovrano ancora l'urgente carità del Comandamento Nuovo.

A lungo si è parlato e scritto, qui tra noi, delle nostre sventure d'immigrati; abbiamo accusato, con voci autorevoli e oscure, ma con un cuor solo, la cinematografia spesso malevola, il libro e l'articolo spesso inconsulti, la conversazione e la diceria spesso ironiche, la malafede e il vilipendio sempre spudorati, e abbiamo accusato anche noi stessi, forse incapaci di far, concordi e forti, quel che altri fanno per il prestigio della lor terra d'origine.

Ma cessino oggi i sordi rancori e le infeconde lagnanze, perché una grande gloria s'è aggiunta al diadema delle nostre glorie italiche: la consacrazione del primo Vescovo italiano di New York.

Mark Pietralunga • *"Divagando* with Giuseppe Tusiani"

Il cinque Maggio scorso, proprio nella Cattedrale di San Patrizio, è stato elevato alla pienezza del Sacerdozio cattolico Mons. Giuseppe Maria Pernicone, nativo di Regalbuto (Sicilia). Non so quanti abbiano avuto la gioia di veder l'Italia rappresentata nella solennissima cerimonia liturgica, dall'ambasciatore e dal console.

Il maggior tempio di New York era gremito di fedeli e di dignitari politici ed ecclesiastici: un mareggiare di colori sgargianti e un unico fremito d'entusiasmo. Fuori, a pochi passi, rigurgitava la vita multanime della Fifth Avenue col suo solito e sempre nuovo sfrecciare di macchine e passare di gente affaccendata in mille cure; ma solo lì, nella chiesa più grande della metropoli, avveniva ciò che noi non avevamo mai veduto ed avevamo sempre sognato ed auspicato; lì, in San Patrizio, veniva celebrato l'evento più nobile nella storia dell'Italia nomade; perché lì, in quel momento, due vecchietti nostri, della nostra terra generosa, piangevano di gioia, essi che, come noi, avevan versato lagrime di dolore per anni ed anni. Ma quel pianto compensava ogni amarezza e forse per la prima volta addolciva ogni accorata nostalgia.

La cerimonia fu lunga; ma alla Signora Petromilla Pernicone non isfuggì alcun particolare. Con occhi umidi di lagrime ella guardava ora i trentadue Vescovi, ora il Cardinale consacrante, ora gli accoliti, e sempre il figlio, il suo Giuseppe, e spesso il labbro si moveva a formare due sillabe care, appena percettibili: "Figlio!" e il Signor Salvatore Pernicone, il padre del nuovo Prelato aveva lo sguardo basso e sembrava quasi impacciato di esser lì, al posto d'onore. O forse si guardava con orgoglio le mani callose che non avevano tremato per nessuna fatica e che ora tremavano dalla commozione? Ah, in quel remito era il monito d'Italia e l'apoteosi del lavoro italiano in America.

In italiano, Mons. Griffiths, il vescovo che tessè l'elogio del novello l'astore, conchiuse il suo sermone:

> Desidero felicitarmi coi genitori del Vescovo Pernicone per aver dato alla Chiesa un simile figlio, così pieno di rare virtù umane e spirituali. Egli è stato consacrato questa mattina, cinquant'anni dopo che un'altra grande immigrata italiana, la Santa Cabrini, entrò attraverso gli ampi portal di bronzo di questa Cattedrale per ricevere la benedizione prima di intraprendere la sua nobilissima missione fra gli immigranti italiani. E desidero

altresì congratularmi col Vescovo-eletto Pernicone, a cui auguro lunghi anni di vita e di ministerio.

Tutto il discorso di Mons. Griffiths fu un inno alato all'emigrazione italiana; ma queste parole in italiano toccarono il cuore di tutti, perché sembrò che l'Italia avesse così il riconoscimento ufficiale della sua grandezza.

Lontano dalla Cattedrale, nel rione italiano di Fordham, per più giorni sventolò da ogni finestra una bandiera italiana, ed ancor oggi si vedono ritagli di giornali orgogliosamente spiegati in ogni angolo della 187.ma Strada, e qualche articolo appare tra fregi bianchi rossi e verdi, messi a matita da qualche intelligente e nostalgico sognator del tricolore. E nei crocchi, caratteristici dei nostri quartieri italiani, continuano i commenti, per lo più in quel sapido dialetto siciliano che oggi può giustamente vantare la nuova gloria di esser la lingua del primo Vescovo italiano a New York.

5 maggio 1954: data indelebile nell'albo degli Italiani d'America.

Quando, dopo l'imponente recessione rituale, i genitori commossi si fermarono al fianco del Figliuolo e di Sua Eminenza il Card. Spellman, i fotografi e le machine televisive poterono ritrarre e fissare pei posteri la parte più bella del miracolo di quel giorno: la dignità di una famiglia italiana resa grande dal dolore e rimasta semplice nella gloria.

Orgogliosa dei suoi figli, plaudiva l'Italia.

Il Vescovo Joseph Maria Pernicone fotografato dopo la cerimonia della consacrazione insieme al Card. Francis Spellman ed i genitori signori Salvatore e Petronilla Pernicone.

Mark Pietralunga • *"Divagando* with Giuseppe Tusiani"

Un Libro del nostro Prof. Tusiani sui Sonettisti Americani

GIUSEPPE TUSIANI

Gli emigrati che giungano alla baia di New York volgono lo sguardo alla colossale Statua della Libertà, che, erta sull'angustia di Bedloe's Island, svetta nei cieli e annunzia al mondo la libertà della terra di Washington e di Lincoln. Ma sanno essi che sul piedistallo della più grande statua del mondo è scolpito un sonetto, da molti definito più grande della statua stessa? Son cinquant'anni ormai che milioni di visitatori, prima di salire (preferibilmente con l'ascensore interno) sulla statua gigantesca, alta 305 piedi sul mare, leggono il nome di Emma Lazarus; ma quanti sanno che soltanto un'ebrea poteva scrivere questi quattordici versi alla Dea Libertà?

Non come il cupo ellenico gigante
Sovra ogni sponda desposta predace;
Qui, su le soglie ove son l'onde infrante
Sorgerà la gran Donna dalla face
Che fe' prigione il lampo, e un nome santo
Avrà: Madre degli Esuli. Il vivace
Suo faro invita il mondo, e il pio sembiante
Scruta il mar che tra due città si giace.
Antiche terre, - ella con labbro muto
Grida - a voi la gran pompa! A me sol date
Le masse stanche e povere e assetate
Di Libertà! A me l'umil rifiuto
D'ogni lido, i reietti, i vinti! A loro
Io mostro il lume su la porta d'oro.

Quando il sonetto, il cui titolo è "The New Colossus" (Il nuovo Colosso), fu composto, Emma Lazarus non aveva veduto la Statua; ed è perciò mirabile il fatto che ella la sognasse si viva nel suo spirito commosso e con tanto profetico calore ne vedesse la funzione pacificatrice, paragonandola, per antitesi, al Colosso di Rodi. Coi quattordici versi della Lazarus l'America parla al mondo, oggi più che ieri. Ma come nacque questo sonetto? Chi era questa Emma Lazarus, tanto infelice e tanto innamorata dell'Italia? E perché mai ella si credeva prigioniera del padre e del mondo?

A queste domande risponde un capitolo del volume *Sonettisti Americani* di Giuseppe Tusiani, il quale, con quella lucidità di giudizio caratteristica di ogni altra sua monografia critica, esamina lo sviluppo logico e cronologico del sonetto in America. Al lettore egli presenta così l'avventura letteraria di Edgar Allan Poe sonettista non felice, la chiarità dei sonetti migliori del Longfellow, il mondo nostalgico e antiamericano di Edwin Arlington Robinson, la tempesta del desiderio erotico nella poesia di Edna St. Vincent Millay, la giovinezza ardente e scapigliata di Alan Seeger, la morbosa autobiografia di William Ellery Leonard, il canto epico e mistico di Thomas S. Jones, e la fama contestabile di qualche vivente.

Tutti i più importanti giornali di Italia, dal *Corriere Mercantile* di Genova a *La Gazzetta del Mezzogiorno* di Bari, dal *Quotidiano* di Roma al *Tirreno* di Livorno, da *L'Arena* di Verona al *Mattino* di Napoli, dal *Messaggero Veneto* alla *Voce di Calabria*, dalla *Gazzetta* di Padova al *Foglietto* di Foggia, dall'*Alto Adige* di Bolzano alla *Riviera* di Napoli, hanno parlato entusiasticamente del nuovo libro del Tusiani. Nella sua Introduzione, scrive Frances Winwar, la massima biografa letteraria d'America, che, con questo suo studio, il Tusiani entra in un campo vergine, "chè, in più di duecento anni di significativa attività poetica (una notevole parte di essa proprio nel sonetto), nessun critico di America ha mai pensato di compiere un tale studio". Nel *Mattino* (17 settembre 1954), Cesare Foligno, il dantista di fama mondiale, scrive: "Il Tusiani acutamente tratteggia le figure di questi poeti. Le sue versioni lo dimostrano fedele e felice traduttore, e c'è tanto in questa raccolta da incuriosire chi tenga l'occhio all'intricato giuoco degli scambi culturali tra paese e paese". Lionello Fiumi, celebre poeta e critico, scrive nel Corriere Mercantile (10 agosto 1954): "Se c'è erudito che sappia rendere interessante la sua materia, è proprio il Tusiani, il quale ci parla, sì, del sonetto americano con rara perizia (è egli stesso poeta), e moltissimi ne traduce egregiamente nel suo libro; ma la sua diagnosi letteraria egli inserisce, con lodevole procedimento, nella biografia stessa dei suoi personaggi; sicchè ne viene una galleria di "vite" mosse, aneddotiche, appassionanti. Non uno dei capitoli di questo libro scade d'interesse umano, oltre che letterario. Caso raro per un'opera critico-esegetica, esso si fa leggere veramente, come suol dirsi, d'un fiato: quasi fosse un romanzo." Alfredo Galletti, il successore di Giovanni Pascoli a Bologna, nella *Fiera Letteraria* del 3 ottobre scorso ha dedicato ben quattro colonne a questo libro del nostro collaboratore Tusiani, contributo di uno studioso italiano verso la letteratura di America. Così, tra l'altro, scrive il Galletti: "Le traduzioni del Tusiani sono fatte da un poeta che ha il senso ed il rispetto della poesia altrui".

Per la prima volta, in questo libro, viene presentata agli Italiani la tragica e quasi allucinante storia di William Ellery Leonard (1876-1944), professore di greco e umanista, il quale, stanco di una vita di dolore, un gior-

(Continua a pagina 25)

Mark Pietralunga • *"Divagando* with Giuseppe Tusiani"

reale aumento del peso. Quel che li deforma, invece che adipe, è una massa di liquido indebitamente trattenuto dai tessuti, o per difettosa circolazione sanguigna (malattie del cuore e dei reni, turbe neurovegetative ecc.) o per incompleta eliminazione dei prodotti di rifiuto del ricambio organico — soprattutto gli acidi urico, lattico ed ossalico — che una rallentata circolazione linfatica mantiene troppo a lungo nell'organismo, con effetti di vera intossicazione del sottocutaneo (celluliti diabetiche, delle malattie di fegato, e simili). Questi, ed almeno un'altra mezza dozzina di malanni, si rivelano soltanto a un occhio esperto, e spesso solo dopo una serie di esami di laboratorio. Il pericolo dunque sta nel credersi senz'altro e semplicemente "infarciti" di grasso, quando le probabilità di indovinare sono soltanto una su tre, troppo poche per giocarsi la salute.

Che cosa accadrebbe a un nefritico, non grasso, bensì gonfio di liquido che i suoi reni malati non riescono ad eliminare, e che il medico obbligherebbe subito alla classica dieta bianca, di acqua, latte allungato, patate e brodo di verdura, se in seguito ad una erronea valutazione del suo "peso", si costringesse a mangiare giornalmente i 150 grammi di carne fritta, le due uova, la pancetta affumicata, il mezzo pollo arrosto, i sedani e i peperoni crudi di una dieta dimagrante secondo Hauser? Probabilmente un irreparabile disastro. Appunto perchè le diete dimagranti moderne si basano tutte su un generoso consumo di carne, occorre a chi le segue la preventiva sicurezza dell'assoluta integrità del fegato, dello stomaco, dei reni. Nonostante le dozzine di manuali in circolazione, il controllo sanitario preventivo è chiaramente insostituibile, anche perchè l'obesità non si adatta a cure collettive: è un dato squisitamente individuale, forse più ancora che una malattia. Perciò deve essere individuale anche la cura, cioè una dieta oculata scelta dal "tecnico" tenendo conto, oltre che dei fattori vitaminici e delle calorie indispensabili, anche delle abitudini alimentari del paese e dell'ambiente familiare di ogni singolo paziente. Una grave pecca, comune a tutti i più o meno famosi volumi di dietetica dimagrante oggi sul mercato (di regola traduzioni di autori anglosassoni), è quella di prescrivere diete inadatte sia al carattere, sia al modo di vita, sia al gusto raffinato dei popoli latini in genere, italiani in specie. A parte la diversa distribuzione e consistenza dei pasti (gli americani, anche quelli magri, fanno a mezzogiorno solo un leggero spuntino), le stesse ricette contemplano accostamenti di sapori e mescolanze poco meno che orripilanti.

LUIGI ORESTE SPECIANI

Un libro del Prof. Tusiani
(Continuazione da pagina 23)

no cerca una stanza d'affitto tra il verde di una città lacustre, per lavorare tranquillo, e bussa proprio alla porta che schiuderà il suo destino amarissimo. Storia che sarebbe tutta da raccontare a colori cupi: con un vecchio generale vedovo di una povera demente, con la figliola soave e infelice, di cui il poeta s'innamora, e che diverrà la sua fidanzata, ma che un giorno gli rivelerà di essere stata, essa stessa, cinque anni prima, in manicomio, di aver tentato di uccidersi tre volte nelle acque del lago; ed egli sente che solo uno scopo nuovo potrà salvarla, le nozze, un infinito amore; e la sposa; ma non per questo ferma il cammino del Fato sulla Casa della Follia; e una mattina il poeta trova che la sposa s'è avvelenata, e il giorno dopo ella muore in manicomio! Sonetti, quelli del Leonard, che in una incalzante sequenza riflettono con commossa semplicità la sua storia freudiana e che ai quattordici versi affidano, come dice il Tusiani, uno spasimo nuovo: l'introspezione psicanalitica, anzi patologica.

Gli Italiani d'America sono orgogliosi del fatto che sia stato uno di loro, prima ancora degli stessi Americani, ad affrontare con competenza il vasto e delicato problema del sonetto d'America.

In *Sonettisti Americani* (Clemente & Sons, 2905 North Natchez Ave., Chicago 54, Illinois, $2.00) ogni amante di poesia e di arte, ogni curioso di avventure d'amore in questo o quel poeta, ogni cultore di studi comparati fra l'Italia e l'America, troverà certamente il "suo" libro. ARGO

Contributors

EMILIO BANDIERA (Professor of Latin Philology, Latin Metrics, Latin Language and Latin Literature in the Faculty of Letters, University of Lecce ITALY) retired in November 2006. His publications concern the theme of *otium* in archaic Latin literature, the legends of Aeneas prior to the work of Virgil, the technique of the Latin dactylic hexameter, the political ideology of Tibullus. He has contributed to the all'ENCICLOPEDIA VIRGILIANA e ORAZIANA, published by the Treccani Institute of the Italian Encyclopedia. Having met Joseph Tusiani in the early 1980s, he engaged in the analysis of Tusiani's Latin poetic production. Numerous volumes followed, comprising the complete edition of Tusiani's Latin poetry with an introduction, the editing of the text, the Italian translation, and various indexes. He has published in a complete volume Tusiani's English poetic production spanning the period 1983-2004, as well as other three English works, with an introduction and translation into Italian. These volumes of Tusiani's Latin and English poems (10 titles) were accompanied by 18 critical essays published in Italy, the USA, Belgium, France, Germany. A passionate lover of history, poetry and local music (he studied piano and organ), he has published four volumes and numerous articles on these topics.

LUIGI BONAFFINI has published numerous articles and books, including *La poesia visionaria di Dino Campana* and translations of works by Dino Campana, Mario Luzi, Vittorio Sereni, Giose Rimanelli, Giuseppe Jovine, Achille Serrao, Eugenio Cirese, Albino Pierro, Cesare Ruffato, Antonio Spagnuolo, Luciano Troisio, Stephen Massimilla, Giancarlo Pontiggia, Attilio Bertolucci, Pier Paolo Pasolini, and others. He has edited five trilingual anthologies of dialect poetry and has translated widely from various Italian dialects. He edited or co-edited *A New Map. A Bilingual Anthology of Migrant Writers in Italy* (2011); *Poets of the Italian Diaspora* (2013); *La letteratura italiana nel mondo. Nuove prospettive* (2015); *Isernia che non c'è più* (2018); *Poeti della diaspora italiana* (2019). He has received several awards for his translations, including the Italian National Translation Prize, given by the Italian government, and the translation award by the Academy of American Poets for his translation of Attilio Bertolucci's *La camera da letto / The Bedroom*. He recently received the Catullo Prize from the Accademia Mondiale della Poesia. He is the editor of *Journal of Italian Translation*

RYAN CALABRETTA-SAJDER is Assistant Professor and Section Head of Italian at the University of Arkansas, Fayetteville, where he teaches Italian, Film, and Gender Studies. He is the author of *Divergenze in celluloide: colore, migrazione e identità sessuale nei film gay di Ferzan Özpetek* (Mimesis) and

"Contributors"

editor of *Pasolini's Lasting Impressions: Death, Eros, and Literary Enterprise in the Opus of Pier Paolo Pasolini* (Fairleigh Dickinson UP), and co-editor of *Italian Americans On Screen: Challenging the Past, Re-Theorizing the Future* (Lexington Books), and *Italian Americans on the Page* (under review). His research interests include the integration of gender, class, and migration in both Italian and Italian American literature and cinema, as well as teaching Italian language and culture through Digital Humanities and Virtual Reality. In Spring 2017, he was a Fulbright Scholar for the Foundation of the South at the University of Calabria. He is currently working on two authored books, one exploring the Italian American gay author Robert Ferro who died of AIDS in 1988 and the second on the Algerian Italian author Amara Lakhous. He is President of the American Association of Teachers of Italian, President of *Gamma Kappa Alpha*, and founding editor of *Diasporic Italy: Journal of the Italian American Studies Association*.

GAETANO CIPOLLA, Professor Emeritus at St. John's University, is a well-known scholar, translator and publisher. Some of his scholarly work on Dante, Petrarca, Pirandello, Calvino and others is contained in *Labyrinth: Studies on an Archetype*. He has devoted much of his career to the promotion of the language and culture of Sicily. He is President and Editor of Arba Sicula. His *Siciliana: Studies on the Sicilian Ethos* contains his work related to Sicily. He wrote *The Sounds of Sicilian*, now included in his *Learn Sicilian / Mparamu lu sicilianu*, a modern college textbook already in its third reprint and in use at some universities, and he is currently working on an advanced second-year textbook, focusing on the different *parrati* of Sicilian. As editor of Legas, he founded three series: *Sicilian Studies* with 30 volumes in print, *Poets of Arba Sicula* with 17 bilingual volumes, and *Italian Poetry in Translation* with 16 volumes in print. He has translated works by Meli, Veneziano, Tempio, Martoglio, Di Marco, Mazza, Carbone, Provenzano, Ancona and others. Prof. Cipolla is the recipient of many prizes including the Telamone Prize from Agrigento, the Pigna d'Argento, the Proserpina Prize, and Sicily's Ambasciatori Siciliani nel mondo.

LUIGI FONTANELLA, born in Salerno, Italy, in 1943, studied at the University of Rome under the guidance of Giacomo Debenedetti and at Harvard under the guidance of Dante Della Terza, where he earned a Ph.D. in Romance Languages and Literatures. Fulbright Fellow (Princeton University, 1976-1978), he has taught at Columbia, Princeton, and Wellesley. He is currently Professor Emeritus of Italian at Stony Brook Universiy. President of I.P.A. (Italian Poetry in America), Fontanella is the founder and the Senior Editor of *Gradiva*, an international journal of Italian Poetry. He has published fifteen books of poetry, four books of fiction, and nine books of criticism. His most recent collection of poetry *L'adolescenza e la notte* (Firenze: Passigli, 2015) was awarded the Pascoli Prize and the Viareggio-Giuria Prize and has been translated into French by Philippe Démeron (Éditions RAZ, 2017), and into English by Giorgio Mobili (Fomite Press, 2021). Forthcoming books *Raccontare la poesia 1970-2020. Saggi, ricordi, testimonianze critiche* (Moretti & Vitali, 2021), and *Tre Passi nel Desiderio* (three one-act plays, Neos Edizioni, 2021). In 2004 President Carlo Azeglio Ciampi nominated Luigi Fontanella *Cavaliere della Repubblica Italiana*. luigifontanella02@gmail.com

PAOLO A. GIORDANO is the Neil E. Euliano Distinguished Professor of Italian and Italian American Studies Emeritus at the University of Central Florida. He has served as president of the American Association of Teachers of Italian (AATI) and as Associate Editor of the Association's journal, *Italica*. He is also co-founder of Bordighera Press and the journals *Voices in Italian Americana* and *Italiana*. His research interests are in the literature of Italian emigration, the Italian Renaissance, and 20th-century Italian Literature. His essays and articles on Italian literature and art, and Italian-American studies, have appeared in Italian and American journals. His most significant publications are *From the Margin: Writings in Italian Americana*, edited with A. Tamburri and Fred Gardaphé, re-released as second edition (Purdue UP, 1990/2000); *Beyond the Margin* (Fairleigh Dickinson UP, 1998), and *Joseph Tusiani: Poet Translator Humanist* (1994). In addition to his work on Italian-American authors, he has published on Cesare Pavese, Beppe Fenoglio, Rodolfo Di Biase, Gabriello Chiabrera, and Piero Davanzati. Giordano was honored by the Italian government as *Cavaliere, Stella della Solidarietà Italiana*. In 2004, Southern Connecticut State University named him "Distinguished Alumnus," and the AATI gave him its "Distinguished Service Award." He was recognized by the City of Bordighera (Italy) with the "Parmurelu d'oru" (Golden Palm) for lifetime achievement.

JOHN T. KIRBY (PhD, University of North Carolina at Chapel Hill) is Professor of Classics at the University of Miami, where for six years he served as inaugural Chair of the Department of Classics and designed its curriculum and undergraduate major. He was previously Professor of Classics and Comparative Literature at Purdue University, where he also founded and chaired the interdisciplinary Program in Classics, and subsequently served as Chair of the interdisciplinary Program in Comparative Literature. Kirby has authored dozens of articles, encyclopaedia entries, and book reviews, which range across a wide field of interests including classical rhetoric and poetics, ancient philosophy, metrics, textual criticism, religious studies, structuralist and poststructuralist literary theory, ancient and modern aesthetics, and visual media. He has also published five books, including *Secret of the Muses Retold: Classical Influences on Italian Authors of the Twentieth Century* (University of Chicago Press, 2001); *The Comparative Reader* (Chancery Press 1998); *The Roman Republic and Empire* (Gale Group 2001); *Classical Greek Civilization* (Gale Group 2000); and *The Rhetoric of Cicero's Pro Cluentio* (Gieben, 1990). His current research focuses on what he calls 'comparative classics,' investigating classical Chinese and Sanskrit literatures in light of the Greek and Roman classics, and vice versa.

MARIA C. PASTORE PASSARO is a professor of Italian at Central Connecticut State University since 1989. A Medieval and Renaissance scholar, Prof. Passaro has published widely on Italian literature. Her publications include translations of Longfellow's *Michael Angelo*, Tusiani's *Gente Mia and Other Poems*, *Rind and All*, *The Fifth Season*, and Tasso's *King Torrismondo* (Fordham University Press, 1997). She is the author of *Representation of Women in Classical, Medieval, and Renaissance Texts* (Mellen, 2005), co-author of *Selected Writings of Girolamo Savonarola: Religion and Politics 1490-1498* (Yale University Press, 2006), contributed three essays to the *Encyclopedia of Italian Literary Studies*, and an essay to the *Guide to the Historical Reception of Augustine* (Oxford UP, 2010). She is also the translator of Tasso's *Love Rhymes*, Pagano's *Corradino*, and the author of *A Selection of Italian Medieval Literary Texts* (NY: Legas, 2019). She was the recipient of the "Excellence in Teaching Award," and of many other academic honors from: AATI, MLA, NEH, NIAF, Yale, and Fulbright.

MARK PIETRALUNGA is the Victor B. Oelschläger Professor of Modern Languages and Linguistics and specializes in 20th century Italian Literature and Culture, with a particular focus on post war novel and translation. His research interests include Italian American Studies. He has served as Chair of the Department of Modern Languages and Linguistics, resident associate director and as summer director of Florida State University's study abroad program in Florence, Italy, as well as coordinator of the Italian Studies Program. He is a former long-serving book review editor for the journal *Italica* and is currently one of its associate editors. He has served as a member of the Executive Committees of the American Association of Teachers of Italian (AATI), the American Association of Italian Studies (AAIS), and the South Atlantic Modern Language Association (SAMLA). He has also served as chair of the Modern Language Association's Honors and Awards Committee. He has received two Outstanding Teaching Awards and a Teaching Incentive Award from Florida State University. His authored, edited, and translated books include: *An Absurd Vice: A Biography of Cesare Pavese* by Davide Lajolo (1983); *Beppe Fenoglio*

"Contributors"

and English Literature: A Study of the Writer as Translator (1987); *Beppe Fenoglio e l'esaltante fatica del tradurre* (1992); *Prometeo slegato: Pavese traduttore di P. B. Shelley* (1998); *Quaderno di Traduzioni: Beppe Fenoglio* (2000); *Cesare Pavese and Anthony Chiuminatto: Their Correspondence* (2007); *Cesare Pavese: A Critical-Analytical Study* by Giose Rimanelli (2019); *Italians in America* by Amerigo Ruggiero (2020).

GIOSE RIMANELLI (1925-2018) was the winner of the prestigious American Book Award for his avant-garde novel, *Benedetta in Guysterland*. He has authored numerous novels, poetry collections, collections of essays, and innumerable journal articles and reviews. His debut novel, *Tiro al piccione* (1952; *The Day of the Lion* [1954]), is a fictionalized account of his journey through Italy's Civil War was translated into eight languages, it was later made into a highly acclaimed movie by Giuliano Montaldo. In 2008, he received the Premio Acerbi career award in special recognition of his contribution to Italian American literature, in Castel Goffredo, Italy. Rimanelli was considered a writer of two worlds, Europe, and America; and he wrote in Italian, English, and his molisano dialect. All his writings deal with the abuse and misuse of power. Over the years, he wrote numerous novels, poetry collections, essays, screenplays, journal articles, and reviews. He was, in addition, a long-time painter in both oils and watercolor. Having taught at Yale, Sarah Lawrence, UCLA, and British Columbia, ultimately, he was for many years Professor of Comparative Literature at SUNY Albany. He divided his later years between Lowell, Massachusetts, and Pompano Beach, Florida, with frequent trips to Italy in the meantime.

ILARIA SERRA was born in Venice, Italy, and is Professor of Italian and Comparative Studies at Florida Atlantic University (FAU) in Boca Raton, Florida. She is the author of several articles and chapters on Italian cinema, literature and migration, and the books, *Immagini di un immaginario: L'emigrazione italiana negli Stati Uniti fra i due secoli: 1890-1925* (Cierre 1997), *The Value of Worthless Lives: Writing Italian American Immigrant"* (Fordham University Press, 2007 & 2010), and *The Imagined Immigrant. Images of Italian Emigration to the United States between 1890 and 1924* (Farleigh Dickinson UP, 2009). She authored the language and culture book, *Italia cantata: Two Centuries of Italian History Through Music* (Rylan, 2021) and has finished a manuscript in English on the same topic. At FAU, she coordinates the digital humanities projects, "Italian American Oral History Archive," "Italian American Memories Documentary Archive" and "Floritalians." She also organizes the FAU Italian and Italian American Film Festivals and the annual the International Symposium

"Italy in Transit." In 2008, she founded a six-week summer study abroad program in Venice, Italy, that she leads every year. She collaborates with the Gallio Film Festival delle Opere Prime, which takes place on the Asiago plateau every July.

COSMA SIANI lives in Rome. A high-school teacher as well as a teacher-trainer in the Italian school system, he also taught English at the universities of Cassino and Roma Tor Vergata for many years. He was the author of textbooks for the teaching of English as a foreign language for the Zanichelli and La Nuova Italia publishers. A president of TESOL Italy, an affiliate of TESOL International, in the 1990s. He is a contributor to the Italian book-review monthly *L'Indice dei libri del mese*, and a member of the editorial board of the *Journal of Italian Translation* edited by Luigi Bonaffini. Among the books he authored or edited are *Lingua e letteratura. Esplorazioni e percorsi nell'insegnamento delle lingue straniere* (1992); *Libri all'Indice e altri*, a collection of reviews (2001); *Un luogo in cui vivere. Letture e scritture italoamericane* (2012); *Jim Longhi. Un italoamericano fra Woody Guthrie e Arthur Miller* (co-author Mariantonietta Di Sabato, 2012); Arthur Miller, *Monte Sant'Angelo* (trans. Di Sabato and Siani, 2019). His numerous writings about the life and works of Joseph Tusiani include the books *Le lingue dell'altrove. Storia testi e bibliografia di Joseph Tusiani* (2004); *Baretti a Londra e altri saggi su Joseph Tusiani* (2013).

ANTHONY JULIAN TAMBURRI (PhD, University of California, Berkeley) is Distinguished Professor of European Languages and Literatures and Dean of the John D. Calandra Italian American Institute (Queens College, CUNY). He is past president of the Italian American Studies Association and of the American Association of Teachers of Italian. His sixteen authored books include: *Una semiotica della ri-lettura: Guido Gozzano, Aldo Palazzeschi, Italo Calvino* (2003); *Narrare altrove: diverse segnalature letterarie* (2007); *Una semiotica dell'etnicità: nuove segnalature per la letteratura italiano/americana* (2010); *Re-reading Italian Americana: Specificities and Generalities on Literature and Criticism* (2014); *Un biculturalismo negato: La letteratura "italiana" negli Stati Uniti* (2018); *Scrittori Italiano[-]Americani: trattino sì trattino no* (2018); and *Signing Italian/American Cinema: A More Focused Look* (2021). His co-edited volumes include: *Italoamericana: The Literature of the Great Migration, 1880-1943* (2014); *From The Margin: Writings in Italian Americana* (1991/2000); edited the entry "Aldo Palazzeschi 1885-1974" in *Twentieth-Century Literary Criticism*. Ed. Lawrence J. Trudeau. Vol. 316 (2015). He is executive producer and host of Calandra's TV program, *Italics*, and co-founder of Bordighera Press, which was established in 1989. In June 2010, the Hon. Giorgio Napolitano, President

"Contributors"

of Italy, conferred upon him *motu proprio* the recognition of *Cavaliere dell'Ordine al Merito della Repubblica Italiana*.

BEA TUSIANI is a freelance writer published in *The New York Times* and *Newsday*, among many other magazines and newspapers, including *Attenzione* and *Ambassador*. She has written a memoir, *Con Amore* (in its second printing), and a children's book, *The Fig Cake Family*, both strongly rooted in her Italian heritage. Bea founded the Writer's Network of Long Island, the Frances Hodgson Burnett Collection at the Manhasset Public Library, and the Italian Welfare League's charitable "I Nostri Bambini Program." She also wrote *Remnants of a Life on Paper: A Mother and Daughter's Struggle with Borderline Personality Disorder*, a moving story of her daughter's struggle with BPD. Together with her family, she established the "Borderline Personality Disorder Resource Center" at New York-Presbyterian Hospital. A native of Brooklyn, she grew up in the Bushwick section where her four grandparents emigrated from Santa Margherita Belice, Sicily.

Index of Names

Agro, 264, 264n15
Aguglia, Mimi 7
Alfieri, Vittorio 44, 49, 60
Alifano, John 6
Alighieri, Dante ix 8, 32, 38, 43, 59, 60, 83, 116, 118, 149-158 (as character in novel), 148, 174, 221, 229, 254n22
Antonini, Luigi 13
Aquinas, Thomas 149
Arguropoulos, Ioannes 113-114
Ariosto, Lodovico 86, 117
Atwood, Margaret 197
Auden, W. H. 59
Auerbach, Erich 147, 147n2
Augustine 116

Bach, Johan Sebastian 82
Baldi, Diana 7
Balducci, Carolyn Feleppa 89
Ballerini, Luigi 83
Bandiera, Emilio 94n4, 95, 95n6, 97, 98, 99, 99n10, 101, 102, 103, 119n16, 213n23
Baretti, Giuseppe 239-258 (also as character)
Basile, Giambattista 139, 140
Basini, Vesare 31n56
Bellanca, Augusto 13, 18
Bembo, Pietro 117
Bergin, Thomas 89
Berlioz, Hector 44, 210
Bernardi, U. 126n10, 137n32, 137n33
Bianco, Orazio 96
Block de Behar, Lisa 111n4
Boccaccio, Giovanni 22, 27, 59
Bocchimuzzo, Vincent 32, 32n59
Bogan, Louise 59
Boiardo, Matteo maria 85

Bonaffini, Luigi vii, 89, 187n6
Borgese, Giuseppe Antonio 16, 16n30, 17-20, 17n32, 20n38, 57, 75
Bracciolini, Poggio 115n11
Bramante, Donato 114
Brevini, Franco 121, 121n1, 123-124, 123n5, 125n7, 128n15, 128n16, 130n19, 136n31
Brother Juniper 149
Browning, Elizabeth 22
Browning, Robert 22
Brunelleschi, Filippo 115
Bugliani, Paolo 255
Buonarroti, Michelangelo 49, 60, 83, 86, 149, 160, 255
Burckhardt, Jacob 112n5
Bynner, Witter 59
Byron, Lord 22

Cabrini, Francesca Saverio 147, 149-158 (as character in novel), 149n6, 150, 152, 153
Caesar 50, 116
Caimi, Gino 7
Calabretta-Sajder, Ryan 167n2, 179n4
Calabretta-Sajder, Ryan vii
Calitri, Antonnio 8-9, 9n13 11, 259, 263n13
Capasso, Nicola 139
Capasso, Roberta 56, 57, 58
Caradonna, Nino 6
Carpi, Adziaro 7
Carravetta, Peter 168, 172-173
Carravetta, Peter 83
Carrera, Alessandro 83
Caruso, Enrico 10-11, 10n15, 31, 34-35
Castiglione, Baldassare 117

Catullus 119
Cavalli, Gianni 104, 104n17
Cecchini, Mimi 7
Celemente, Egidio 16-17
Cennerazzo, Armando 7
Chaucer, Geoffrey 256
Chersterton, G.K. 34
Chiesa, M 133n24
Cicero 116, 116n13
Cicolella, Luca 164
Cima, Michele 137
Cipolla, Gaetano vii
Citati, Pietro 88
Clements, Robert L. x
Coco, Peppino 161
Coleridge, Samuel Taylor 22
Colombo, Furio 98, 98n8, 213, 213n24
Colum, Padraic 34, 201, 201n4
Columbus, Christopher 66-69
Condini, Ned 83
Congedo, Mario 97, 102
Contini, Gianfranco 82
Cordiferro, Riccardo 6
Cortese, Giulio Cesare 139, 140
Crialese, Emanuele 223n9
Crivello, Antonino 14
Croce, Benedetto 20
Cross, Donatella 28, 28n51
Cuomo, Andrew 76

D'haen, Theo 111n4
D'Amaro, Sergio 83
D'Annunzio, Gabriele 27-28, 28n50
da Vinci, Leonardo 114
Damrosch, David 111n4
De Amicis, Edmondo 32
de Bosis, Lauro 17
De Luca, Dino 7
De Martino, Ernesto 124
De Martino, Francesco 104

de Palchi, Alfredo 83
De Sanctis, Francesco 27
De' Liguori, Alfonso Maria 139
de' Medici, Cosimo 113, 114, 114n9
degli Agli, Antonio 114
Della Terza, Dante 82
de Saussure, Ferdinand 225n10
Di Biasio, G. 125n7
Dickinson, Emily 262
di Donato, Pietro 64n16, 153n8
di Giacomo, 123
Dreiser, Theodore 10-11
Dryden, John 160
Dunsany, Lord 34
Durham Peters, John 170
Duse, Eleonora 28

Eisenstein, Elizabeth L. 115n10
Eliade, Mircea 147n1
Eliot, George 113n7, 254n22
Eliot, T.S. 4
Elman, Misha 25, 161
Erasmus 117

Farrell, James T. 34
Ferrucci, Franco 82
Ficino, Marsilio 114, 114n9, 115n11, 116
Fiedlia, Alma 6
Fiumi, Lionello 28n50, 28n51
Flamma, Ario 6
Foligno, Cesare 4n4, 28n50, 214
Fontanella, Luigi vii, 55n2, 83, 121n2, 167n1, 179n4, 196n8, 204, 204n10, 215, 215n2, 216n5, 229n11, 237n13
Franchi, F 125n7, 135n28
Frassica, Pietro 82

Galassi, Jonathan 88
Galdieri, Rocco 139

Galletti, Alfredo 197
Galletti, Alfredo 28n50
Gambara, Veronica 86
Gemistos, Georgios (Plethon) 113-114, 113n6
Gemito, Vincenzo 9, 12, 56n3
Gianfreda, Maestro M. 161
Gianfreda, Massimo 96
Giannini, Federico 114n9
Gigli, Beniamino 31
Giglio, Sandrino 7
Giordano, Paolo A. vii, 99n10, 103n16, 118n15, 176, 176n3, 174, 181, 181n5, 183, 203-204-205, 204n9, 204n11, 205n12, 218n7, 239, 239n3
Giotti, 123
Giovannitti, Arturo 12, 12n20, 13-16, 14n24, 16n29, 56, 56n3, 57, 71, 75, 150
Giustiniani, Enzo 6
Giusto, Nicola 5n8
Grafton, Anthony 115n12
Greco, Francesco 6
Greco, Pietro 6
Gregory, Horace 59
Gunther, John 25n43
Gutenberg, Johannes 115

Hall, Donald 59
Hollander, Robert 82
Holmes, John 59
Horace 119

Iacovella, Mary 6
Iannace, Carmone Biagio 32, 32n60
Iannella, Maria 7
IJsewijn, Jozef 91, 92, 93, 95
Incalicchio, Giuseppe 6

Jeffers, Robinson 59

Johnson, Samuel 239-258 (also as character)
Juvenal 119, 119n16

Kadir, Djelal 111n4
Keats, John 22
Keller, Helen 10-11
Kennedy, John Fizgerald x, 59
King, Martin Luther 75
Kirby, John T. vii, 111n2, 111n3, 111n4, 118n15, 119n16
Koch, John 25
Kock, Dora 26

La Guardia, Fiorello 5n5, 10
Lacan, Jacques 168-169, 178
Laderman, Ezra 160
Landino, Cristoforo 114
Lawrence, D.H. 21
Leoaprdi, Giacomo ix, 86, 230-231, 232n12, 235
L'Episcopo, Charles 261n5
Levertov, Denise 59
Livy 116
Loi, Franco 131n21, 136n31
Lombardi, Antonietta 75
London, Jack 11
Lorch, Maristella 82
Lucarelli, Lorenzo 6, 6n9
Luotto, Andrè 259-261, 261n4

Machiavelli, Niccolò 149
Macy, John 34
Maeterlinck, Maurice 34
Magno, Pietro 231
Mann, Thomas 34
Marazzi, Martino 74
Marcantonio, Vito 5n5
Marchand, Jean-Jacques 121n2, 204n10
Marchegiani, Irene 88, 89
Marcone, Maria 164

Marin, 123
Marino, Giambattista 86
Martin de Porres 149, 149n6
Matteo, Sante 194
Maurois, Andre 34
Maynard, Thomas 153, 153n8, 157
Mazzitelli, Oscar 11
Meli, Giovanni 137
Meneghello, Luigi 123, 123n4
Meucci, Antonio 30-31
Milton, John 121
Miranda, Lin-Manuel 246
Montale, Eugenio ix, 262
Montana, Pietro 14
Moore, Marianne 59
More, Thomas 117
Moroni, Mario 83
Morse, Margaret 174
Mother Antonietta della Porta, 153n8
Motta, Antonio 162, 251
Moult, Thomas 29

Naficy, Hamid 166, 168, 169-170, 177-178
Nardella, Tommaso 17n32
Nicholl, Louise Townsend 75
Nicolardi, Edoardo 139
Novasio, Pietro 259-260, 261, 263
Noventa, 123
Nuzzi, Bernardo 114

Ong, Walter 222
Ovid 113, 119

Pagano, Nunziante 139
Palma, Michael 86
Pane, Remigio Ugo 3, 82
Paolucci, Anna 89
Paone, Nicola 7
Pascoli, Giovanni 82, 136, 136n31

Pastore Passaro, Maria C. vii, 203, 203n8
Peirce, Charles Sanders 225n10
Pernicone, Giuseppe Maria 263, 273-275
Perosa, Alessandro 117n14
Perretta, Pasquale 23
Petrarca, Francesco 59, 115n12, 117, 118
Piccirilli, Attilio 10, 10n17, 56n3
Pietralunga, Mark vii
Pisone, Angelo 28n50
Pisone, Maria (Tusiani's mother) 82
Plato 114
Poliziano, Angelo 86
Pomeroy Harrington, Karl 117n14
Pope John XXIII 148
Praz, Mario 4n4
Prezzolini, Giuseppe 5-6, 6n8 9
Pucci, Joseph 117n14
Pucelli, Rodolfo 6
Pulci, Luigi ix, 43, 44, 85, 142
Puzo, Mario 149n7

Quasimodo, Salvatore 262

Ragusa, Olga 82
Raine, Kathleen 200
Reynolds, Joshua 244
Rimanelli, Giose 83
Riviello, Tonia 83
Ruotolo, Onorio 9-10, 9n12, 10n17 11-12, 12n20, 13-14, 16-20, 24, 56-57, 56n3, 71, 75, 259, 261-262, 261n5-7, 262

Sacré, Dirk xii, 92, 93-94, 95, 99, 100-102, 212n22
Saint Catherine of Siena 149
Salvemini, Gaetano 17

Sand, George 20
Santoro, Daniel 30-31
Savonarola,
Schena, Nunzio 95
Schipa, Tito 31
Scilla, Guglielmo 14
Serra, Ilaria vii
Serrao, Achille 139
Sgruttendio da Sclafani, Filippo 139, 142-144
Shakespeare, William 38
Shelley, Percy Bysshe 8-9, 22
Siani, Cosma 60, 99n10, 162-163, 240, 241, 243, 256n25
Socrates 50
Sparrow, John 117n14
Speciale, Emilio 83
Spezzano, Lia 6, 31, 31n57
Stanco, Italo 6, 263n13
Stefanile, Felix ix, 240
Sterni, Giuseppe 7 24
Sturzo, Luigi 17
Swenson, May 59

Tagore, Rabindranath 50
Talese, Gay 149n7
Tamburri, Anthony Julian vii, 56, 68-69, 99n10, 103n16, 172-173, 181n5, 196n8, 215n1, 216n4, 218n6, 239-240, 245, 245n15
Tarchiani, Alberto 222n8
Tasso, Torquato ix, 43, 49, 86, 162
Tesio, G. 133n24
Testi, Nicola 32, 32n58
Thompson, George 59
Thrale, David 243n9, 244, 244n11, 250
Toscanini, Arturo 25, 161
Tresca, Carlo 17
Trilussa, 137

Tusiani, Michele 7n10, 7n11

Ungaretti, Giuseppe 262

Valentino, Rodolfi 7n10
Valesio, Paolo 83, 84
Van Doren, Mark 59
Vecchione, Mario 6
Verdi, Giuseppe 13
Vergil 119
Verrazzano, Giovanni 30-31
Vigilante, Matteo 162
Viola, Salvatore 263n13
Viviani, Alberto 13-14, 259, 266-267, 267n17

Williams, William Carlos 59
Wilson, Nigel 115n12
Winwar, Frances 10n16, 20-26, 29-35, 34n62, 56-58, 71, 75, 161, 167, 262-263, 264
Wolfe, Thomas 165, 196
Wordsworth, William 4n4, 12, 22, 121

Zanzotto, Andrea 125n7, 135, 135n29
Zappulla, Giuseppe 6

SAGGISTICA

Taking its name from the Italian—which means essays, essay writing, or non-fiction—*Saggisitca* is a referred book series dedicated to the study of all topics and cultural productions that fall under what we might consider that larger umbrella of all things Italian and Italian/American.

Vito Zagarrio
  The "Un-Happy Ending": Re-viewing The Cinema of Frank Capra. 2011. ISBN 978-1-59954-005-4. Volume 1.
Paolo A. Giordano, Editor
  The Hyphenate Writer and The Legacy of Exile. 2010. ISBN 978-1-59954-007-8. Volume 2.
Dennis Barone
  America / Trattabili. 2011. ISBN 978-1-59954-018-4. Volume 3.
Fred L. Gardaphè
  The Art of Reading Italian Americana. 2011. ISBN 978-1-59954-019-1. Volume 4.
Anthony Julian Tamburri
  Re-viewing Italian Americana: Generalities and Specificities on Cinema. 2011. ISBN 978-1-59954-020-7. Volume 5.
Sheryl Lynn Postman
  An Italian Writer's Journey through American Realities: Giose Rimanelli's English Novels. "The most tormented decade of America: the 60s" ISBN 978-1-59954-034-4. Volume 6.
Luigi Fontanella
  Migrating Words: Italian Writers in the United States. 2012. ISBN 978-1-59954-041-2. Volume 7.
Peter Covino & Dennis Barone, Editors
  Essays on Italian American Literature and Culture. 2012. ISBN 978-1-59954-035-1. Volume 8.
Gianfranco Viesti
  Italy at the Crossroads. 2012. ISBN 978-1-59954-071-9. Volume 9.
Peter Carravetta, Editor
  Discourse Boundary Creation (LOGOS TOPOS POIESIS): A Festschrift in Honor of Paolo Valesio. ISBN 978-1-59954-036-8. Volume 10.
Antonio Vitti and Anthony Julian Tamburri, Editors
  Europe, Italy, and the Mediterranean. ISBN 978-1-59954-073-3. Volume 11.

Vincenzo Scotti
Pax Mafiosa or War: Twenty Years after the Palermo Massacres. 2012. ISBN 978-1-59954-074-0. Volume 12.

Anthony Julian Tamburri, Editor
Meditations on Identity. Meditazioni su identità. ISBN 978-1-59954-082-5. Volume 13.

Peter Carravetta, Editor
Theater of the Mind, Stage of History. A Festschrift in Honor of Mario Mignone. ISBN 978-1-59954-083-2. Volume 14.

Lorenzo Del Boca
Italy's Lies. Debunking History's Lies So That Italy Might Become A "Normal Country". ISBN 978-1-59954-084-9. Volume 15.

George Guida
Spectacles of Themselves. Essays in Italian American Popular Culture and Literature. ISBN 978-1-59954-090-0. Volume 16.

Antonio Vitti and Anthony Julian Tamburri, Editors
Mare Nostrum: prospettive di un dialogo tra alterità e mediterraneità. ISBN 978-1-59954-100-6. Volume 17.

Patrizia Salvetti
Rope and Soap. Lynchings of Italians in the United States. ISBN 978-1-59954-101-3. Volume 18.

Sheryl Lynn Postman and Anthony Julian Tamburri, Editors
Re-reading Rimanelli in America: Six Decades in the United States. ISBN 978-1-59954-102-0. Volume 19.

Pasquale Verdicchio
Bound by Distance. Rethinking Nationalism Through the Italian Diaspora. ISBN 978-1-59954-103-7. Volume 20.

Peter Carravetta
After Identity. Migration, Critique, Italian American Culture. ISBN 978-1-59954-072-6. Volume 21.

Antonio Vitti and Anthony Julian Tamburri, Editors
The Mediterranean As Seen by Insiders and Outsiders. ISBN 978-1-59954-107-5. Volume 22.

Eugenio Ragni
After Identity. Migration, Critique, Italian American Culture. ISBN 978-1-59954-109-9. Volume 23.

Quinto Antonelli
Intimate History of the Great War: Letters, Diaries, and Memoirs from Soldiers on the Front. ISBN 978-1-59954-111-2. Volume 24.

Antonio Vitti and Anthony Julian Tamburri, Editors
  The Mediterranean Dreamed and Lived by Insiders and Outsiders. ISBN 978-1-59954-115-0. Volume 25.
Sabrina Vellucci and Carla Francellini, Editors
  Re-Mapping Italian America: Places, Cultures, Identities. ISBN 978-1-59954-116-7. Volume 26.
Stephen J. Belluscio
  Garibaldi M. Lapolla: A Study of His Novels. ISBN 978-1-59954-125-9. Volume 27.
Antonio Vitti and Anthony Julian Tamburri, Editors
  The Representation of the Mediterranean World by Insiders and Outsiders. ISBN 978-1-59954-113-6. Volume 28.
Philip Balma and Giovanni Spani, Editors
  Translating for (and from) The Italian Screen: Dubbing and Subtitles. ISBN 978-1-59954-141-9. Volume 29.
Antonio Vitti and Anthony Julian Tamburri, Editors
  The Representation of the Mediterranean World by Insiders and Outsiders. ISBN 978-1-59954-142-6. Volume 30.
Anthony Julian Tamburri, Editor
  Interrogations into Italian-American Studies. The Francesco and Mary Giambelli Foundation Lectures. ISBN 978-1-59954-143-3. Volume 31.
Giose Rimanelli
  Cesare Pavese's Long Journy. A Criticial-Analytical Study. Edited with an Introduction by Mark Pietralunga. ISBN 978-1-59954-133-4. Volume 32.
Susanna Nanni and Sabrina Vellucci, Editors
  Circolazione di idee e di persone: Integrazione ed esclusione tra Europa e Americhe. ISBN 978-1-59954-155-6. Volume 33.
Sian Gibby, Joseph Sciorra, and Anthony Julian Tamburri, Editors
  This Hope Sustains the Scholar: Essays in Tribute to the Work of Robert Viscusi. ISBN 978-1-59954-167-9. Volume 34.
Antonio Vitti and Anthony Julian Tamburri, Editors
  Mediterranean Encounters and Clashes. Incontri e scontri meditteranei. ISBN 978-1-59954-171-6. Volume 35.
Wendy Pojmann
  Espresso. The Art and Soiuld of Italy. ISBN 978-1-59954-168-6. Volume 36.

www.ingramcontent.com/pod-product-compliance
Lightning Source LLC
Chambersburg PA
CBHW071958220426
43662CB00009B/1179